A HISTORY AND CRITIQUE OF THE ORIGIN OF THE MARCAN HYPOTHESIS 1835–1866

NEW GOSPEL STUDIES 8

A HISTORY AND CRITIQUE OF THE ORIGIN OF THE MARCAN HYPOTHESIS 1835–1866

A Contemporary Report Rediscovered

a translation with introduction and notes of
Geschiedenis en critiek der Marcushypothese
(History and Critique of the Marcan Hypothesis)
by
Hajo Uden Meijboom
at the University of Groningen, 1866

translated and edited by
John J. Kiwiet

PEETERS   MERCER

ISBN 0-86554-407-7   MUP/H330

A History and Critique
of the Origin of the Marcan Hypothesis, 1835–1866.
A Contemporary Report Rediscovered.
Copyright ©1993
Mercer University Press, Macon, Georgia 31207 USA
All rights reserved
Printed in the United States of America

Library of Congress Cataloging-in-Publication Data

Meyboom, H. U. (Meijboom, Hajo Uden), 1842–1933
[Geschiedenis en critiek der Marcushypothese. English]
A history and critique of the origin of the Marcan hypothesis, 1835–1866 :
a contemporary report rediscovered / translated and edited by John J. Kiwiet.
xl+236 pages. 6x9" (15x23cm.) — (New gospel studies : 8).
"A translation with introduction and notes
of Geschiedenis en critiek der Marcushypothese
(History and critique of the Marcan hypothesis)
by Hajo Uden Meijboom at the University of Groningen, 1866."
Includes bibliographical references and indexes.
ISBN 0-86554-407-7
1. Bible, N.T. Mark—Criticism, interpretation, etc.
2. Bible, N.T. Mark—Criticism, interpretation, etc.—History—19th century.
3. Synoptic problem.
I. Kiwiet, John, 1925– .   II. Title.   III. Series.
BS2585.2.M43513   1992
226.3'066'09034—dc20   91-32869
                              CIP

Table of Contents

Foreword

The service of bringing important books from the continent of Europe into the mainstream of scholarly discussion within the English-speaking world through translation has largely been performed by the British. But beginning in 1972, with the translation by Robert Kraft and Gerhard Krodel of the second edition of Walter Bauer's *Orthodoxy and Heresy in Earliest Christianity*[1], a considerable share of the initiative, particularly in the specialized field of Christian origins, shifted to the western shores of the Atlantic. In the even more specialized field of the history of gospel criticism, that initiative was matched nine years later with the translation by Donald L. Niewyk of Hans-Herbert Stoldt's *History and Criticism of the Marcan Hypothesis*[2]. Both these German books were published by the eminent house of Vandenhoeck & Ruprecht, Göttingen. In both cases, translation into English has resulted in a more widespread influence for these works. Following the appearance of Stoldt's book in English, the public debate between Professors David Dungan and Howard Kee at the Society of Biblical Literature meetings in New Orleans over whether Stoldt had or had not succeeded in disproving Marcan priority represented a high-water mark in public discussion of the Synoptic Problem.

The prompt attempt of Professor Hans Conzelmann in 1978 to discount the important achievement of Stoldt had been critically rejected on both sides of the Atlantic before the English translation was published.[3]

Meanwhile, however, something else had happened that deserves recording in order to understand how the original nineteenth-century Dutch version of the book before us first came into the twentieth-century discussion, and why, once it did, translation into English was mandated.

At a conference held in Cambridge, England, in August 1979, scholars gathered to discuss a series of papers that, subsequently amplified, was published under the title *New Synoptic Studies: The Cambridge Gospel Conference and*

---

[1]Philadelphia: Fortress Press; original German 1934[1], 1964[2] edited and supplemented by Georg Strecker.

[2]Macon: Mercer University Press, and Edinburgh: T.&.T. Clark; German original, 1977.

[3]See my introduction to Stoldt's *History and Criticism of the Marcan Hypothesis,* xiv-xvii.

Beyond[4] C. M. Tuckett, who participated as an observer in this conference, had recently made known his doubts about the weight Stoldt gives to reaction against Strauss's *Leben Jesu* in explaining the demise of the Griesbach hypothesis. Stoldt, who himself was unable to be present for the conference, prepared a vigorous response in writing to Tuckett. Stoldt's written response lay on a table with other unpublished materials relevant to the theme of the conference.

One of the participants at the conference was Professor K. H. Rengstorf of Germany, who chaired the session where Professor J. D. Kingsbury presented his paper on "The Theology of St. Matthew's Gospel according to the Griesbach Hypothesis." When Rengstorf returned to Münster, he mentioned to his seminar the disagreement between Tuckett and Stoldt over the relevance of the reaction against Strauss for understanding the demise of the Griesbach hypothesis. A doctoral candidate from Holland responded by drawing attention to a little-known work by Hajo Uden Meijboom, which he said would offer support to Stoldt in this matter under dispute. In this way, a book written in Dutch in 1866, which was received virtually stillborn by the wider scholarly world of the time, was rescued from near oblivion by an international German-speaking circle of scholars in Münster, more than a century after its initial publication.

It would be easy to underestimate the prodigious amount of work that has been put into the translation, editing, and publication of this book. It would not be wrong to say that this English version is in significant respects an improvement over the original. This is certainly the case as far as the incomplete bibliographical information given in the footnotes of the original is concerned. Nonetheless, the reader who has access to the Dutch original and who has a mastery of that language will no doubt find it possible at not a few points (though none of crucial importance) to find the original less explicit than Kiwiet has made it. For there are places in Meijboom's text where Professor Kiwiet, with the help of colleagues whose technical expertise supplemented his own, had to amplify in order to make clear the mind of the author. On the whole, however, this translation gives the reader of English a reliable working knowledge of a most remarkable book, which to read will certainly lead one to ponder how this book could have gone unattended until now.

For example, although it offers a devastating analysis of Holtzmann's *Die synoptischen Evangelien. Ihr Ursprung und geschichtlicher Charakter*[5], a careful examination of the Berufungs-Akten (appointment documents) preserved in the archives of Strasbourg University, indicates that if this scholarly exposé of the unscientific character of Holtzmann's work was known in Strasbourg and Berlin, it was completely ignored in all official correspondence. Stoldt exposed the

---

[4]Ed. William R. Farmer (Macon: Mercer University Press, 1983).
[5](Leipzig: Verlag von Wilhelm Engelman, 1863).

critically untenable character of Holtzmann's book in 1977, but until Professor Rengstorf brought attention to Meijboom, contemporary students of nineteenth-century Gospel criticism did not know that this had been done quite independently as early as 1866, eight full years before Holtzmann received the prestigious appointment to Strasbourg.

At a high-level, small-scale conference bringing together for the first time historians at German universities in the nineteenth century with experts on the history of biblical criticism, a sociohistorical discussion of Holtzmann's appointment was initiated. The venue for this conference on "Kulturpolitik and the Entrenchment of Marcan Primacy in the German Universities 1860–1914" was St. Vincent's College in Latrobe, Pennsylvania, and the year was 1990. Professor Graf Reventlow presented a paper on Holtzmann and gave a preliminary report on the correspondence between Berlin and Strasbourg.

This discussion was continued at a follow-up conference held at Bochum University in Germany in 1992, where important additional light was thrown on the social history of nineteenth-century Gospel criticism in Germany. At this conference, Meijboom's book played an even wider role than at Latrobe, through a paper by Professor David Peabody on the work of key members of the French school of Gospel criticism in Strasbourg.

Meijboom's contemporary account of the continental discussion of the source question in Gospel studies is revolutionizing our twentieth-century understanding of nineteenth-century developments. No less important is the light his work casts on the text of Mark, including, among other topics, Meijboom's theological assessment of the Gospel. There are few, if any, twentieth-century treatments of Mark that are more refreshing or intellectually and theologically insightful than the work of this brilliant young Dutch scholar.

Like a book born out of due time, Meijboom's work has been largely overlooked. Now, thanks to Professor Kiwiet's prolonged labor of love, this book is being reborn. Its publication in the monograph series New Gospel Studies is long awaited and most welcome.

Dallas, Texas
October 1992

William R. Farmer

Translator's Preface

When William Farmer suggested a translation of Meijboom's document in 1980, I did not realize the implications. Not only was the Dutch text more than a hundred years old, but also its composition was cryptic in nature. I had to divide the materials into paragraphs and develop an outline in order to be able to follow Meijboom's line of thought. In the present version below, this outline precedes the translation and appears in bold type or captions throughout the text. Also, I had to add connecting sentences in order to assist the reader in understanding. These inserts are clearly marked by brackets ([. . .]) so the critical scholar can assess the correctness of the connecting statements. I have rendered the New Testament quotes in Greek text wherever necessary[1] and followed the Revised Standard Version for text translations.

The historical introduction to the issue of the Marcan hypothesis and to Meijboom as a contemporary observer was prepared originally for lectures at Southern Methodist University in Dallas as well as at Southwestern Baptist Theological Seminary in Fort Worth. It is appropriate to express a few words of appreciation to all those colleagues and friends who had a share in this project.

First of all, William R. Farmer should be recognized as the initiator and patient supporter of this project. Many Saturdays were spent in careful analysis of Meijboom's text. In close coordination with Dr. Farmer, Professor David L. Dungan should be mentioned. As executive secretary of the International Institute for the Renewal of Gospel Studies, he was instrumental in providing financial assistance during the initial stages of this project. During those initial stages, Dr. W. Nijenhuis of the University of Groningen was helpful in unearthing biographical details concerning Dr. Hajo Uden Meijboom. Several scholars read all or part of Meijboom's text in translation, including Dr. Lorin L. Cranford and Dr.

---

[1][Readers consulting the Greek N.T. occasionally will note slight discrepancies between the Greek as cited by Meijboom and as occurring in current editions. In 1866, of course, Meijboom would probably have used some critical edition of the Stephanus/Elzevir printed Greek text. Current texts, based on much broader manuscript evidence, are often at variance with the former standard texts. For example, while current texts almost always opt for the form $\epsilon\mathring{\upsilon}\theta\mathring{\upsilon}\varsigma$ in Mark, Stephanus/Elzevir almost invariably (36 of 38 occurrences, 4 other times omitting the word altogether) chose $\epsilon\mathring{\upsilon}\theta\acute{\epsilon}\omega\varsigma$. (The change regarding this particular variant [$\epsilon\mathring{\upsilon}\theta\mathring{\upsilon}\varsigma$→$\epsilon\mathring{\upsilon}\theta\acute{\epsilon}\omega\varsigma$] occurred with the editions of Tregelles [1857–1879] and Tischendorf [1869–1872], too late for Meijboom's use in 1866.) Such variations between former and present critical texts, however, affect Meijboom's argument not at all. (See also 167n.21, below.) —ed.]

E. Earle Ellis, both professors of New Testament at Southwestern Baptist Theological Seminary; the late Dr. John Jansen of the Austin Presbyterian Seminary in Austin, Texas; Dr. Frans Neirynck, dean and professor at the University of Leuven, Belgium; Dom Bernard Orchard O.S.B. of Ealing Abbey, London; and Dr. David B. Peabody of Nebraska Wesleyan University. Dr. Karl E. Snyder, emeritus professor of English at the Texas Christian University in Fort Worth, Texas, went over the translated text in order to protect the fine nuances of English style.

When a project covers such a span of time several secretaries could be mentioned for their share. I trust they will not mind I only mention my recent secretaries, Mrs. Laura P. Cook and Miss Amy McNeil, who have retyped the complete text incorporating the numerous corrections. Since most of the research and translation had to be done "after hours" the burden was carried by my family as well. My wife, Margaret, has faithfully dedicated her time and interest to projects and friends allowing me to plod through this intricate material. Meijboom closed his study with the hope that there might be at least one reader who would read his complete manuscript. After his book fell into oblivion for more than a century I, at least, have read every sentence of his book several times. I hope that many other readers will benefit from this contemporary report on a major theological battle during the nineteenth century.

The fact that sociopolitical and philosophical factors were so dominant in religious debate should not deter us from active involvement in it during our own day. It seems to me an implication of the incarnation that the Spirit of God is communicated to us through the realities of human existence. We would not have the normative Christological creeds had it not been for the political tensions during the early years of the Constantinian empire. Not only political factors have inspired theologians and dogmaticians, also socioeconomic issues, cultural developments, and scientific discoveries have played a role in adjustments of biblical interpretation. If the Gospel addresses the total man, we should not expect otherwise in our own history. We do have the obligation, however, to review the human accretions to divine revelation. The issue of the so-called "Two-Document Hypothesis," for example, may be up for review within a new historical context.[2]

Southwestern Baptist Theological Seminary   *John J. Kiwiet*
Fort Worth, Texas   Professor of Theology

---

[2][In English publications Meijboom's name is often anglicized as *Meyboom* (see the CIP data on p. iv, above). Students researching English publications, then, should search for *Meyboom*. In the present text, the spelling *Meijboom* is retained throughout. —ed.]

Translator's Introduction

HISTORICAL INTRODUCTION TO THE DEBATE REGARDING THE SEQUENCE OF THE SYNOPTIC GOSPELS

The synoptic problem has vehemently disturbed the minds of biblical scholars ever since the controversial publication of *Das Leben Jesu, kritisch bearbeitet* by David Friedrich Strauss in 1835–1836 (ET *The Life of Jesus Critically Examined,* 1846). The author compared the reaction to his book to "a wailing of terrified women after hearing the sound of a gunshot in their vicinity."[1] Even deep into the American frontier, revival preachers for more than a century afterward would blast the supposed demonic attack of higher criticism. Strauss not only questioned the historical data of the New Testament, but its theological content as well. The Gospel, he contended, did not give the message of Jesus in the first place, but rather the historical interpretations of the authors.

Introduction

Crucial to this confrontation was the "two-document hypothesis," also called the "Marcan hypothesis." The opponents of the Tübingen School, which followed Strauss, saw in this hypothesis a valid argument for the historicity of the data presented by the synoptic gospels. They interpreted a statement by Papias[2] as a reference to two historic documents, namely an earlier form of Mark and a *Logia* ("Sayings") document, with which the later hypothetical *Quelle* ("Source") or Q-document is sometimes identified. Thus the Marcan hypothesis claimed to defend the historical reliability of the New Testament. This interpretation of history clashed with that of the Tübingen school, whose adherents attempted to discover the historical tendencies of the gospel writers, a view later described as "Tendency Criticism."

---

[1]See below, Hajo U. Meijboom, "History and Critique of the Marcan Hypothesis," 11.
[2]See below, Meijboom, "History and Critique," 17, cf. 67ff.

Over against a documentary history came a doctrinal history, which reflected the situation during the decades following the cross and the resurrection. The Hegelian dialectic provided a convenient pattern for this history, as Professor Bo Reicke has described.[3] The Jewish original Gospel of Matthew was counteracted by the Hellenistic Gospel of Luke, which Mark—as the new catholic gospel—then synthesized.

Conservative scholars welcomed Marcan priority, while liberal theologians, valuing the ethical norms of the Sermon on the Mount, claimed traditional Matthean priority. The debate was fanned by the sociopolitical tensions of early mid-nineteenth-century Germany. Conservative forces wanted to maintain and extend the Prussian establishment, while liberal forces hoped to achieve a more democratic pattern of government and society. Originally the center of the debate was the newly established University of Berlin, founded by the Prussian King Friedrich Wilhelm III in order to revamp the German spirit by establishing a bulwark against the rising revolutionary tide of the French Revolution. Two of the leading protagonists were Georg F. W. Hegel and Friedrich E. D. Schleiermacher.

The Royal University of Berlin
The Politics of Reaction, 1810–1835

It should not be difficult, then, to trace the philosophical and political factors affecting the German debate regarding the otherwise purely historical-theological issue of the sequence of the Gospels. For the German intelligentsia the nineteenth century began with a sequence of unsettling events. The French Revolution of 1789, which initially seemed a mere thunderstorm on the horizon, became a dramatic reality with the advance of the audacious and young emperor Napoleon into Germany.[4] Hegel described his feelings of awe and fear as he watched this little but powerful man ride into Jena in the year 1806.[5] Hegel had his completed manuscript on the *Phenomenon of the Spirit* in his coat pocket and became convinced more than ever of the power of the Spirit at work in man. That same

---

[3]See Bo Reicke, "From Strauss to Holtzmann and Meijboom," *Novum Testamentum* 39/1 (1987): 6, 7.

[4]Napoleon Bonaparte proclaimed himself emperor of the French in 1804; he defeated the Austro-Russian forces in the battle of Austerlitz in 1805; Prussia declared war on France in 1806 and was defeated by Napoleon that same year at Jena and Auerstädt. Napoleon entered Berlin victoriously. Also in 1806 Napoleon decreed the official end of the Holy Roman Empire by forcing Francis II, last Holy Roman emperor and emperor of Austria, to become King Francis I of Austria.

[5]Hans Küng, *Does God Exist. An Answer for Today* (New York: Doubleday & Company, 1980) 144.

year Napoleon entered Berlin; the proud Prussians had been defeated and the Holy Roman Empire under Francis II in Vienna had formally come to an end.

The Prussians felt deeply humiliated by the devastating defeat in Jena on 14 October 1806. During that very year a number of militant clergymen took the initiative in rallying the citizens to volunteer for the hastily organized national guard, the "Landwehr." Surprisingly, the romantic Friedrich Schleiermacher volunteered for the army. Since he was not accepted as a soldier, he turned to volunteer services and used his pulpit for the national cause. He was called the "first great political preacher of the Germans since Luther."[6] Napoleon's troops were defeated in Leipzig in 1813 and two years later thirty-nine states united in Vienna as the German Federation.[7]

Since there was little governmental organization and since there were no political parties,[8] the universities were the only agencies to sort out the amalgam of Enlightenment, revolution, politics, and religion. In most towns church buildings were the only gathering places for larger meetings, while of course taverns remained the places for small talk and debate.[9] Universities mostly had only a few halls available in various parts of the town. The Prussian king, Friedrich Wilhelm III, converted his court library into the later famous Royal University of Berlin during the year 1810. He invited men of renown for the purpose of revitalizing the German spirit.[10] Friedrich Ernst Daniel Schleiermacher became the first dean of the theological faculty, while Georg Wilhelm Friedrich Hegel was called in 1818 to lay the philosophical foundations of a stable social order.[11]

Both Schleiermacher and Hegel contributed to the issue of gospel history. Although they did not directly take sides among the emerging polarities, these

---

[6]Statement by Schleiermacher's contemporary, Bishop R. F. Eylert, as quoted in Robert M. Bigler, *The Politics of German Protestantism: The Rise of the Protestant Church Elite in Prussia, 1815–1848* (Berkeley: University of California Press, 1972) 29.

[7]For the above information, see Bigler, *The Politics of German Protestantism,* 19-29.

[8]The first political fraternity consisted of a group of aristocrats gathering around the Gerlach brothers in the Maikäferei Club in 1815. See Jacques Droz, *Europe between Revolutions, 1815–1848* (New York: Harper & Row, 1967) 14; see also Bigler, *The Politics of German Protestantism,* 78.

[9]Edward Robinson, professor at Andover Theological Seminary, in the journal of which he was founding editor, published an eyewitness report about university education in Germany, in which he explained that the pulpit and lectern were the only opportunities for expression of public opinion since courts and senate were conducted behind closed doors; see *American Biblical Repository* (ABR)1/1-4 (1831): 41.

[10]Robinson, ABR 1/1-4 (1831): 19.

[11]One of Hegel's first books published after 1818 was his *Naturrecht und Staatswissenschaft im Grundrisse* (1821; 2nd ed. as *Grundlinien der Philosophie des Rechts,* ed. E. Gans, 1833; ET *The Philosophy of Right,* 1896ff.). In this publication Hegel sought to lay the theoretical foundation for a stable social order.

two Berlin professors caused or encouraged various theological tensions with
their different approaches to history. Schleiermacher searched for concrete historical data, as evidenced in his study of the Papias statement concerning the
"Logia." He understood "Logia" to mean a "collection of words" of Jesus rather
a message of Jesus in general.[12] With Schleiermacher begins the search for documents leading ultimately to the two-document hypothesis. Since an early edition
of Mark was the second "source" document, this theory was also called the
"Marcan Hypothesis."[13]

Hegel, on the other hand, recommended his dialectical philosophy as a hermeneutical key for each area and aspect of history. Consequently, the beginnings
of Christianity and of the gospels were defined in a dialectic manner, all during
the nineteenth century up until Adolf von Harnack's *Das Wesen des Christen-
tums* in 1900.[14] The three synoptic[15] gospels were an easy target for such dialectic speculation. In antithetical fashion one gospel would be written in opposition
to another, while the third would synthesize the two opponents. This deductive
method led to an affirmation of Matthean priority, which had been the traditional
conviction since Augustine.

The issue of Matthean or Marcan priority entailed a decisive sociopolitical
stance hotly debated during the crucial decades preceding the institution in 1870
of the united German Empire under the chancellor Otto von Bismarck. Confront-
ing each other were the historical and the Hegelian approach, inductive over
against deductive reasoning.[16] The political and religious conservatives identified
with the historical-inductive approach. They affirmed Marcan priority, since it

---

[12]F. D. E. Schleiermacher, "Über die Zeugnisse des Papias von unseren beiden ersten
Evangelien," *Theologische Studien und Kritiken* 5 (1832): 735-68. Schleiermacher's ideas
were extended in 1835 by Karl Lachmann, who combined the logia concept with Lessing's hypothesis of an original gospel preceding the Synoptics. See William R. Farmer,
The Synoptic Problem: A Critical Analysis (New York: Macmillan, 1964; corr. rpt. Dills-
boro NC: Western NC Press; distr. Mercer University Press, 1976) 3-17.

[13]In 1838 two representatives broached this hypothesis almost simultaneously: Christian Hermann Weisse (1801-1866), in *Die evangelische Geschichte kritisch und philosophisch bearbeitet (The Gospel History Critically and Philosophically Interpreted)*, 2 vols.
(Leipzig: Breitkopf und Härtel, 1838); and Christian Gottlob Wilke (1786-1854), in *Der
Urevangelist, oder, exegetisch kritische Untersuchung über das Verwandtschaftsverhältniss der drei ersten Evangelien (The Ur-Evangelist, or an Exegetical-Critical Investigation
of the Interrelatedness of the Three First Gospels)* (Dresden and Leipzig: Gerhard
Fleischer, 1838). For details see Hans-Herbert Stoldt, *History and Criticism of the Marcan
Hypothesis,* trans. Donald L. Niewyk (Macon GA: Mercer University Press, 1980) 27-68;
see also below, Meijboom, "History and Critique," 12ff. and 20ff.

[14](Leipzig, 1900); translated as *What Is Christianity* (London, 1901).

[15]Johann Jakob Griesbach (1745-1812) formulated the concept of "synopse" and
coined the term "synopsis" sometime before 1774; see Stoldt, *History and Criticism,* 2.

[16]Reicke, "From Strauss to Holtzmann and Meijboom," 1-21.

seemed the earliest and most concise of the gospels. The Hegelian dialectic was taken up by the politically progressive minds who tended to follow a Matthean priority. Also the more socially relevant Matthean Sermon on the Mount appealed to the liberal mind. But after 1870 liberals shifted and began to embrace the Marcan hypothesis as Matthew became identified with ultramontanism. Some liberals such as Hilgenfeld and Zeller continued to hold to Matthean priority. And eventually, only two scholars, and they of a conservative disposition, publicly rejected Marcan primacy, namely, Adolf Schlatter and Theodor von Zahn.[17]

The Tübingen School
The Politics of Change, 1835–1850

The nationalistic movement was especially strong in the universities. In Jena a national student organization was formed under the influence of one of the professors. In October 1817 they organized the Wartburg festival in celebration of the victory over Napoleon and of the anniversary of Luther's posting of his ninety-five theses. Soon this movement got out of hand. In 1819 one of their radical members, Karl Sand, murdered the reactionary poet August Kotzebue. A sudden and long-range reaction by the government followed. The national student movement was dissolved, inspectors were appointed at the universities, and professors were dismissed. The democratic constitutions of various German states were revoked by the Austrian imperial government, especially in the Rhineland area. The culmination was the dissolution of the Hannover constitution, where seven resisting professors of the University of Göttingen were dismissed. Among these was Heinrich Ewald, who later played a theologically conservative role in the promotion of the Marcan Hypothesis.[18]

Against this backdrop the publication of David Friedrich Strauss's *Life of Jesus* in 1835 was experienced as an exploding bombshell not only in Württemberg, where Tübingen was located, but throughout all Germany. The Pietist professor August Tholuck concluded that the mythical hermeneutics of Strauss reflected the rebellious spirit of the times, "respecting no God in heaven and no rulers on earth."[19] Strauss himself (as mentioned above) described the reaction

---

[17]Stoldt, *History and Criticism,* 238; Farmer, "State *Interesse* and Marcan Primacy, 1860–1914," forthcoming in Frans Neirynck Festschrift (Leuven, Belgium: Peeters), refers to the importance of "ultramontanism" in winning support for Marcan primacy.

[18]The above information was taken from Droz, *Europe between Revolutions, 1815–1848,* 143-59; see also Marilyn Chapin Massey, *Christ Unmasked: The Meaning of the Life of Jesus in German Politics* (Chapel Hill: University of North Carolina Press, 1983) 37-55.

[19]Bigler, *The Politics of German Protestantism,* 118.

to his publication as "the wailing of terrified women after hearing the sound of a gunshot in their vicinity."[20] This characterization of the response shows Strauss's scorn toward his opponents. According to Strauss, the theologians of his day did not have the courage to be consistent in their biblical criticism.

The Old Tübingen School had, indeed, practiced a form of literary criticism. Its founder, Gottlob Christian Storr (1746–1805), had also been the first to deal theologically with the synoptic problem.[21] His objective had been "to substantiate the authority of the Bible through historical investigation and reasoned argument," according to Harris in his study of the Tübingen School.[22] In order to achieve this, Storr had suggested the priority of Mark as early as 1794, because it seemed to him the most "rational" gospel. Mark leaves off the supposedly mythical infancy stories, including the virgin birth, as well as the resurrection appearances to the disciples. Even so, the Württembergers who were largely pietistic in their beliefs were yet proud of their university and its sophisticated theological faculty.[23] There was a peaceful coexistence between rationalists and Pietists, because the former merely wanted to rationalize the miraculous rather than to reject it.[24] A colleague of Storr was Ernst Gottlieb Bengel, the grandson of the devout biblical expositor Johann Albrecht Bengel.

Strauss was born, raised, and educated in Württemberg.[25] He reacted, however, to rationalism as well as to Pietism. For Strauss rationalism did not take the Bible seriously, while Pietism repudiated a sound reasonable approach. When Strauss graduated from the University of Tübingen he was "primus" among the students. Yet he was still searching for a more viable exegesis of the Scriptures. During a brief vicariate in the village of Klein-Ingersheim he faced the reality of the economic and political situation and experienced how little a rationalist or pietist message could do in the given circumstances. Horton Harris quotes a sample of one of his sermons in which Strauss attempted to comfort the farmers who had lost their grape crop due to a hailstorm.

---

[20]In the preface to the 2nd ed. of his *Life of Jesus,* and as mentioned in Meijboom, "History and Critique," below, 11 and 11n.2.

[21]See Stoldt, *History and Criticism,* 137, where two of Storr's relevant books are cited: *Über den Zweck der evangelischen Geschichte und der Briefe Johannis (On the aim of the gospel history and the letters of John*; Tübingen, 1786; ²1810), and *De fonte evangeliorum Matthaei et Lucae (Regarding the Sources of the Gospels of Matthew and Luke*; Tübingen, 1794). Along with Göttingen's J. B. Koppe (1782), Storr (before 1786) was one of the first to advocate Marcan priority.

[22]Horton Harris, *The Tübingen School* (Oxford: Clarendon Press, 1975) 16.

[23]See Bigler, *The Politics of German Protestantism,* 15.

[24]Horton Harris, *David Friedrich Strauss and His Theology* (Cambridge: University Press, 1973) 42.

[25]Harris, *Strauss,* 1-26.

Yes, my friends, better to perish from lack of earthly bread than to suffer from a lack of heavenly manna, the word of God! Better to go without the fruit of our vineyards than the spiritual drink from the rock, which is Christ! And so has it happened to you: The Lord has struck your fields, but not so that you must hunger; and he has preserved for you his word and his Church: therefore with quickened thankfulness let us celebrate this Church festival and close the old Church year! Amen.[26]

After only nine months in the ministry Strauss left for Berlin in order to hear Schleiermacher, and especially Hegel. Both professors attempted to harmonize the Scriptures with modern insight. Schleiermacher did this by advocating an existential historical hermeneutic, while Hegel attempted to develop a dialectic interpretation which would allow for the interaction of the rational and the pietistic or organic approach. Strauss heard only two lectures by Hegel. A few days later his revered professor was snatched away by cholera. Strauss studied his books and joined the young Hegelians in their debates. It was during these discussions that his *Life of Jesus* was conceived.[27]

For Strauss, Jesus represented the divine incarnation, the Spirit in human form. The gospels may not reflect accurate historical data, but the divine-human event as experienced in the early church was reliably reflected in these sacred texts. The only way the biblical authors could give expression to their elation was through mythical narrative and through miracle stories. Marilyn Chapin Massey concluded that "Strauss asked not about the history of the stories but simply whether the stories themselves were historical."[28] For Strauss the historical context of the writers and their documents was of primary importance rather than the facts presented in these gospels.

Marilyn Massey has portrayed in detail the political implications of the Hegelian-mythical approach of David Friedrich Strauss. By rejecting the historical accuracy of the gospels Strauss rejected the foundation of Christian culture in general and of the German nation in particular. He questioned the unity of "Throne and Altar." Hegel had intended to create a divine rationale for the monarchy. As God had become human so the monarch was to be a unifying center. Strauss, however, described himself as a left-wing Hegelian in beginning from below.[29] Politically this translated into beginning with democracy as the unifying principle. Strauss was compared with the sensational novelist Karl Gutzkow, who

---

[26]Harris, *Strauss,* 26. Karl Marx in 1835 had a similar interpretation of suffering before he became a radical atheist in 1841; see Küng, *Does God Exist,* 219.

[27]Massey, *Christ Unmasked,* 14.

[28]Ibid.

[29]Strauss derived the terms "right" and "left" from the French parliament; see Massey, *Christ Unmasked,* 31.

was briefly imprisoned after being convicted of undermining the social and political order by injudicious statements in his journal. Gutzkow's novel entitled *Wally, the Skeptic* was published in 1835, the same year as Strauss's *Life of Jesus.* [30]

Strauss was forced into obscurity, while his teacher Ferdinand Christian Baur applied the Hegelian mythical approach to gospel history. Baur's approach was called the method of "Tendency Criticism" and was promulgated in the Tübingen yearbooks. In his *Paul the Apostle of Jesus Christ* (1845) he applied this method to the Pauline literature. In one of his articles Baur defined his method as follows.

> Since all history is transmitted to us by way of the author who recounts it, the primary question is not to what degree some story informs us about reality, but in what relation this story stands to the consciousness of the author. Through the mediation of the author the historical data become for us objects of research, which is true also for the criticism of Gospel history.[31]

Basically Baur affirmed the position of Strauss, his former student and temporary colleague at Tübingen University. Together they carried the torch of Hegelian idealism. Baur even called this the historic approach, possibly to appease his opponents. He was, however, very clear in not subscribing to "objective" history but to the text-critical history of the documents. Furthermore the Tübingen School remained faithful to the Griesbach hypothesis, which assigned priority to Matthew. The antithesis to Matthew was found in the Gospel of Luke, while Mark established their synthesis.[32] Thus, at this time liberal theologians were associated with the priority of Matthew.

The Göttingen School
The Politics of Restoration, 1850–1870

During the 1840s a feud erupted between the Tübingers and the Göttingen school.[33] The principal opponents were Heinrich Ewald and F. C. Baur. Ewald

---

[30]Massey, *Christ Unmasked,* 6; Gutzkow, *Wally, die Zweiflerin* (repr. Göttingen: Vandenhoeck and Ruprecht, 1965).

[31]Meijboom, "History and Critique," below, 34.

[32]Harris, *The Tübingen School,* 210-12. Adolf von Hilgenfeld from Jena adhered to Matthean priority, but considered Mark the second Gospel; see Farmer, *The Synoptic Problem,* 29-30.

[33]The University of Göttingen was founded by Prime Minister G. A. von Münchhausen in 1737. The university soon became the major German institution for political law.

had been professor of oriental languages at Göttingen since 1831, but was dismissed along with six other professors in 1837.[34] Under pressure of the Austrian chancellor von Metternich several states were forced to repeal their liberal constitutions which had been established since Napoleon. Ewald and his colleagues had protested and were dismissed. Some months later he was accepted at the Tübingen University in the philosophy faculty and in 1841 in the theology faculty. Also in Tübingen Ewald was deeply involved in politics. The objects of his criticism were the Catholics, Pietistic orthodoxy, and the Tübingen School of Baur. In 1848 Ewald returned to Göttingen from where he continued his crusade against Tübingen.

Within two years Ewald published a translation and commentary on the Synoptic Gospels in which he strongly reacted to the Tübingen School. Meijboom quotes Ewald: "The Tübingen School was, indeed, like Satan coming to earth, but then not in order to test the devout Job but rather as a curse on a sinful generation."[35] Ewald's vituperative attacks were not always taken seriously but his persistent criticism drew the attention of the orthodox church leaders and of the leading figures in government. According to Horton Harris, Ewald's attitude may have impeded the spreading of the Tübingen School to England.[36]

Ewald was an advocate of the Marcan hypothesis, although in the context of a complex process. According to Ewald, the synoptic development went through eight stages. Within these stages the Gospel of Mark was the first "original work" which had used some sources. Ewald had no historical data for his theory, but rather referred to the literary qualifications of graphic imagery as proof of originality. Meijboom quotes one of Ewald's extravagant utterances regarding the Gospel of Mark: nowhere else is found to the same degree "this loveliness of fresh flowers, this pure vigorous vitality of the materials."[37] In reaction to the so-called "Tübingen hypothesis," Ewald did not tolerate any theological tendency of the authors to be considered. For Ewald the relation of Mark to Peter was insignificant, and he demoted Luke to the position of an

---

Before the French revolution its students came from the lower and higher nobility. During the 19th century Göttingen University became the school for government administrators, among whom was also the famous Otto von Bismarck. Also because its rulers, the house of Hannover, had resided in England since 1714, the university could maintain a mediate position in politics as well as in theology. See *Religion in Geschichte und Gegenwart* (RGG) (Tübingen: J. C. B. Mohr, 1958) cols. 1676-78; see also Bernd Moeller, *Theologie in Göttingen* (Göttingen: Vandenhoeck and Ruprecht, 1987) 412.

[34]See Harris, *The Tübingen School,* 43-48.

[35]Meijboom, "History and Critique," below, 39.

[36]Harris, *The Tübingen School,* 48. For the influence of Germany's criticism of the gospels on England, see Farmer, *The Synoptic Problem,* 48-198.

[37]Meijboom, "History and Critique," below, 41.

editor adding only a few remarks to materials developed previously. The Gospels were not subjective accounts but rather collections of objective sources. Only Mark, Ewald contended, was the "pure archetype among the early Evangelists."[38]

Ewald's work was imbedded in political and personal conflict. At that time, professors were political authorities and the churches were considered branches of the government.[39] Because of political implications, Baur could not get a position in Berlin, where he would have loved to gain an appointment. Ewald was embroiled in politics also. Political polarities followed the originally French distinction of the left wing being democratic and right wing being aristocratic or monarchial. The Synoptic theories reflected this polarity by the two general options of Matthean or Marcan priority. We see an illustration of the political validity of these options in the career of Albrecht Ritschl. His change from Tübingen via Bonn to Göttingen is equally indicated by a shift from Matthean to Marcan priority.

Ritschl[40] started out as an enthusiastic member of the Tübingen School. At age 23 he already had studied all the writings of F. C. Baur, and he was very excited over being allowed some time for study in Tübingen itself. It was during the winter of 1845–1846 that Ritschl worked on his first book, *The Gospel of Marcion and the Canonical Gospel of Luke* (1846). In this publication he follows Baur's "historical approach" of the dialectical tension between Jews and Gentiles resulting in the prominence of Luke as a reconciler.[41]

When Baur's *Paul the Apostle of Jesus Christ* appeared in 1845, Ritschl felt increasingly dissatisfied with the Tübingen perspective. His critical review of this book caused a definite rift between him and Tübingen's patriarch F. C. Baur. This criticism resulted in an open clash of opinion in Ritschl's next publication, *The Origin of the Early Catholic Church* (1850). Soon after, Ritschl accepted a position at the University of Bonn, where in 1857 he declared his final break with the Tübingers. During that year, a revised edition of his *Origin of the Early Catholic Church* was published, in which his radical break with Tübingen was symbolized by a declaration of his shift to Marcan priority.

In 1864 Ritschl was called to Göttingen as professor of theology. For a period of twenty-five years he was able to build his own "School," which was soon called the "Ritschlian School." Characteristic of the Ritschlian school of thought was a definite distinction between faith and reason, or between value

---

[38]Meijboom, "History and Critique," below, 43.
[39]Bigler, *The Politics of German Protestantism,* 20; Massey, *Christ Unmasked,* 36.
[40]See Harris, *The Tübingen School,* 101-12.
[41]The first publication of this idea was in an article in 1831: F. C. Baur, "Die Christuspartei in der korinthischen Gemeinde," *Tübingen Zeitschrift für Theologie* 5 (1831): 61-206.

judgments and causal judgments. For Ritschl, attempts by the Hegelians to join philosophy and faith had failed. The Hegelians had missed the genuinely religious motivations in the authors of the Scriptures. A second characteristic of the Ritschlian school was its corporate conception of the Christian life and message. Where the Tübingers had dwelt exclusively on individual leaders of the Early Church with their tendentious opinions, Ritschl dwelt on movements and groups of Christians.

Finally Ritschl turned his back on the search for self-consciousness which had so occupied the Idealist theologians and philosophers. Instead, Ritschl underscored the ethical and social aspects of the Scriptures. By so doing he distanced himself from direct involvement in the politics of his day. His theology was called a mediating theology, choosing neither aristocracy nor democracy but rather the well-being of mankind under any political circumstances.

The dictatorial German chancellor Otto von Bismarck was educated at Göttingen. With him a new era dawned for the German nation. Bismarck's objective was more pragmatic in that he used mainly military forces for gaining political power rather than working with philosophical or theological ideas.[42] The new era chose the secular power of the army. A forty-year period of aggressive ideological competition of forces was brought to a close. The academy had attempted to use Hegelian ideology for a promotion of democratic ideals. By contrast the reactionary school of Marcan priority came to the fore in support of aristocracy. Bismarck, however, chose to achieve national unity through "blood and iron."

After 1870 the discussion of the history of the gospels no longer had the same political implications. The final study in Germany was the eclectic analysis of Heinrich Julius Holtzmann in 1863. Since Holtzmann adhered to Marcan priority, this theory prevailed in the succeeding years and was adopted widely, also outside Germany. In a detailed publication Holtzmann summarized the various theories over the preceding eighty years and proposed to select the best of each theory. He wanted to be guided by the text itself rather than by extraneous theories. Yet Holtzmann could not completely disengage himself from the Tübingen perspective. The gospels could not be detached completely from the conflicting parties in the early church. Holtzmann, however, wrote as if the major battle was

---

[42]Otto von Bismarck (1815–1898) underwent a spiritual renewal in 1846 and married a woman from Pietist circles, Johanna von Puttkamer. During his chancellorship (1871–1890) he aimed for a separation of church and state, which evoked the resistance of his emperor Wilhelm I. Bismarck became known for his "Kulturkampf" (1872ff.) against the political power of the Roman Catholic Church. See RGG (1958) cols. 1312-15, and Bigler, *The Politics of German Protestantism,* 142. With the death of F. C. Baur in 1860 the driving force of the Tübingen School had been put to rest. Furthermore, Baur's successor Karl Weizsäcker had adopted, like Holtzmann, the two-document hypothesis; see Farmer, *The Synoptic Problem,* 55.

over. The authors of the gospels had the same pragmatic mindset as their German interpreter. Holtzmann spent most of his time in tracing technical issues, such as the peculiarity of the language of the gospels, and in explaining the reason for double accounts in one gospel.[43]

The Renewed Debate Regarding the History of the Gospels

During the 1960s, the synoptic problem received renewed attention by William R. Farmer who concentrated on discussions by English theologians, especially William Sanday and B. H. Streeter.[44] In 1977 Hans-Herbert Stoldt provided a polemical history and critique of the Marcan hypothesis. Stoldt's conclusion was that "The Marcan hypothesis . . . grew out of theological commitment. It is a theologumenon."[45] During recent years three volumes on this subject were written by Bernard Orchard, his Griesbach Solution to the Synoptic Question trilogy.[46] Some years ago an unpublished dissertation in the Dutch language was discovered at the University of Munich. The author, Hajo Uden Meijboom (anglicized as Meyboom), defended this dissertation for the theological faculty in Groningen, the Netherlands, in 1866. Since other concerns demanded attention, Meijboom's dissertation was forgotten.

In his dissertation, Meijboom traced the interuniversity conflicts influencing the debate on gospel history in Germany and he assumed similar tensions among the authors of the gospels. Since the Dutch sociological and theological context was similar to that of Germany, Meijboom's study can be considered a knowledgeable eyewitness report. As Meijboom was not involved in the political issues of Germany, he could write with a certain objectivity and, given the date of his dissertation, he could include the synthesis of the German discussion by Heinrich Holtzmann in 1863.[47] By this time all the major questions had been raised while

---

[43]See Farmer, *The Synoptic Problem*, 36-47, and Meijboom, "History and Critique," below, 71ff.

[44]See "The Intellectual Climate," in Farmer, *The Synoptic Problem*, 178-90.

[45]Farmer's publication was in 1964; Stoldt's German original was published in 1977 as *Geschichte und Kritik der Markus Hypothese* (Göttingen: Vandenhoeck & Ruprecht) and translated in 1980—see above, p. xii, nn.12, 13.

[46]Bernard Orchard, *Matthew, Luke & Mark*, GSSQ 1 (Greater Manchester: Koinonia Press, 1976; [2]1977); idem, *A Synopsis of the Four Gospels in a New Translation, Arranged according to the Two-Gospel Hypothesis*, GSSQ 2 (Macon GA: Mercer University Press; Edinburgh: T. & T. Clark, 1982 (*A Synopsis of the Four Gospels in Greek* [Edinburgh: T. & T. Clark; Macon GA: Mercer University Press, 1983]); idem, with Harold Riley, *The Order of the Synoptics: Why Three Synoptic Gospels?* GSSQ 3 (Macon GA: Mercer University Press, 1987).

[47]See Farmer, "The Holtzmannian Synthesis," *The Synoptic Problem*, 36- 47.

at the same time the sociological implications were still burning issues. Furthermore, Meijboom included the discussion in France which, even until the present time, has escaped the attention of writers in the field of gospel history.

Meijboom was born in 1842 when F. C. Baur, at the peak of his career, was rector of the University of Tübingen delivering the silver jubilee address on the accession of King Wilhelm I to the throne of Württemberg.[48] The young Meijboom was raised in a pastor's home in the northern part of the Netherlands.[49] His father was a prominent theologian actively participating in the ecclesiastical affairs of the nation. After his studies at the gymnasium in Assen and at the Athenaeum in Amsterdam, Meijboom went to the University of Groningen for his graduate studies. In 1866, at age twenty-four, he defended his doctor's dissertation on the "History and Critique of the Marcan Hypothesis." Then, following twenty-five years of ministry in three congregations,[50] he was elected to the theological faculty of the University of Groningen, where he served for twenty years as professor of church history, theological encyclopaedics, and ethics.

Meijboom had a great zeal for educating the common man in religion and social ethics. He worked for the establishment of libraries and organizations for the underprivileged. His twenty popular books and brochures included textbooks for Bible study in the second grade as well as for high school age; he wrote essays on life insurance, and in 1869, wrote about reconciliation with Rome; he edited a New Testament translation for laymen provided with explanatory observations.

During his twenty-one years of retirement, Meijboom was deeply involved in editing and translating a fifty-volume series on the Church Fathers. His own translations included the Apologists, Irenaeus, Clement of Alexandria, Origen, Tertullian, Eusebius, Hippolytus, and Minucius Felix. Special studies were made on Marcion (1888) and Clement of Alexandria (three volumes, 1902–1912). No listing is available of his many articles in theological journals.[51] When he died in 1933, the rise of National Socialism demanded full attention.

Meijboom was strongly influenced by the Groningen School which in its theological orientation may be compared with the mediating theology of Göttingen University.[52] That is, the theological faculty of Groningen managed to stay free from rationalistic or pietistic movements as well as from rigid

---

[48]Harris, *The Tübingen School,* 39.
[49]In Hornhuizen, Groningen.
[50]Scherpenzeel in Friesland, Veendam, and Assen.
[51]The best bibliography of his works is available at the Royal Library in the Hague.
[52]See "Göttingen," in *Religion in Geschichte und Gegenwart,* 3rd ed. (Tübingen: J. C. B. Mohr, 1958ff.). Defectors from Tübingen were welcomed in Göttingen because of their mediating theology.

orthodoxy.[53] The University of Groningen can claim its roots in the medieval movement of the *Devotio moderna*. At Groningen, Wessel Gansfort (Gansvoort) and the renowned Latinist Rudolf Agricola (Roelof Huysmann) prepared the way for the Christian humanist of the sixteenth century, Desiderius Erasmus.

During the first decades of the nineteenth century the theological faculty created its image as the "Groningen School." Herman Muntinghe, the school's principal founder, wrote a history of Christian culture, and under his influence the school became an advocate of social ethics, tolerance, and progress. Faithful to the Erasmian tradition, the Groningen School considered Christian living to be more important than orthodoxy; for God's revelation in Christ had first of all an ethical meaning.

Several professors at Groningen, including Meijboom, were directly involved in matters of public education and social concern. Their distinctive theological contribution at Groningen stood in contrast to the views of other Dutch universities. The University of Leiden represented a more naturalist position like that of Tübingen. The University of Utrecht, representing a mixture of pietism and orthodoxy, had some resemblance to the early Berlin University. The strictly orthodox Free University was founded in 1880 in Amsterdam by the theologian and politician, Abraham Kuijper (Kuyper).

It is not known why Meijboom chose the "Marcan hypothesis" as the subject of his dissertation. Perhaps he was influenced by a French publication of Albert Réville which, just a few years before, had been awarded a prize by the Society for the Humanities at the Hague.[54] Or, since the gospels were thought by Baur to have originated during the second century,[55] Meijboom may have considered this area as an appropriate entry into patristic studies. It may be, of course, that Meijboom had developed an interest in the debate between Heinrich Ewald of Göttingen and Ferdinand Christian Baur of Tübingen.

As was demonstrated above, Ewald's style was most lively and vituperate, personal as well as political, and he vented feelings of strong rejection against Baur: "Herr Baur, in my opinion, is neither a Christian . . . nor one of the better heathen. He is one of the literary Jews, this present-day pest of our poor Germany. . . . The atheism which he transfers from the theory of his beloved School into practice . . . bears its fruit a thousandfold." Ewald wrote this one

---

[53]Information on the University of Groningen was received from W. Nijenhuis, who wrote the article on Groningen in the recent edition of *Theologische Realenzyklopädie* (Berlin, New York: Walter de Gruyter, 1985) 14:264-66.

[54]French title: *Études critiques sur l'évangile selon Saint Matthieu* (Leiden: D. Noothoven van Goor, 1862).

[55]See Harris, *The Tübingen School*, 237.

year after the March revolution of 1848.[56] As the three enemies of Germany, Ewald lists "the Catholics, the orthodox led by Hengstenberg, and the abominable Tübingen school of Baur.[57] He regarded the priority of the Gospel of Mark as the answer against the Tübingen School and the Roman Catholics.

Meijboom has the distinct quality of referring to the irenic French scholars of Strasbourg as well. Eduard W. E. Reuss developed his own approach to Marcan priority already in 1842. He was succeeded by Edmond H. A. Scherer, Albert Réville, and finally by Michel Nicolas.[58] In contrast to Heinrich Ewald these scholars showed no trace of political or academic polemics. As a minority group in France operating from one university, these scholars demonstrate a merely professional interest in the issue of canon history. Even though Meijboom does not agree with their conclusions,[59] he admires their "dispassionate and impartial" approach.[60] Eduard Reuss is described as a "composed, honest, and systematic" scholar.[61] The Marcan hypothesis found acceptance in the Netherlands basically through Albert Réville.[62]

Although not emphatically expressed, Meijboom conveys the conviction that the Germans were weakened by their political and adversarial approach, while the French scholars provided ingenious insights, which could be discussed on purely exegetical and historical grounds.

Meijboom's Analysis of the Marcan Hypothesis

This brings us to Meijboom's analysis of the Marcan hypothesis.[63] In the first section of his dissertation, by way of a historical survey, Meijboom attempts to demonstrate the basic difference of opinion between the Tübingen School and its opponents. At issue is the Hegelian hermeneutical principle of "tendency criticism" launched by F. C. Baur, especially in his *Paul the Apostle of Jesus Christ* (1845).[64] Baur argued that the letters of Paul reflected a tension between Jew and Gentile and that this same tension could be detected in the gospels.

In order to understand these New Testament documents, Baur believed like Strauss that one should look not for recordings of factual data but rather for

---

[56]Quoted in Harris, *The Tübingen School*, 45-46; see also Farmer, *The Synoptic Problem*, 25-29.
[57]Harris, *The Tübingen School*, 44.
[58]See below, "The Development of the Marcan Hypothesis in France," 45-63.
[59]Ibid., 59-63.
[60]Ibid., 53.
[61]Ibid., 45.
[62]Ibid., 55-60, and also 89.
[63]See Meijboom, "History and Critique," below, 9-148.
[64]Baur introduced this idea in his article "Die Christuspartei": see n. 41, above.

indications concerning the author's viewpoint. In the words of Baur, "The primary question is not to what degree some story informs us about reality, but in what relation this story stands to the consciousness of the author."[65] With this reasoning Matthew is a Jewish gospel to which the Gentile gospel of Luke presents an antithesis. Finally, the Gospel of Mark serves as the Catholic keystone to complete the synthesis.[66]

Although Heinrich Ewald originally agreed with this approach, after his conflict with Baur he changed his mind. He believed the text of the gospels contained the story of Jesus' life and work and was to be interpreted at face value.[67] When Jesus says "I am the light of the world," we have a direct quote rather than the confession of the early church. Tendency criticism found itself confronted by literary criticism and the latter prevailed, especially through the support of Albrecht Ritschl when he defected from the Tübingen School in 1857. An absolute Hegelian dialectic did not prove tenable for reconstructing the history of the early church.[68]

Thus, the Marcan hypothesis benefited by Ewald's literary-historical approach. However, since the hermeneutical question was foremost in the minds of Baur and Ewald, neither of the two scholars was genuinely interested in gospel history. If Baur had welded the Marcan hypothesis to his hermeneutical thesis, the outcome would have been quite different.[69]

On the basis of his historical survey, Meijboom suggests, as William Farmer and H.-H. Stoldt[70] have more recently, that the real issues of the Synoptic problem had not been raised. In a concluding statement Meijboom exhorts his readers, "We should not lose sight of the fact that the . . . concurrence among so many theologians [in favor of the Marcan hypothesis] was largely a result of the reaction against Strauss and the Tübingers." Somewhat sarcastically he quotes a jubilant expression by the Zurich scholar Titus Tobler, who observed that "after Ewald's conclusive exposition, the Marcan priority should no more be considered a hypothesis."[71]

---

[65]Quoted by Meijboom, "History and Critique," below, 34. More radical than F. C. Baur was Bruno Bauer (1809–1882) in his *Kritik der evangelischen Geschichte der Synoptiker* (*Criticism of the Gospel History of the Synoptics*) 3 vols. (Leipzig, 1841/1842).

[66]Cf. Harris, *The Tübingen School,* 210; E. Earle Ellis, "Gospel Criticism: A Perspective on the State of the Art," in *Das Evangelium und die Evangelien: Vorträge vom Tübinger Symposium 1982,* P. Stuhlmacher, ed., 27-54 (Tübingen: J. C. B. Mohr, 1983).

[67]Meijboom, "History and Critique," below, 38ff.

[68]Harris, *The Tübingen School,* 225.

[69]One biographer of Baur, indeed, suggested Baur might have accepted Marcan priority had it not been for the political complexities in which he had found himself; see Harris, *The Tübingen School,* 212.

[70]See above, nn. 12 and 13.

[71]Meijboom, "History and Critique," below, 67.

Meijboom then proceeds, in his literary evaluation, to investigate the three major issues or presuppositions of the Marcan hypothesis.[72] According to Meijboom, the first and major issue is the question of whether the shortest gospel is really the oldest document. This presupposition was expressed by Johann Gottfried Herder in 1796[73] as "the natural point of view."[74] Later the idea was popularized by Heinrich Ewald so that it became commonly accepted among New Testament scholars.[75] The assumption behind this idea was "that the purpose of the evangelists was to preserve as many reports as possible about Jesus' life and work."[76]

Meijboom rejected the assumption that the evangelists were simply compiling data for posterity.[77] Forty years before Albert Schweitzer, he already maintained that the eschatological perspective would not allow the early church simply to compose lives of Jesus. The evangelists expected an imminent return of Jesus Christ. According to Meijboom the exhortation in Luke 21:28 provides an insight into the eschatological perspective of the author. When Luke quotes Christ as saying "Look up and raise your heads," it may be inferred that some early Christians were losing their eschatological outlook and were "bending their heads toward worldly concerns."[78]

Meijboom suggests that "the purpose of the evangelists could not simply have been a description of the historical Jesus." Their work was "not historical but rather theological in nature."[79] He is of the opinion that there were four gospels corresponding to the variety of theological and moral needs in the early church and that if this was the case, the authors would be selective rather than exhaustive in their presentation of materials. He concludes, therefore, that there is no convincing proof for the assumption that the shortest gospel would be the earliest document.

The second issue presented by Meijboom also originated with Herder. As Stoldt has shown us, the early Romantic movement discovered "sacred epics" in various classic documents.[80] This literary characteristic was applied by Herder to the Gospel of Mark and was used by Christian Hermann Weisse as a major argument for Marcan priority. Weisse, professor in Leipzig, is credited by both

---

[72]Meijboom, "History and Critique," below, 97-130.
[73]See Farmer, *The Synoptic Problem,* 30-35; Stoldt, *History and Criticism,* 167.
[74]Meijboom, "History and Critique," below, 16-17.
[75]Farmer, *The Synoptic Problem,* 25.
[76]Meijboom, "History and Critique," below, 97.
[77]Meijboom, "History and Critique," below, 103.
[78]Meijboom, "History and Critique," below, 97.
[79]Meijboom, "History and Critique," below, 98.
[80]Stoldt, *History and Criticism,* 167; see also Meijboom's discussion of Gustav Volkmar, in "History and Critique," below, 83-85.

Meijboom and Stoldt as the major founder of the Marcan hypothesis. Weisse's first major work appeared in 1838, three years after the explosive publication of Strauss's *Life of Jesus*.[81] Weisse wrote enthusiastically, almost exactly as Ewald, noted above, about the "fresh liveliness and fullness of picturesque detail" and about the "sweet smell of fresh flowers" in the Gospel of Mark. There was no doubt in Weisse's mind that "Mark was the original gospel possessing priority over Matthew and Luke."[82]

The question for Meijboom was whether Mark's fresh and lively style indicates an eyewitness account or rather a mature Christian author.[83] To Meijboom the smooth succession of events and the psychological and dramatic details in Mark point to the art of a preacher. He concedes that the literary style and content alone cannot ultimately determine an early or late date for a gospel, even though it does testify strongly for the individuality of the evangelist. After discussing other aspects, Meijboom concludes,

> The evangelists must have been brilliant minds who knew how to wield their pen for the sake of the Church and its members. In the public worship services they were frequently engaged in the reading and the exposition of the Scriptures. . . . The memory of the early Christian scholars had not yet been weakened by an overload of literary studies. It was for them, therefore, easier to absorb and retain the content of the Gospel. They were saturated by its message and their lives were influenced by each detail of these gospels.[84]

It is clear that for Meijboom the two major arguments of brevity and literary style are not determinative for either an early or a late date, although his preference is clearly for a late date.

One more argument had to be discussed. The proponents of the Marcan hypothesis were perfectly aware that each of the Synoptic Gospels had so many unique features that they must not have known one another and they could not simply have copied one another.[85] Yet, there is so much commonality that there

---

[81]Meijboom, "History and Critique," below, 12; Stoldt, *History and Criticism,* 47. Weisse's publication was *Die evangelische Geschichte kritisch und philosophisch bearbeitet,* see above, n. 13.

[82]Stoldt quotes Weisse in *History and Criticism,* 168. This argument was also essential for Ferdinand Hitzig, who was of the opinion that John Mark was the author of both the Gospel of Mark and the Book of Revelation; see Meijboom, "History and Critique," below, 12-20. Regarding Herder as the originator of a romantic interpretation of Mark, see Farmer, *The Synoptic Problem,* 25, 26, and 7n7, for important bibliographical reference to Herder's work.

[83]Meijboom, "History and Critique," below, 106; discussion on pp. 105-15.

[84]Meijboom, "History and Critique," below, 166.

[85]This was proposed by J. B. Koppe in 1782; see Farmer, *The Synoptic Problem,* 6.

must have been some common source. Already in 1784 Lessing[86] had referred to an "Ur-Gospel" which was eagerly elaborated by Christian Gottlob Wilke in 1838.[87] Supposedly Papias mentioned this Ur-Gospel in a document quoted by Eusebius.[88] It is not clear, though, whether Papias referred to such an original gospel or to the canonical Gospel of Mark.[89] If the latter were true, his quote cannot be used by adherents of the Marcan hypothesis.

Great efforts were made by various proponents of the Marcan hypothesis to construct some kind of later development which would allow an original priority of Mark. From this discussion resulted the Two-Document Hypothesis.[90] The French scholar Albert Réville argued for a Proto-Mark which was more extensive than any of the Synoptic gospels. According to his theory each gospel was a selection from this large resource of materials. However, the difference in linguistic use and sequence of materials between Matthew and Mark made this option also questionable.[91]

In whatever form the argument is developed, as long as there supposedly are written sources preceding the canonical gospels, a redactor is needed to fashion the gospels in their present form. Meijboom concurred, there must have been copyists who may have contributed minor elements, for instance, the last twelve verses of the Gospel of Mark, whose authenticity is much debated.[92] The Gospel of Mark in its present form, however, is so much a unity that no one other than the original author can be responsible for this.[93]

Summarizing the three major presuppositions of the Marcan hypothesis, Meijboom was of the opinion that neither the argument of brevity nor that of literary imagery carried adequate weight in determining Mark's relation to the other Synoptic Gospels. The need for a redactor, he argued, is created by the Ur-Gospel hypothesis itself rather than by the harmonious style and content of Mark's gospel. Thus the search for an original gospel or document created the greatest confusion among the adherents of the Marcan hypothesis.[94]

---

[86]See Farmer, *The Synoptic Problem,* 4.

[87]In his *Der Urevangelist, oder, exegetisch kritische Untersuchung über das Verwandtschaftsverhältniss der drei ersten Evangelien,* see above, n. 13; for a detailed discussion see Stoldt, *History and Criticism,* 27- 46.

[88]See Meijboom, "History and Critique," below, 124n9 and 127n10.

[89]See Meijboom's discussion in "History and Critique," below, 123-29.

[90]See Farmer, *The Synoptic Problem,* 15-19, 30-47.

[91]Discussed in Meijboom, "History and Critique," below, 55-60.

[92]Meijboom, "History and Critique," below, 116.

[93]Meijboom, "History and Critique," below, 121; for a complete discussion, see 117-23.

[94]For a listing of the various suggestions, see Meijboom, "History and Critique," below, 116-17.

The only convincing argument remaining for Meijboom was Griesbach's hypothesis, which is that Mark used the gospels of Matthew and Luke.[95] By means of a chart Meijboom demonstrated how Mark alternately used Matthew and Luke.[96] With the exception of one hundred verses, the complete Gospel of Mark can be found on the pages of its parallel gospels,[97] and the sequence of Mark's materials is identical to the sequence of the used materials from the other two.[98] Mark combines verses and even words from the other gospels[99] and he also eliminates certain passages.[100] He translates the Hebraisms of Matthew[101] and introduces additional personal names or geographical data.[102]

It is Meijboom's argument that it is easier to understand how one author, Mark, can combine pericopes, verses, and words rather than to suppose the opposite, that two authors, namely, Matthew and Luke, would independently separate texts and words, as it is said they have done, unbeknownst to one another.[103] According to Meijboom, the study of the origin of the gospels has presented us with a radical alternative, the Gospel of Mark is either first or last in the series of Synoptic Gospels. There is for Meijboom no mediating position.[104]

Meijboom has clearly indicated his position and demonstrated the theological consequences of his choice.[105] The Gospel of Matthew presents the Jesus of history, while the Gospel of Mark exalts the Christ of faith.[106] In Mark, Christ, after his baptism, is revealed by God and is recognized by demons.[107] The disciples are far inferior to their master and remain in constant misunderstanding.[108] The "messianic secret" is typical for Mark and to a certain degree also for the Gospel of John. Mark's emphasis is on teaching about Jesus rather than a portrayal of his ministry; Jesus' suffering is a matter of doctrinal interpretation rather than of historical description.[109] Meijboom draws all these aspects together with this con-

---

[95]Johann Jakob Griesbach, *Synopsis Evangeliorum Matthei, Marci et Lucae una cum iis Joannis pericopis: Quae historiam passionis et resurrectionis Jesu Christi complectuntur,* 2nd ed. corr. (Halle Saxonum: Jo. Jac. Curtii Haeredes, 1797; [1]1774–1776).

[96]Meijboom, "History and Critique," below, 151-53.

[97]Meijboom, below, 159.

[98]Meijboom, below, 154-55.

[99]Meijboom, below, 165-74.

[100]Meijboom, below, 159.

[101]Meijboom, below, 86ff.

[102]Meijboom, below, 107, cf. 199ff.

[103]Meijboom, below, 184.

[104]Meijboom, below, 227.

[105]Meijboom, below, 131-48.

[106]Meijboom, below, 133-36, 137-39.

[107]Meijboom, below, 134, 145-46.

[108]Meijboom, below, 144-45.

[109]Meijboom, below, 140-42.

clusion: "Such a christological image certainly cannot boast an early date. The Gospel of Mark is not a statement of first impressions like the Gospel of Matthew," but rather a mature christology comparable to the Gospel of John.[110]

Concluding Evaluation

In Meijboom's subsequent ministry, the Jesus of history would be equally as meaningful as the Christ of faith. The Sermon on the Mount would for him always precede a glorying in salvation. Meijboom would be neither for revolution nor for supporting the status quo, but rather for promoting a healthy mediating position of genuine progress combined with meaningful tradition.

By means of his dissertation Meijboom was introduced to the history of the early church. He perceived in this church a certain dramatic development, a courage in the face of persecution, a bold initiative in integrating Greek and Jewish culture, and a sense of the high calling of being a new people of God. Accordingly, Meijboom gives a positive and imaginative picture of Marcion. He views his religion as a consistent form of New Testament Christianity, a religion free from the law and the Old Testament, a genuine form of pre-Catholic, nonhierarchic Christianity.[111] Along these same lines Meijboom also took a special interest in Clement of Alexandria. He wrote a two-volume novel, an academic publication, and a translation of all available texts of Clement for a series of early Christian writings.[112] Furthermore, Meijboom was greatly intrigued by the implications of Christianity for astrology and geography, for marriage and the role of women, for dieting and clothing, and for multiple other aspects of life which had to be incorporated into a Christian lifestyle.

The same enthusiasm motivated Meijboom as a pioneer and cofounder in 1866 of the Protestant Union (*Protestantenverein*), instituted in order to promote a cooperative effort of all Protestants in matters of social concern.[113] In one of his sermons Meijboom asserted, "Personal morality must become a divine calling to such a degree that being religious and being ethical become two designations for the same cause."[114] The Incarnation meant for him that God has come and is

---

[110]Meijboom, below, 147.

[111]Hajo Uden Meijboom, *Marcion en de Marcionieten* (Leiden: P. Engels, 1888) 249.

[112]Hajo Uden Meijboom, *De Clemens Roman*, 2 vols. (Groningen: J. B. Wolters, 1902–1904); idem, *Clemens Alexandrinus* (Leiden: P. Engels, 1912) 255; idem, ed., *Clemens Alexandrinus, Werken*, 12 vols. (Leiden: P. Engels, 1913–1915).

[113]Hajo Uden Meijboom, *De Oude Kerken en De Nieuwe Tijd* ("The Early Churches and the New Era") (Amsterdam: A. W. Sijthoff, 1881) 72; reference to the "Protestanten Bond" ("The Protestant Union") on 67.

[114]Hajo Uden Meijboom, *Ter Nagedachtenis, Een Tiental Toespraken* (Amsterdam: A. W. Sijthoff, 1879) 9.

at the same time in process of coming today. "The love of Christ," he said, "is to conquer the hearts of men at home, in school, and in society."[115] Such was the message of Christ interpreted by the Groningen School of which Hajo Uden Meijboom was a faithful disciple.

---

[115]B. P. Hofstede de Groot, *Vijftig Jaren Theologie* ("Fifty Years of Theology") (1870) 29.

An Outline of the Translation

Part 2
Critique of the Marcan Hypothesis

Chapter 4
The Three Theses of the Marcan Hypothesis

Part 3
Exegetical Assessment of the Gospel of Mark

History and Critique
of the Marcan Hypothesis

Academic Dissertation
in fulfillment of the degree of
Doctor of Divinity
at the University of Groningen

By the authority of the Rector Magnificus
F. Z. Ermerins
D.Lit., Med.D., Prof. Med. Studies

To be defended publicly by
Hajo Uden Meijboom
from Hornhuizen
on Thursday, September 27, 1866, at noon

Amsterdam
Kraay Bros.
1866

Introduction

The "Marcan hypothesis" has been known among New Testament scholars for quite some time. Concerning its general intent there is not the slightest uncertainty. Immediately one or another of the many forms of this hypothesis comes to mind suggesting an explanation for the origin of the Synoptic gospels. The Marcan hypothesis has in general commanded great interest among a wide circle of theologians and has gained a dominant position in the field of Gospel criticism. Major objections arise, however, when one attempts to be more specific about the meaning of this hypothesis and its theological import.

A survey of the work of the advocates of this theory reveals that because of their various theological orientations, their common position has been worked out quite differently. C[hristian] G[ottlob] Wilke is considered one of its defenders, but it is obvious that this scholar differs strongly from the French scholar Albert Réville, in starting point as well in final result. Similarly, one does not need to search long for the difference between Chr[istian] Hermann Weisse and Heinrich Ewald or between Eduard Reuss and Heinrich Julius Holtzmann. Yet all these men are to be considered adherents of the one Marcan hypothesis. What then is this hypothesis, and where can it be found in its purest expression?

Definition of the Project

For a description of this hypothesis one should consult its history. In order to arrive at an accurate definition of this hypothesis we have to listen to those who have been mentioned as its adherents or who have identified themselves as proponents of this hypothesis. It is essential to learn what these scholars taught concerning the origin of the gospels and to note their points of agreement and difference. Within the diversity of these viewpoints one must find their common denominator, that is, the distinctive traits that must be present if a scholar is to be considered an adherent of the Marcan hypothesis. Only after we have worked our way through the history of the Marcan hypothesis and have ascertained the place it has received in the history of Gospel criticism will it be possible to give this hypothesis an accurate definition. As a general description to be used for a guideline in this investigation I would like to propose the following formulation: The Marcan hypothesis attempts to use the second gospel as a key to the explanation of the origin and the interrelatedness of the Synoptic gospels.

Theories Concerning the Synoptic Question

It is, however, necessary to make one further delineation. It is common knowledge that the synoptic problem has played a role in various theories over a considerable period of time. The traditional effort at harmonization of the gospels finally ended with no other result than the recognition of the frustration of its attempts. After this failure scholars eagerly began to devise and apply a great variety of explanations for the complex interrelatedness of the Synoptics. [These explanations can be reduced to four basic theories.]

There was first of all the theory that all three gospels have stemmed from a common root, [namely an original written gospel] (the Ur-Gospel hypothesis, see [below]); another was the theory of a fixed oral gospel from which the three gospels stem (the Tradition hypothesis [generally called the Oral Gospel hypothesis]); thirdly, there was the hypothesis that features the idea of written fragments that have been differently unified by the synoptic evangelists (the Fragment hypothesis, see [below]); finally, providing one does not rule out the possibility that one evangelist knew the work of another, the theory was advanced that the evangelists used one another's work (the Utilization hypothesis).

In each case one attempted to find the sequence in which the synoptic gospels were written by comparing synoptic parallels. Consequently, also the Gospel of Mark became recognized as being the first gospel in the series of the Synoptics. In this case one could easily designate such a position as a form of the Marcan hypothesis. But priority in sequence alone is not sufficient to identify a scholar as a proponent of the Marcan hypothesis.

The Initiative of Historical Criticism

One would do injustice to the advocates of the Marcan hypothesis if one would include all those who in an earlier era gave priority to Mark. At most one can speak of precursors, for almost any acceptable hypothesis had its antecedents a hundred or more years earlier. All the theories mentioned above belong to the era of criticism which came to an end with David Friedrich Strauss (1808–1874). Before his day there had been a period of abstract reasoning using methods of explanation for the interrelatedness of the gospels that were extraneous to the gospels themselves and alien to their historical content. When Strauss called the critics back to the concrete reality, however, the situation changed. Since that day scholars have studied the gospels increasingly from a historical perspective. Thus an earlier merely literary quest gradually changed into a historical quest.

The narrative content of the gospels as well as historical data [from the early Christian era] were taken into consideration for the understanding of the problem of canon history. This has become the common characteristic of the various trends in gospel criticism practiced since the 1830s.

A description of the Marcan hypothesis has to concentrate upon the group of scholars since Strauss, who were of the opinion they found a remarkable agreement between the tradition of the early Christian era concerning Mark and what could be derived from the characteristics of the Marcan Gospel and its relation to the other gospels. Consequently, they uphold the priority of the second gospel in order to find there, or in its antecedent, the stem onto which the other gospels have been grafted.

Outline and Procedure

It is my intention to investigate in this dissertation the value and validity of the Marcan hypothesis. In part one I will give an exposition of the history of this hypothesis with the following threefold objective: in the first place, it should yield an accurate and complete definition of my subject; secondly, it should give me an outline according to which I can deal with the strengths and weaknesses of this hypothesis; finally, it should provide the unifying characteristics in my search for the common elements among the diversity of approaches. This will also afford an opportunity to eliminate immediately certain arguments that are found only among a few of the adherents of the Marcan hypothesis, and are therefore not part of the common characteristics of all its advocates.

In part two I will first analyze the three major arguments upon which the Marcan hypothesis hinges, namely, the brevity of the Gospel of Mark, its literary quality, and the redaction of its original text. Since this literary analysis is not altogether conclusive I propose to conclude this part with a theological analysis of the Gospel of Mark. Even though neglected by the proponents of the Marcan hypothesis, the theological tenets of the Gospel of Mark provide more conclusive evidence of a later development than [does] a purely literary evaluation.

Part three will deal with literary and textual issues that seem to indicate Marcan posteriority. For the most part these passages have been discussed by the advocates of Marcan priority in order to explain them within the context of their hypothesis. The study of this controversy in the interpretation of canon history is a genuine challenge to contemporary research. I am confident that the importance of the issue will create more interest among my readers than the method of my procedure.

Part One

The History
of the Marcan Hypothesis

Chapter 1

The Origin
of the Marcan Hypothesis

The Prelude

Literary Criticism in the 1830s

If we are to begin at the point when the Marcan hypothesis presented itself as a distinctive theory, we will have to go back to the period beginning with Strauss. Let us concentrate upon the ethos of those days.

Long before the storms of the spring of 1835 swept over the land, there were indications amid apparent quietness and serenity in the intellectual world that could have prepared the observer for what was to come. The science of criticism had moved along two lines during the preceding years. These two progressed independently without the one adequately communicating with the other. On the one hand there was a [purely harmonistic] inquiry after the origin and the mutual relationship of the gospels; on the other hand an investigation was launched into the historical character of the gospels. Both approaches in isolation had to lead to a dead end.

The question of the mutual relation of the gospels had occupied the minds of scholars for a considerable time without taking seriously into consideration how to find the answer in their literary content and in the data of history. After numerous abstract possibilities had been attempted without lasting results, the conclusion that one had to acquiesce in a confession of ignorance was obvious.

Furthermore, without scholars being aware of it, the question of the historical validity of the gospels had emerged. The study in classic mythology had evoked an interest among many scholars. A remarkable agreement had been discovered between several features of the Old Testament and the imagery from Greek and Roman mythology. Considerable parts of the historical writings of the Old Testament had already been consigned to the category of mythology. A cautious attempt had also been made to enter the realm of the New Testament; especially in the opening narratives and in the closing stories of the gospels, sections were singled out for a mythical interpretation. Even in the account of the historical ministry of the Lord, scholars meant to discover elements over which they would have liked to pronounce a similar mythical verdict, supposedly without endangering the belief in the miraculous power of the Lord. Thus the fear was not unfounded that eventually the last trace of historical evidence would be wiped out by the flood of doubt which increasingly threatened the whole area of New Testament history.

The Achievement of David Friedrich Strauss (1835)

The man in whom the achievements of both literary and historical criticism merged to their mutual benefit—although to the shock and dismay of Europe— was David Friedrich Strauss. No fear for the honor of Jesus impeded this follower of Hegel in his critical research, as had been the case among his predecessors. His critical approach could harm neither the form nor the content of the faith he had adopted. With the intention of being absolutely unbiased, he set to work.

To deem the gospels historically valid by definition was considered by Strauss a lukewarm approach which could not be tolerated by sound scholarship as long as their historical validity had not been verified. The movement of rationalism had rejected the supernatural character of biblical history in order to bring into focus its purely historical elements. The question of the historical validity of the gospels was now to be raised.

Strauss had followed the discussion of the mythical conception outside as well as inside the circle of theological studies. He deemed it weakness when theologians hesitated to apply the mythical question to the area of gospel history. To use the mythical option consistently also in that area seemed to him the challenge of his day. Strauss felt at liberty to meet this challenge by publishing his *Life of Jesus* in 1835.

The Mythical Interpretation by Strauss

Even though for Strauss all historical evidence had vanished, he expected his successors to rediscover gradually, after the confusion of radical questioning had resided, which data in the gospels had historical validity.[1] Although under compulsion to question all historical facts, Strauss nonetheless felt that rejection could not have the last word. Thus he posed a new challenge for New Testament criticism.

In Strauss the balance had swung in the direction of the mythical view, while historical evidence was hardly available; to reaffirm the historical position

---

[1] David Friedrich Strauss, *Das Leben Jesu, kritisch bearbeitet*, 2 vols., 3rd ed. rev. (Tübingen: Osiander, 1838–1839) 1:124.

became a concern for everyone. Soon the realization made itself felt that, in the first place, it was necessary to have certainty concerning the origin and nature of the gospels.

Had Strauss contented himself with the attempt of a mythical interpretation of the gospels from the characteristics of the writings themselves as well as from external testimonies, such a negative achievement would not have been satisfactory. As long as the necessity of mythical interpretation has not been demonstrated, one is entitled to search for evidence, or for even the necessity, of recognizing and finding history in the gospels.

The obligation to find historical evidence was felt, therefore, in all circles of critical scholarship in general as well as in gospel studies in particular. Because theologians before Strauss had neglected the historical question, adverse consequences were bound to result. The publication of the *Life of Jesus* was [the result of] one of the major reactions to prior neglect. Not only were New Testament scholars rudely awakened from their peaceful slumber, but they were also compelled by Strauss to descend from the clouds of abstract reasoning. He caused them to face up to historical reality and to lay new foundations for a more solid construction of canon history.

The Response to Strauss

In the endeavor to establish a critical-historical approach to the gospels, two major schools of thought developed—the "Tübingen school" and the proponents of the Marcan hypothesis.

The polemics against Strauss, in reaction to his first publication, [Strauss said,] "were not much different from the wailing of terrified women after hearing the sound of a gunshot in their vicinity."[2] Strauss had hoped for a more creative effort by his opponents in proposing a gospel history.[3] To a degree this hope was met by the two groups just mentioned, although in a different and more theological sense. The internal difference between these two responses was considerable, however, and it was far from accidental that one school saw the most accurate proclamation in the Gospel of Mark, while the other school, the Tübingen school, was of the opinion that Matthew was the most original gospel.

Because we are investigating only the Marcan hypothesis, we will refer to the adherents of the Tübingen school only insofar as is necessary to explain the modifications in the Marcan hypothesis occasioned by the publications of this school.

---

[2]Ibid., preface to the 2nd German ed. (Tübingen: Osiander, 1837) xiv.
[3]Ibid., xv.

The Establishment of the Marcan Hypothesis (1838)

Christian Hermann Weisse, Founder of the Marcan Hypothesis

As I mentioned above, it is only since the period of New Testament criticism following Strauss that we can speak of a "Marcan hypothesis." The person who brought this hypothesis into being was very much aware of the innovation of his conception of the gospels. I am referring to Chr. Hermann Weisse, who in his publication *The Gospel History Critically and Philosophically Interpreted*,[4] devoted a separate section to the origin and interrelatedness of the gospels. The idea of a book [referring to the mythological elements in the gospels] had been with him for a considerable time, even before Strauss published his *Life of Jesus*. Because Weisse recognized the disturbing effect that inevitably would follow such a book, he might never have carried out such a project.[5] But once the less desirable work had been completed by Strauss, Weisse felt it was essential to present a more positive and complete picture of the entire sacred New Testament history.

Weisse stated he welcomed the publication of the *Life of Jesus* for still another reason. A disease, which had spread unnoticeably over a long period of time in Gospel criticism, had now come into the open, [namely, the disease of abstract literary speculation]. The presupposition [of the Oral Gospel hypothesis] that tradition was the source from which the evangelists drew their information had suddenly yielded its implications and thereby demonstrated its weaknesses. Once the disease had been diagnosed, the opponents of Strauss clearly faced their target.[6] If tradition is considered the source of history, historical uncertainty must of necessity be the consequence. If certainty is desired, one must look for more dependable sources. Weisse was sure he had found these.

His hypothesis was that the Marcan Gospel is the oldest record of historical facts made by an eyewitness. He was convinced that this gospel became the basis for Matthew and Luke, except for some elements from other sources and from later tradition. It is this persuasion which became the new hypothesis, which Weisse felt free to recommend because of its alleged internal and external probability. In his preface he expressed the hope that through further research it would prove to be the right hypothesis, a fact that would enable him to present a gospel with a constructive meaning.

One notices immediately the perspective from which the hypothesis and its

---

[4]Christian Hermann Weisse, *Die evangelische Geschichte kritisch und philosophisch bearbeitet,* 2 vols. (Leipzig: Breitkopf and Härtel, 1838).
[5]Ibid., preface, 1:iv.
[6]Ibid., 1:7.

"discovery" should be regarded. It has close ties with the search for historical certainty. What this entails becomes clear when one traces the development the process took for Weisse personally. His investigations into the value of the gospel stories had already led him to believe that he could retain a considerable part of their content as more or less historical. He was already equipped to write his criticism of gospel history when he was overtaken by the new approach of historical criticism by Strauss. In reexamining how far adjustments in his previous studies were needed because of this approach, he noticed a remarkable agreement. The new approach of historical criticism gave him the opportunity to prove scientifically what he had assumed as true previously.

How did Weisse make the connection between the historical validity of the gospels and the editorial content of Mark? Weisse speaks repeatedly of his "critical sense," which supposedly gave him certainty concerning the earlier date of some sections of Mark in comparison with similar passages in the other gospels. This "critical sense," to be sure, is a nonrational perception; it is a critical touch, a norm, that ultimately determines the value of historical sources. Especially the issue of the gospels is a sensitive matter. The validity of this critical norm, however, is closely related to the scientific factors of which it is the result. When we become aware of the ideas Weisse brings along before the inception of his study, his "critical sense" diminishes considerably in value, however boldly he places his confidence in it.

Assumptions of Weisse's Historical Criticism

Three basic assumptions are to be taken into consideration. Proceeding from the correct observation that there is an inner relation between the workings of the mental powers of man and his physical organism, Weisse concluded that one may assume extraordinary physical powers among people with unusual spiritual gifts. According to Weisse this proposition, a result of experience in a higher sense,[7] is not in conflict with the law of cause and effect. This law is for him as well as for Strauss a norm for historical research[8] and its purpose is to explain the various miracles, even healings from a distance, that are reported in the gospels.

Secondly, Weisse assumed the possibility that metaphorical expressions by Jesus had been reported in such a way that they obtained the characteristics of factual reports. This possibility, which as such is indisputable, was posed in order to make acceptable those miracle stories that could not be explained on the basis of kinetic or psychic magnetism.

---

[7]Ibid., 1:337.
[8]Ibid., 1:335.

Finally, Weisse cautioned against the expectation of literal exactness among our evangelists. For instance, he considered it quite possible that Mark, because of his observation of the highly effective healing power of Jesus, was unwittingly tempted to occasional exaggeration. Also, mindful of the miracles by the Old Testament prophets, Mark may have imperceptibly conformed the miracles of Jesus to Old Testament patterns.[9]

Thus Weisse undertook his investigation on the basis of these three presuppositions. Their validity would have to be tested, however, by application to specific stories. It is obvious one can not safeguard oneself completely against an arbitrary application of such presuppositions. Naturally Weisse obtained from the gospels an account that he could genuinely consider complete and historical. It is also understandable and quite natural that by this method he would opt for an early date for Mark and for its close affinity with an eyewitness account.

Since the content of the Gospel of Mark can be found almost completely in the pages of the other two Synoptic gospels, it could easily lead to the conclusion that Mark was the source for the other gospels. Furthermore, the vivid imagery in the Gospel of Mark leads easily to the conclusion of its primary role. In addition to such initial impressions Weisse had the three above-mentioned assumptions available, which he could alternately apply to counter arguments that might rise from the text of Mark's Gospel itself. Thus he could easily find followers who would uncritically accept his position.

An Example of Weisse's Hermeneutics: The Mountain of Transfiguration

The following example will illustrate the above-mentioned suggestion regarding the subjective and arbitrary character of Weisse's hermeneutics. The account of the transfiguration is one of the gospel stories where the critic shows most clearly his true colors in the process of interpretation. Weisse, in agreement with Strauss, recognized that a completely nonmythological explanation, made merely for the sake of retaining a supposed historicity of the account, loses all theological value.[10] In other words, for the sake of maintaining a historical structure [for example, assuming a historical mountain] one loses the ideological content [that is, the meaning of the story].

On the other hand, in contrast to Strauss, Weisse could not attach great value to a consistent mythological interpretation by leaving only a minimum of historical fact. Thus, without accepting the miraculous character of the account in a literal sense, Weisse set out to preserve sufficient historical material.

---

[9]Ibid., 1:361.
[10]Ibid., 1:534ff.

According to Weisse, the portrayal of the transfiguration was originally a vision. During the six days after the profession of Peter—"Thou art the Christ!"—Jesus must have commented in more detail on his role as Messiah. He must have focused especially on those of his disciples whom he esteemed most receptive to such information. These must have been the three who were reported as witnesses of the transfiguration. The intention of that instruction must have been a demonstration that Jesus was in fact the Christ, and that in him all the prophecies were being fulfilled in a higher sense.

This proclamation, impressed upon the three confidants, this surprising news which was so totally different from the political expectations they had shared with the Jews of their day, transported them into a certain "spiritual inebriation,"[11] which is the visionary experience recorded in the gospel. The historical possibility of the vision thus is created by what Weisse read between the lines of the gospel accounts. The various details are interpreted in agreement with his overall approach to the story. The mountain is not to be found on the maps of Palestine, but rather in "the depths of the spirit" and to be understood from the "heights of cognition." The metamorphosis of Jesus is the expression of the illumined idea of the Messiah. And the cloud corresponds to the vagueness in which this still-floating idea is perceived by the disciples, in danger of being obscured at any moment.

What about Peter's offer to build tabernacles? This agrees strikingly with the dogmatic and aggressive character typical for this disciple. He immediately felt the desire to define the new idea theologically and to press it into a formula for further proclamation. This dogmatic desire is expressed by his offer [to build three tabernacles]. If one wants to know how the peculiar offer of the building of tabernacles came into the account of the vision, one can avoid both a purely mythological origin, as well as a pejorative historical description revealing a less favorable side of Peter. The reference [to the building of the tabernacles] may simply have been a figurative manner of speaking by Jesus when he rejected the desire of Peter to tell others about the messiahship in dogmatic formulas (Mark 9:9).

The Conclusive Point for Weisse

The example above is an illustration of Weisse's attempt to find a solution for a "potential problem" [in explaining historically the transfiguration of Jesus] which could give occasion to an objection to his hypothesis concerning the origin of the Gospel of Mark.[12] This approach is characteristic for Weisse, and is

---

[11]Ibid., 1:538.
[12]Ibid., 1:543.

closely related to his method in general. In the recognition of Jesus by the demons Weisse mentions that he is tempted to see the influence of a poetic saga.[13] He declares, however, that he cannot resist believing in the historicity of this piece of information in the gospel account.

Thus in spite of his firm assurances some hesitation appears when the content of the gospels creates difficulties for his subjective "critical sense." These problems have "to be removed." Such a remark is decisive for an evaluation of Weisse's "discovery," which is the conclusive point, the *punctum saliens* from which his hypothesis concerning the priority of the Gospel of Mark is drawn.[14] It refers to his observation that the historical nucleus, after all the critical observations, roughly equals the vivid imagery of the text of the second gospel. It was this surprising "discovery" that caused him to search for evidences within and without the gospels that would give him the right to affirm his conclusion concerning the priority of Mark which already had forced itself upon him. Let us consider the evidences he regarded as vital.

The Priority of Mark according to the Ur-Gospel Hypothesis

To support his convictions concerning his innovating opinion Weisse could refer to predecessors who like himself saw in Mark the earliest gospel. This persuasion reached back to Gottlob Chr. Storr[15] in 1794. At that time the concept of Marcan priority appeared as a replacement of the old harmonization process, as it in turn had evolved from the inspiration theory. Storr had no faith in a revealed text anymore, although he did not cease believing in the absolute validity of the gospels and the historical character of the gospel account. His literal approach [based on an Ur-Gospel] allowed him more freedom in the reconstruction of a gospel history.

The two methods that enabled him to achieve this reconstruction were the assumption that Mark was the oldest gospel, and that Matthew was writing without sequential coherence.[16] The origin of the first assumption can be explained from what Herder some years later called "the natural point of view."[17] By this

---

[13]Ibid., 1:356.

[14]Ibid., preface, 1:v.

[15]Gottlob Christian Storr, "De fonte evangeliorum Matthaei et Lucae commentarii theologii," in *Commentationes Theologiae,* 6 vols., ed. J. C. Velthusen (Leipzig, 1794–1799) 3:140-72.

[16]Ibid., 158; further developed in his book *Über den Zweck der evangelischen Geschichte und der Briefe Johannis* (Tübingen: J. F. Heerbrandt, 1786) 64. [I have not been able to consult this work.]

[17]Johann Gottfried Herder, *Sämtliche Werke zur Religion und Theologie* (Karlsruhe, 1820–1821) 44:19.

Herder meant that among writings of such close affinity as the gospels, the briefest must be considered the earliest document, if it were to keep its right of existence.[18] A more simplistic explanation is hardly imaginable! Even Weisse himself in reference to this opinion of both Storr and Herder, speaks of it as a limited viewpoint which had already become too narrow for the scholarship of his day.[19]

The Priority of Mark according to the Fragment Hypothesis

Of a more complex nature was Marcan priority formulated with the help of the so-called Fragment hypothesis. According to this hypothesis the gospels originated as a collation of various small writings or fragments (*Diegesen*).

It would be an overstatement to assert that Friedrich D. E. Schleiermacher shed a total new light on gospel history through his study "On the Testimonies of Papias Concerning Our First Two Gospels."[20] In the first place Karl A. Credner had independently arrived at the same opinion during his research for his *Introduction to the New Testament;*[21] secondly, however, their alleged discovery was merely the result of the Fragment hypothesis.

As often as an attempt was made to explain the origin of the gospels from one or more possible sources, which as such is an appropriate proposition, the tendency has always been to go to extremes. The reason is apparent. With such sensitive questions as are being raised by gospel critics, not much more is needed than a certain predisposition toward a hypothesis in order to become prejudiced and so to lose a sense for historical accuracy.

As soon as the possibility of a plurality of sources had been broached the search was on, with the result that several different sources were discovered. It is well known how Schleiermacher analyzed the Gospel of Luke. Similarly, Karl K. F. W. Lachmann[22] discovered in the Gospel of Mark five fragments which allegedly originated from tradition or from other writings.

When one looks outside the gospels in the patristic literature, then there also shows up an evidence of sources of which one may expect evidence in the present gospels. This actually occurred in Schleiermacher. In the publication mentioned above he formulated his opinion, which since then has become widespread, about the Logia and the original text of Mark. He himself was not

---

[18]Storr, "De fonte evangeliorum Matthaei et Lucae," 142.

[19]Weisse, *Die evangelische Geschichte,* 1:45.

[20]Friedrich Daniel Ernst Schleiermacher, "Über die Zeugnisse des Papias von unseren ersten beiden Evangelien," *Theologische Studien und Kritiken* (1832).

[21]Karl A. Credner, *Einleitung in das neue Testament* 2 vols. (Halle: Verlag der Buchhandlung des Waisenhauses, 1836) 1:vii.

[22]Karl K. F. W. Lachmann, "De ordine narrationum in evangeliis synopticis," *Theologische Studien und Kritiken* (1835): 570.

able to implement a further development of his discoveries.

Four years later Credner published a study in which he attempted to demonstrate to the scholarly world how the composition of the gospels could be explained from the two documents mentioned by Papias. This approach safeguarded itself against the unsatisfactory solution of the Tradition hypothesis and against the unlikely solution of the Ur-Gospel hypothesis. Credner's exposition, however, was no more than a directive; a detailed analysis of the gospels would have to be carried out by higher criticism.[23] The new idea, which had been launched by both men, was the recognition that the priority of Mark was related to the testimony of Papias, which in turn caused a more profound research into tradition and information that could be derived from it.

Still a third element was introduced into the arena. It was Lachmann who gave special attention to the sequence of the stories in the gospels. Like Credner he agreed with Schleiermacher concerning the conception of the term "Logia" to such a degree that Credner's further information concerning this issue seemed almost superfluous to him.[24] Furthermore he noticed that both other gospels follow so closely the sequence of Mark, that only for an urgent reason did they allow themselves to deviate from it. From this phenomenon he concluded that a traditional sequence had developed that basically gave the present form to our Synoptic gospels. According to Lachmann, the sequence in Mark seemed to be most in agreement with the traditional sequence, although the same Mark allowed five different *corpuscula* (fragments) of oral or written nature to be incorporated in his gospel.

Weisse's Evaluation of Previous Arguments

In Weisse these various arguments took quite a different shape as a result of his own study. He frequently referred to the sequence of the stories in the gospels when dealing with his subject material, but he used this without special emphasis for his hypothesis. He merely pointed to the fact that the thread of Mark runs through both of his synoptic editors. The fact that this thread allowed so much variety is to explained from the nature of the Gospel of Mark which indeed depicts the life of Jesus as a unit, but yet in a somewhat loose connection of events.[25]

Against Schleiermacher he maintained strongly and emphatically the earlier conception of Papias's testimony, namely, that his reference to Mark pointed to our canonical Mark. This assertion meant, to be sure, a definite step forward.

---

[23]Credner, *Einleitung,* §89.
[24]Lachmann, "De ordine narrationum," 577.
[25]Weisse, *Die evangelische Geschichte,* 1:71.

What had been accepted routinely in earlier days had now been subjected to investigation.

For the Marcan hypothesis, the studies of Schleiermacher and Weisse had opened two parallel ways of research, along which it would proceed depending on circumstances. Henceforth, either the "Ur-Mark" of Schleiermacher or the canonical Mark of Weisse would be acknowledged as the source for Matthew and Luke. The contours of both conceptions of Mark would approach one another very closely at times and then again they would keep at a distance from each other. This vacillating process, however, would not produce obviously different results.

Weisse spoke with less conviction when drawing upon the internal evidences of the gospels themselves, "in which indeed, more than in any external evidence, the true motivations for a decision about priority are to be found."[26] He called his "impression" the final authority which had convinced him. To be more specific, he meant by this impression the graphic imagery and the traces of Petrine tradition, which for him had gained conclusive evidential support. The literary imagery seemed to him so vivid that one must come to the conclusion that this gospel was written by some one who was in close contact with eyewitnesses.

Yet Weisse did not want to draw the conclusion that the detailed description in Mark was "definitely to be considered as a perfect reproduction of the experience of the eyewitness Peter."[27] Petrine traits are scattered throughout this gospel, so that Peter consistently is mentioned as one of the foremost disciples; it is Peter who preferably is the spokesman for the other apostles; the whole content of the gospel account concentrated with some exceptions on events of which Peter could have been an eyewitness.

Yet Weisse considers it possible to accord unwarranted importance to this observation;[28] moreover, one should not overlook the objections which can be made by comparing this aspect from the other gospels.[29] These two arguments, namely, the graphic imagery and the Petrine character of Mark, can be regarded as serving the same function as the considerations which brought Herder to his recognition of the priority of Mark. One can, indeed, consider these arguments equally insignificant. Yet Weisse's argumentation is of a totally different quality and of a much higher level, because he has derived his observations from the gospels themselves. His statements have a more solid footing than the questionable suggestions by Herder.

---

[26]Ibid., 53.
[27]Ibid., 65.
[28]Ibid., 59.
[29]Ibid., 62.

An Appraisal of Weisse's Marcan Hypothesis

Weisse belongs therefore, indeed, to the critical era which began at the time of, and through the instrumentality of, David Friedrich Strauss. Through Weisse the Marcan hypothesis obtained a truly scholarly quality. His Marcan hypothesis resulted from merging the conclusions of the research concerning the internal nature of the gospels as well as of the gathering of the external data of history. The graphic imagery of Mark and its so-called Petrine character led accumulatively to the same conclusion as the investigation concerning the testimony of Papias. The Mark whom the tradition portrayed as a follower of Peter was the man to whom we owe the second gospel. The interrelatedness of the Synoptics can clearly be explained when Mark is considered the source of both other gospels.

Very significant for the characteristic quality of this hypothesis is that the apparent result of historical research strikingly agrees with its presupposition. As soon as one feels compelled to accept the verdict of nonoriginality pronounced over the other three gospels, the desire concerning the possibility of a historical account in the remaining gospel is most welcome. This desire was a powerful inducement for Weisse to give his support to Marcan priority. Weisse's consciousness of the originality of his own discovery must be derived mainly from the fact that he was first in identifying the value of Marcan priority as a basis for the reconstruction of an original and historical gospel.

The reason we look to Weisse for the origin of the Marcan hypothesis is his scholarly and critical approach. He was the first critic and scholar since Strauss to establish by this method the recognition of Mark as the oldest gospel; in the same manner he argued for a dependence on Mark by the two other Synoptics. It was Weisse who related the priority of Mark to the study of the historical content of the gospels in general and to the construction of a canon history in particular.

The Hypothesis of a Marcan Ur-Gospel by C. G. Wilke (1838)

Arguments for a Common Literary Source

It is not altogether accidental that the Oral Tradition hypothesis was contested by another study published in the same year as Weisse's work. In that year, 1838, C[hristian] G[ottlob] Wilke completed *The Ur-Evangelist, or an Exegetical-Critical Investigation of the Interrelatedness of the Synoptic Gospels.*[30]

---

[30]Christian Gottlob Wilke, *Der Urevangelist, oder, exegetisch-kritische Untersuchung über das Verwandtschaftsverhältniss der drei ersten Evangelien* (Dresden and Leipzig: Gerhard Fleischer, 1838).

In the introduction Wilke devoted a large portion of his voluminous work to a critical evaluation of the Oral Tradition hypothesis.

According to Wilke the conclusion had been reached that the endeavor to explain from a fixed oral tradition both the difference and agreement between the Synoptics had been unsuccessful. Whereas previously the close agreement of the gospels was felt as an objection against the Oral Tradition hypothesis, Wilke on the contrary derived from the differences his most decisive argument against that hypothesis. For him the unusual variety in both content and form of the gospel accounts defied a simple natural statement, which one would expect of an oral tradition.

This observation is certainly correct, but it does not altogether support Wilke's own concept of written tradition. In distinction from Weisse, who subsumed under the concept of tradition all ideas including the mythologizing elements, Wilke had a fixed doctrinal structure in mind. This source had been developed and standardized in a written form by the apostles in order to be transmitted for the benefit of the preachers.

Wilke would have no objection against a fixed tradition in oral form if there would not remain too many differences that could not be harmonized with such a creedal form. Rejecting an oral tradition in favor of a written code would allow for differences and would solve the issue of style and variety among the evangelists. According to Wilke the gospels are primarily literary documents [calling for a creative approach with individual articulation in form and content].

In spite of this correct assumption there remains an extraneous element in Wilke's reasoning, [namely, that a written document would allow more freedom of expression than an oral tradition]. This explains the nature of Wilke's study, which is strictly a result of the Ur-Gospel hypothesis. He considered the following question the cardinal issue: "To what degree should the common element of the three Synoptics be granted an independent existence?"[31]

Wilke focussed especially on this common element which must provide the answer to the questions concerning its essence and its relation to the particular approach of each of the Synoptics. Once an affirmative conclusion had been reached it was no longer difficult for Wilke to make a choice between an oral or a written Ur-Gospel. Since an oral apostolic tradition would, according to Wilke, not allow for deviations, a written source would invite a more creative involvement by its editors. These two considerations can only partly exist side by side, as was mentioned above. Thus, the Ur-Gospel theory asserts that what is common to the Synoptic gospels should be derived from a written source!

---

[31]Ibid., 20.

The Critical Approach by C. G. Wilke.

Wilke provided the arguments for his thesis in such a manner that Holtz-mann credited him with the merit "to have made us aware how long and trying the exploratory journey through the gospels is."[32] By way of a long list of "data" Wilke demonstrated that in every case deviations from the common source could easily be identified and isolated. The context everywhere supposedly exhibits signs of a bringing together [of the common source and personal creativity:] where two authors are more elaborate, the third one lacks in clarity; where two authors are shorter the third one betrays his additional statements by the wealth of his material. In each of the three gospels the deviating elements show a pecu-liar character by which they distinguish themselves from the common source.

This general result makes one feel uneasy. How peculiar that every detail be-trays the existence of an Ur-Gospel! This arouses the suspicion that Wilke cannot be relied upon at every point.[33] This suspicion is reinforced by the definition he gave of this common source. He attributed to this source, and, therefore to this original document, the parallel texts of the three Synoptics expanded by what within certain limits is shared equally by two gospels. Wilke rejected Eichhorn's approach which traces back to the Ur-Gospel merely what is common to all three of the Synoptics. He regarded this as "a selection which produces only an inco-herent whole."[34] Thus the delineations drawn by Wilke are wider; but this raises the question whether there is not something arbitrary in the drawing up of these delineations. Could one not equally suppose the possibility that only one of the gospels is to be identified with the Ur-Gospel? And would not the acceptance of such a proposition affect the outcome?[35]

The Exegetical Approach by C. G. Wilke

There is yet another point which affects Wilke's theory negatively. The exe-getical process to which the gospels are subjected by him looks very much like an anatomical analysis. The gospels are taken apart as if they were dead docu-ments without any unifying idea. The Ur-Gospel hypothesis, the principle idea

---

[32]Heinrich Julius Holtzmann, *Die synoptischen Evangelien: Ihr Ursprung und geschichtlicher Charakter* (Leipzig: W. Engelmann, 1863) 31.

[33]Further evaluation of Wilke's arguments by Friedrich Karl Albert Schwegler, "Die Hypothese vom schöpferischen Urevangelisten in ihrem Verhältnis zur Traditionshypoth-ese," *Theologische Jahrbücher* (Tübingen, 1843): 203; see also Wilke, *Der Urevangelist*, 452: "Zwanzigstes Datum."

[34]Wilke, *Der Urevangelist*, 316.

[35]Wilke had indeed to allow for this possibility later, for the sake of his Ur-evangelist Mark.

of this work, has made itself felt especially by rejecting an oral tradition. Wilke combated such oral origins strongly and attempted to demonstrate clearly the dependence on a written source. To this end he had to point to the difference between speeches that easily can be remembered in unaltered form, and stories or meditations that are the work of the authors and therefore had to turn out differently for each one of them.

True as this may be, separating words and sayings from stories and connecting thoughts, and consequently treating each of them differently, is detrimental to sound exegesis. On the whole Wilke's arguments for the existence of an original written document have not been derived from the theological content of the gospel material. They rather have been derived from the literary form involving the length or the copiousness of the narratives.[36] His criticism of Griesbach is therefore that according to the latter's hypothesis, Mark alternately elaborated or abbreviated the material of his sources. Wilke regards this an arbitrariness that cannot be relied upon.[37] He considers it impossible to suppose that Mark would have left out details from the narratives in Luke, as some scholars have alleged that Mark did with the Logia from Matthew. With the suggestions that Mark did not want to adopt these details, "one loses all solid ground," according to Wilke.[38] Motives for redaction other than copiousness or preciseness, did not occur according to Wilke. He scarcely mentioned the cause for the modifications made by the various authors in their common source, beyond their being the result of rearrangement and insertion. Modifications are considered to be merely unexplained peculiarities of the authors!

An Appraisal of Wilke's Ur-Gospel Hypothesis

Meanwhile this naive literary conception of gospel literature need not surprise us. It is in complete agreement with the ethos of the era to which the work of Wilke belongs. The Tübingen school had not yet appeared on the scene in full force and the voice of Strauss was not yet able to interfere with Wilke's "independent research."[39] It is indeed surprising in such a copious and even detailed publication to find no reference at all to the vehement perturbation initiated in the theological world by Strauss three years earlier.

Also [Wilke] does not seem to have been acquainted with Schleiermacher's suggestion concerning the direction of the subsequent Marcan research. This is the more surprising since both approaches could have been used for their mutual

---

[36]Which is the quantitative conception of the Gospels.
[37]Wilke, *Der Urevangelist,* 385.
[38]Ibid., 549.
[39]Ibid., 22.

benefit. The Papias reference is completely disregarded, including all external historical references; merely the internal traces of relatedness are used in the decision for the existence of a common Ur-Gospel.

The idea Wilke seemed to have developed concerning "independent research" was to reach a conclusion on the basis of nothing else than the reading of the gospels irrespective of external influences. Taking into consideration that he invested more that ten years in his work[40] and that its inception therefore preceded the new era by more than seven years, one must acknowledge that the publication of this work after Strauss was merely a coincidence. According to its form and content it belongs rather to an earlier era, since the whole procedure of study betrays a certain predisposition for the Ur-Gospel hypothesis in the form it took in [Johann Gottfried] Eichhorn.

The question comes to mind, what connection Wilke has with the Marcan hypothesis. Indeed, the connection is tenuous. When F[erdinand] C[hristian] Baur claims that Wilke was primarily the man who "with great exactness and scholarship attempted to introduce the Marcan Gospel as the common root and basis of the synoptic text, while considering both other gospels as extensions and partly redactions of Mark's portrayal,"[41] he brings together positions which do not exactly correspond.

Baur conceded that Wilke's approach was not new, but he maintained that it had gained new meaning through the critical research of his day. We certainly agree that Wilke posited Mark as the original Gospel. It is true also that his opinion received new impetus because of the state of the synoptic issue at the time. But that Wilke promoted these ideas for the sake of, and in the awareness of, the new meaning it had obtained, cannot truthfully be maintained. It was most coincidental that his Ur-Gospel hypothesis showed similarities with the Marcan hypothesis.

Wilke had indeed a great aversion for the followers of Griesbach, but this had not been caused by his love for Mark but rather for his Ur-evangelist, who ultimately would be closely associated with Mark. Wilke's polemic against the followers of Griesbach becomes more explicit to the degree that his conviction becomes more outspoken.[42] His attempt to keep up so emphatically the honor of Mark is made less for Mark as an author than for the sake of a gospel writer who has the fame to be a "rational author"[43] who is not accused of being

---

[40]Ibid., iii.

[41]F. C. Baur, *Kritische Untersuchungen über die kanonischen Evangelien, ihr Verhältnis zu einander, ihren Charakter und Ursprung* (Tübingen: L. F. Fues, 1847) 68.

[42]Wilke, *Der Urevangelist*, 431, 443, 549.

[43]Ibid., 443.

narrowminded.[44]

That Wilke had been persuaded to consider Mark the earliest factual account was neither because he wanted to obtain a reliable source for the knowledge of Jesus' history nor because he had observed a historical relationship between this gospel and Peter or the Petrine tradition; his conviction was merely the result of his conception of what is common in the Synoptic gospels.

The Canonical Mark Identified as the Ur-Gospel by C. G. Wilke

In the existing relationship of the Synoptics, Wilke pursued the thread of Mark through the other two Synoptic gospels up to the end: at one time it runs through Matthew, at another time through Luke, or through both of them at the same time. If that which is found only in two gospels be considered also part of the common source, the resulting body of material is about equal to the total content of the Gospel of Mark. In that case it would be obvious to see in Mark the Ur-evangelist.

Already the discovery that Mark almost always shares in the agreement of the two other gospels should direct our attention to this author, according to Wilke.[45] The proportion of the common elements in view of the particular traits of each gospel persuaded him to accept the existence of an Ur-Gospel.[46]

The scarcity of individual traits in the second gospel caused Wilke initially to consider it [close to] an original text that had been most accurately rendered by Mark. Originally Wilke proceeded no further than the assumption of a document preceding the canonical Gospel of Mark. The insignificance of its individual qualities gave Wilke finally the liberty also to cross the last border by simply declaring the canonical Gospel of Mark as the Ur-Gospel.

As soon as the minor peculiarities of this canonical gospel have been noted to be the work of a second hand, which therefore can be separated from the main body of material,[47] one is faced with the question of authorship. Wilke observed that these peculiarities are merely repetitions or statements that can easily be disengaged from the context. They seem to serve only to strengthen the imagery of this gospel. In sum, the peculiarities are to be considered part of the shell rather than of the kernel.[48]

According to Wilke, these observations must of necessity lead to a choice, whether one accepts the canonical text of Mark as his own work including the

---

[44]Ibid., 401.
[45]Ibid., 296.
[46]Ibid., 324.
[47]Ibid., 325.
[48]Ibid., 677.

nonessential additions, or whether one associates his name with the original writing. The immediate implication of this alternative requires that the canonical writer is not given a too significant position. "One cannot suppose that the author Mark after having derived the kernel of his account from elsewhere, would merely devote his zeal to the embellishment of the shell"[49] task good enough for an unknown redactor. [Therefore, Mark is to be considered the author of the Ur-Gospel.]

[In this connection Wilke raised the question] concerning data which Matthew and Luke have in common, but which are not found in the Marcan text. In such cases one should, according to Wilke, begin with the explanation of the places where Luke's text shows a more original reading than Matthew. This phenomenon gave Wilke ground to suggest the possibility that Matthew used Mark as the basic source for the composition of his own gospel and that he further consulted Luke's redaction of Mark.[50]

With this proposition all objections seem to have been removed. The Ur-Gospel has been brought to light and has even received a biblical name, [namely, Mark]. This name, however incidental and unessential for the Marcan hypothesis itself, is the reason Wilke's work has been included by us in the history of that hypothesis. At this point Wilke has actually left the territory of Eichhorn, [who was the first to propose that the text of the Ur-Gospel could be reconstructed from the common elements of the Synoptics]. The Ur-evangelist really has lost his title as soon as he becomes identified with one of the canonical gospels.

Mark remains Mark, however little or much he has been pruned. This remains the dominant idea among the proponents of the Marcan hypothesis and for that reason alone, Wilke may be counted among them. In his recognition of Mark as the source of the two other Synoptics, Wilke took the liberty of conceiving the Gospel of Mark in a flexible manner and of freeing it of seemingly nonessential elements as circumstances might require. [It was this form of redaction criticism that gave him a role among the proponents of the Marcan hypothesis].

---

[49]Ibid., 677.

[50]Ibid., 462, 693. [See also David B. Peabody, "Chapters in the History of the Linguistic Argument for Solving the Synoptic Problem: The Nineteenth Century in Context," *Jesus, the Gospels, and the Church,* ed. E. P. Sanders (Macon: Mercer University Press, 1987) 47-68, for a critical evaluation of Wilke's mistaken methodology and its influence on Holtzmann and his successors. —ed.]

The Question of Authorship of the Second Gospel (1843)

John Mark the Author of the Second Gospel,
according to Ferdinand Hitzig

With more justification we may deal with the form the Marcan hypothesis attained under Hitzig in his book *About John Mark and His Writings.*[51] In order to understand him well the purpose of his book needs to be taken into account. Hitzig started from the proposition that the fourth gospel and the book of Revelation are not by the same author but that both were written by a person named John. Since Hitzig considered the gospel a document written by the apostle John his question focussed initially on the authorship of the book of Revelation. The New Testament mentions two men by the name of John: the apostle John and John surnamed Mark. By recognizing the authenticity of the fourth gospel and by taking into account only names that occur in the New Testament, the answer had already been decided. Since Hitzig believed in the tradition that a certain John was the author of the book of Revelation and because he discovered a similarity of style in this book and in the Gospel of Mark, his selection of John Mark as the author of both the Gospel of Mark and the book of Revelation seems [to Hitzig] sufficiently proven.

[Hitzig's] argumentation for the identity of authorship is conducted in a pleasing manner by demonstrating agreement in the selection of words, morphology, declension, theological principle, and poetic composition. Hitzig is amusing in his many humorous and peculiar conjectures. But he felt that one possible objection needed to be addressed immediately. According to the opinion of Griesbach and his followers, Mark would have compiled his gospel from the two other Synoptic gospels. Such a conception would be in conflict with the original character typical of the author of the book of Revelation.[52] A certain predilection for Mark can, therefore, be expected from Hitzig. Had Mark simply "nailed or pieced together" his gospel from materials derived from others, he would have little or nothing in common with the ingenious author of the Apocalypse. Hitzig considered it a point in his favor that nothing other than prejudice and manifest partiality was found among the advocates of the Griesbach theory. Hitzig claimed they had no valid argument which even remotely had any force of proof.[53]

---

[51]Ferdinand Hitzig, *Über Johannes Marcus und seine Schriften* (Zürich, 1843) 224.
[52]Ibid., 37ff.
[53]Ibid., 39.

The Marcan Hypothesis, according to Hitzig

Hitzig proceeded to demonstrate the originality of Mark and to confirm the thesis that Mark has been used as a source by the other Synoptics. He largely used the current arguments, although he placed little emphasis upon the brevity of the second gospel, which nonetheless was an argument of importance for him.[54] Moreover, Hitzig discovered traces of misunderstanding in Matthew and Luke, which traces he traced back to Mark. They failed to include, for instance, the deaf and dumb spirit (Mark 9:25) in the story of the boy with a demon (Matt 17:14-21, Luke 9:37-43). Matthew and Luke supposedly did not understand that the word "deafness" used in connection with an evil spirit was nothing else than the stubborn refusal to leave after exorcism or threat. Hitzig alleged that snake charmers sometimes use that expression for obstinate snakes.[55] Had not the disciples attempted to heal the boy in vain?

Hitzig detected misunderstanding also in the way the question of the coming of Elijah was discussed in Matthew (17:9-12 cf. Mark 9:10-13).[56] First Hitzig emended the Greek reading for "restoring all things," in Mk. 9:12, from ἀποκα-θιστάνει to ἀποκαθιστάναι, so it then looks like a Hebrew construction where the infinitive is governed by the participle "coming" (ἐλθών). Then he explained the train of thought in this pericope of Mark as follows: Jesus forbids his disciples to mention the transfiguration on the mountain before the event of the resurrection, by which Jesus meant his own resurrection. The disciples, according to Hitzig's rather unclear presentation, understood this to refer to the eternal life-giving power of God, which is to be distinguished from the resurrection of the Son before and in the parousia, according to John 5:21, Rom. 4:17, and 2 Tim 2:18.

Hitzig argued the disciples must have had this thought in mind since one cannot suppose they were uncertain about the resurrection of Jesus from the dead (the ἀνάστασις ἐκ νεκρῶν). The Pharisees, who had no notion of a suffering Messiah, could hardly have associated the coming of Elijah with the resurrection of Jesus either.[57] Thus the disciples must have asked, according to Hitzig, concerning the relationship between the life-giving power of God and the coming of Elijah. Jesus' answer, however, returns to his actual intention, namely, his own resurrection following his suffering and death. This answer reduces a restoration (ἀποκατάστασις) by Elijah to an implausibility, since suffering would not be possible in a restored world order.

While Luke left the whole "thorny question" out, Matthew only eliminated

---

[54]Ibid., 60.

[55]Ibid., 52.

[56]Ibid., 47ff.

[57]Namely, when πρῶτον must be considered to refer here to the resurrection.

the uncertainty of the disciples by leaving out their question concerning the rising from the dead (see Mark 9:10, τί ἐστιν τὸ ἐκ νεκρῶν ἀναστῆναι). In doing so, however, Matthew had interrupted the train of thought [as it is found in Hitzig's interpretation of Mark].

At this point I could mention that this interpretation is weakened first of all by the peculiarity of such a misunderstanding between Jesus and his disciples, and secondly by a text emendation, which is not supported by any manuscript. I do not want to suggest at this time another interpretation of this significant account. The reference to this place in Hitzig's work merely serves to convey the manner in which he found everything in Mark "clear and in the right order."[58]

The Hebraic Origin of Mark, according to Hitzig

These and similar remarks are also closely connected with another assertion, which is of great importance for Hitzig's overall approach, namely, that in his opinion the Marcan text is preeminently Hebraic. This phenomenon is first of all relevant for his John Mark hypothesis,[59] but it also suggests that this gospel must have an earlier date than the two other Synoptic gospels,[60] and finally it serves excellently to explain the vacillating character of the Marcan text itself.[61] These last two points belong together.

Attempts have been made to explain the unsteady character of the Marcan text from its conflated nature. The issue, however, according to Hitzig, is that later copyists as well as the two redactors, Matthew and Luke, were not satisfied with Mark's Hebraic style and replaced it therefore by their more-Greek readings. The Hebraic style of the first Christian writers certainly must have preceded the purer Greek style, which implies for Hitzig that the more Hebraic the writings are, the earlier must be their date.

This observation, however, has always appeared to me to be of little value. Even if the first thesis concerning the Hebraic element is true, it does not have to lead to the succeeding inference of dating the gospels. Firstly, by isolating the Hebraisms (which, it is asserted, Matthew adopted from Mark), one attempts to set up an argument with the help of the points at issue themselves. Secondly, one should take into account the unequal stages through which this process of purifying the language must have gone. Thirdly, a disparity is caused by influences such as the parentage of the author, his study of the Old Testament, and of the translation of the Septuagint. Finally, during the rather short span of

---

[58]Hitzig, *Über Johannes Marcus und seine Schriften*, 57.
[59]Ibid., 34.
[60]Ibid., 37.
[61]Ibid., 29.

time in which the New Testament came into being, the development of language must have been almost imperceptable.

As long as some independence is ascribed to an author in addition to the use of his sources, one will attach little weight to the phenomena [of linguistic transition] in deciding the date of a document. In particular one will not confuse the Aramaic words in Mark with Hebraisms[62] nor deem it more likely that Mark wrote the Hebrew word for teacher (ῥαββουνί) instead of the Greek word (κύριε).[63] But Hitzig's contribution to the Marcan hypothesis is that scholars since his day have paid attention to the style of the evangelists; also vocabulary and idiom have been studied in order to gain insight into the interrelatedness of the synoptic authors. Later we will come upon more accurate research in this area of study.

The Graphic Imagery of Mark, according to Hitzig

For Hitzig the first and major evidence of Mark's originality is Mark's style and imagery. "When I took up this question independently for the first time I discovered immediately the originality of the Marcan Gospel on the basis of its descriptiveness alone."[64] It is essential to take note of the space this part of Hitzig's argumentation takes up in his book and consequently in the history of the Marcan hypothesis. While in the book of Revelation everything is described in "glowing colors" the Gospel of Mark at least shows the initial stirrings of imagination. The pollen of blossoms (*Blütenstaub*) is attached to this gospel. The author is rich in literary description. His style is poetic, his prose noble and pure.

In case a friend of historical certainty should feel uneasy with these remarks and lose confidence in this author, he may abandon his concern. The early origin of this gospel and its recognition as a useful source by Matthew and Luke are guarantees of its historical reliability. That is to say, "in general,"[65] as Hitzig observed, because at some points he found Mark in error, as the following statements may illustrate: the Last Supper of Jesus was moved erroneously to the evening of the Passover; Mark added to the description of the execution of John the Baptist motivations and circumstances as they seemed likely to him; he showed less interest in doctrine than in descriptions, which was especially due to his poetic mind; and the evangelist arranged all of the public ministry of Christ within the time span of one year in order to create a harmonious unit.

It is obvious at this point that the recognition of the authenticity of the fourth

---

[62]Ibid., 34.
[63]Ibid., 31.
[64]Ibid., 41.
[65]Ibid., 121ff.

gospel on the one hand and the identity of Mark with the author of Revelation on the other hand forced Hitzig to adopt theses with implications of which he was not quite aware. What remains of the historical reliability of this gospel (a) when one cannot depend on temporal data; (b) when the arrangement of the facts is the work of the author;[66] (c) when the descriptive imagery is just the result of his imagination; (d) when the camel's passing through the eye of a needle is ascribed to indulging imagination; (c) when there is place for the gaining of the whole world as well as for a faith like a mustard seed; or (f) when the limited addresses of Jesus are to be considered as sources for Mark's own theology?[67]

In a word, Hitzig unconsciously allows to escape from his own hands the guarantees which a friend of historical reliability would certainly need for his faith. Even though Hitzig declared a potential for doubt unfounded, he did not contribute very much to suppress this doubt. His zeal for John Mark has carried him beyond his intentions.

The Initial Traces of Tendency Criticism in Hitzig

This brings us to a further consideration. Already Wilke had undertaken "the endeavor to take into consideration every conscious idea and intention, every trace of reflection, and every direction of thought, in order to establish the major factor for understanding the interrelatedness of the gospels."[68] The same may be said to a greater degree of Hitzig. According to Hitzig, the reader is removed from the Palestinian soil into the mind of the New Testament writers from whom the gospel story emerged more directly. The writers were the medium through which the imprints of the reality had to be transmitted in order to be released into manuscript on paper. The condition of that medium would evoke increasing attention and become a point of new research.

In Hitzig this process was already strongly manifest in the ranks of the proponents of the Marcan hypothesis. It occurred, however, without a clear self-consciousness. This could be attained only after the issue had been studied in wider circles; it was to be connected with a completely new view of the situation of the Christian church in the earliest period of its development. It would find a number of representatives in the Tübingen school who adopted this approach as a project of research. But then it also would become evident to what degree the Marcan hypothesis could genuinely be harmonized with the principle of Tendency Criticism, and what adjustment the hypothesis had to undergo because of it.

I pointed out above that the Tübingen school as well as the advocates of the

---

[66]Ibid., 124ff.
[67]Ibid., 130ff.
[68]Baur, *Kritische Untersuchungen über die kanonischen Evangelien,* 68.

Marcan hypothesis had their reason for existence chiefly insofar as they both attempted to lay a more solid groundwork for the construction of a gospel history. [It had to be more historical in orientation] since the old foundations had turned out to be weak and the erected walls had been brought down by the trumpets of Strauss. Both endeavors soon came into conflict with one another, however. The temple builders of Jerusalem [referring to Tübingen], did not tolerate Samaritan help [advocates of Marcan priority] to join hands and the relation between the two parties soon came to be such that Strauss seemed to have received new auxiliary troops while the proponents of the Marcan hypothesis were facing a new enemy.

At this point we have approached the moment when the Marcan hypothesis can be considered to have entered a new era. Before we pursue the forms it took during its subsequent period of development, we have to call to mind the ideas of the Tübingen school in order to understand the shift that took place in the form of the Marcan hypothesis.

The Approach of Tendency Criticism

The Subjective Approach to History by Bruno Bauer (1841)

First another study should be mentioned which had some connection with the Marcan hypothesis, namely, Bruno Bauer's *Critique of the Gospel History of the Synoptics.*[69] It is not an overstatement when I assert that Bauer's notorious book had some connection with the Marcan hypothesis, although the qualification "some" is of importance as well. Indeed, this connection is only accidental and merely a result of the nature of this study and the time of its publication. Not satisfied anymore with the notion of a God-man and his miracles as these are found in the gospels, Bauer rejected their historical validity and derived the emergence of this notion of the God-man in Hegelian fashion from the growing awareness of the religious mind during that period of history when Christianity made its beginning. Such awareness of mind was not possible without its concretization into the notion of a God-man in whom the recognition of a miraculous power was of necessity contained.[70]

According to Bauer the content of the gospels did not have the imprint of historical reality, but was the result of a thought process. The Gospel stories were the forms in which those thoughts were projected concretely. Such a conception of the essence of the New Testament story is hardly compatible with the acknowl-

---

[69]Bruno Bauer, *Kritik der evangelischen Geschichte der Synoptiker,* 3 vols. (Leipzig, 1841–1842).
[70]Ibid., 1:69, 82; 2:157ff.

edgement of objective history in the gospels. Bauer, on the contrary, demanded of critical scholars that they deduce the total content of the gospel stories from the mind of the authors [that is, that nothing was to be assumed to have come from factual history]. Bauer's idea about progress in criticism was that critics attribute greater influence to the creative effort of the evangelists than to historical data.

Bauer assigned himself the task of implementing this method of criticism. In order to understand its relevance for the Marcan hypothesis we have to consider how Bauer visualized the process of the religious mind. Initially one would conclude that the mythical conception in its full development would have satisfied Bauer completely. The mythical theory also operated from the assumption that the initial religious and moral experience among a number of persons is gradually projected as history and then as external reality. However, Bauer rejected the mythical approach and objected to the need for a group of persons creating objective history emerging from their personal convictions. He especially rejected the idea that this process would have to take place subconsciously.

The Evangelist Mark, the Origin of a Hegelian Dialectic

The recent results of Gospel criticism, especially of the Marcan hypothesis, were avidly used by Bauer to make his point. The amazing discovery of Weisse had been confirmed conclusively by Wilke, according to Bauer. He considered it demonstrated that Mark was entitled to the name of Ur-Evangelist. When Weisse had assumed a second source in the Logia mentioned by Papias, Wilke had again removed this by demonstrating that Matthew had used Mark and Luke as his sources. [Thus Bauer could use the latest results of research for his dialectic thesis.] One author of a gospel had raised the consciousness of another in such a manner that from the tension of both new ideas could further develop in concrete fashion. Thus the origin of gospel history could be explained from the nucleus in the most simple way.

Because of its simplicity the Marcan hypothesis could serve Bauer's Hegelian approach to interpretation quite well. The original intention of this hypothesis to gain certainty concerning biblical history provided Bauer with the occasion for taking advantage of it for his critical interpretations of a totally different nature. The connection between Bauer and the Marcan hypothesis is no more than a mere association. Just as his book is of little value for the explanation of the origin of Christianity, so his significance for the Marcan hypothesis is not to be esteemed very highly. His conception of Mark does not reflect personal study;

and new arguments have not been introduced by him.[71]

The Tendency Criticism of F. C. Baur

In [Bruno] Bauer the same approach is present which manifested itself increasingly in his day, that is, to take into consideration the personal attitude of the authors in interpreting their works. In Bauer this approach had been fully developed, or rather, it had become a caricature. Such degeneration does not prevent us, however, from noting a certain progression in the history of Gospel criticism. This would appear after it had been channeled in the right direction and after it had gained its own territory. To quote Ferdinand Christian Baur,

> Since all history is transmitted to us by way of the author who recounts it, the primary question is not to what degree some story informs us about reality, but in what relation this story stands to the consciousness of the author. Through the mediation of the author the historical data become for us objects of research, which is true also for the criticism of Gospel history.[72]

This conviction became, indeed, the maxim of the day. Thus far it had been applied only to the form of the gospels; those who went further than that had no awareness of the consequences. In a certain way Bruno Bauer was right when he claimed also the content of the gospels for this new method of interpretation. Its validity merely had to be demonstrated and the limits of its territory had to be established. This then was to be implemented by the Tübingen school, where the possibility of its implementation was provided by the results of historical research.

The "Historical Approach" of F. C. Baur (1845)

The direction F. C. Baur's study was to take could have been anticipated even before the book by Strauss had been published. In his study of the Letters to the Corinthians, Baur's attention was attracted to the relationship of Paul to the early Christian churches and to the original apostles. It occurred to Baur that this relationship had been entirely different from the prevailing notion of his day. Baur devoted all his interest to this aspect and discovered everywhere traces of tension and conflict. Other writings from the apostolic era were consulted; the homilies of Clement in particular were carefully scrutinized.

Increasingly the apostolic era appeared to Baur as a scene of vehement

---

[71]So also Schwegler, "Die Hypothese vom schöpferischen Urevangelisten," *Tübinger [Theologische] Jahrbücher* (1843): 241ff.

[72]Baur, *Kritische Untersuchungen über die kanonischen Evangelien*, 73ff.

conflict instead of the supposedly serene epoch posited by tradition. Baur saw this conflict resolved in a union of the opposing parties by way of Catholicism. This discovery shed new light upon the origin and value of the book of Acts. Further research in the Gnostic movement and a deeper insight into the mind of the great Apostle to the Gentiles would lead to a totally different view of the origin of the Pauline letters. Already in 1845 the various results of Baur's studies could be embodied in his book on Paul.[73]

These various studies had occupied Baur so completely that not much time was left him for Gospel criticism. But when the studies on Paul had been completed new light had been kindled by which the gospels could be interpreted from a totally different perspective. With even more zeal Baur assumed the second part of this labor as he felt challenged to try his new approach in view of the development of the Gospel criticism of his day. Numerous hypotheses had superseded one another. Scholars had turned from one gospel to another in order to find the beginning of gospel literature, without arriving at a firm conclusion that could bear fruit for a historical evaluation of the gospels. Strauss had used a most defective approach to Gospel criticism, which had not failed to produce harmful consequences. If everything was not to remain fruitless, a criterion would have to be found by which the historical worth of the gospel accounts could be measured.

Baur was of the opinion he had discovered exactly this criterion as a result of his own historical investigations. Baur reasoned that in order to answer the question of the historical validity of any writing, one must first establish whether the author actually set himself the task of writing history, or whether other motivations guided him in his work. To that end one must seek primarily for the occasion and the purpose of any document and the ensuing character it received. In order to obtain conclusive evidence, one must engage in a most careful inquiry into the historical circumstances in which the particular document came into being.

Where the object of the writer's interest was of such nature that it exerted a profound influence on circumstances and movements of all sorts, one may expect that those circumstances reciprocally exerted influence on the purpose and structure of his document. These considerations, plus the newly achieved conception of the situation of the early Christian church, caused Baur to view the gospels from a totally different perspective.

---

[73]F. C. Baur, *Paulus, der Apostel Jesu Christi. Sein Leben und Wirken, seine Briefe und seine Lehre. Ein Beitrag zu einer kritischen Geschichte des Urchristenthums* (*Paul, the apostle of Jesus Christ. His life and activity, his letters and his teachings. A contribution to a critical history of primitive Christianity*) (Stuttgart, 1845) 398; idem, *Kirchengeschichte des neunzehnten Jahrhunderts* (Tübingen, 1862) 395.

The new insight into the mutual relationship of the apostles and their initial followers had to assert its influence. It was unlikely that the traces of the vehement conflict, which was reflected in so many documents of antiquity, would not equally be found in the gospels. At least, it was most likely these traces could be anticipated. Baur therefore investigated the particular nature of the gospels in order to discover the reflection of contemporary situations and whether the authors showed other objectives than pure historical ones in their writings.

Baur expected three issues to be resolved as a result of this investigation: (1) the place in the literary history to be assigned to each of the gospels; (2) the more or less explicit secondary intentions the authors betrayed in form or content; and (3) the degree of historical credibility of the gospels.[74]

The answers Baur found to these various questions are known. They were successively presented to the theologians in the *Tübingen Yearbooks,* and since then collected in his *Critical Investigations.* The method he recommended was called the "historical approach." Baur saw its relevance for critical scholarship in the fact that it would provide a means of overcoming the ambivalence [concerning a historical criterion] which existed since the days of Strauss.

An Appraisal of F. C. Baur

Under the influence of Baur's ideas Schwegler had already in 1843 suggested a way to reach a solution in the difficult issue of gospel history. He proposed a consideration of "the Synoptic Gospels in connection with the complications and contentions by which the early Christian church was plagued, as this is known to us from other sources."[75] Also independently from Baur, the Anonymous Saxon[76] had already applied this criterion. The historical approach [from external sources] was thus promoted from all sides.

It should be conceded that the development of Baur's studies, which had taken its starting point in John as the most spiritual gospel, had a somewhat negative influence on his view of the Synoptics.[77] It should be stated also that the new way of thinking did not stay free from some exaggeration. The historical approach had, however, demonstrated the justification of its claims. The validity

---

[74]Baur, *Kritische Untersuchungen über die kanonischen Evangelien,* 620.

[75]Schwegler, "Die Hypothese vom schöpferischen Urevangelisten," 235.

[76]*Die Evangelien, ihr Geist, ihre Verfasser, und ihr Verhältniss zu einander: Ein Beitrag zur Lösung der kritischen Fragen über die Entstehung derselben* (Leipzig: Otto Wigand, 1845). [The author probably is to be indentified as Christian Adolf Hasert.]

[77]David Friedrich Strauss, *Das Leben Jesu für das deutsche Volk bearbeitet,* 2 vols. (Leipzig: F. A. Brockhaus, 1864 ed.) 1:109. [This was Strauss's *second* "Life of Jesus," freshly written, and not just a later version of his first "Life," the 4th edition of which had been published in 1840.]

of each conclusion in critical studies would henceforth be dependent on its taking account of the historical question.

The presupposition which had to underlie all research since Baur was that each gospel had its individual character. As a result the necessity of this historical quest was felt by all scholars working critically with the texts of the Gospels.

The Marcan Hypothesis Confronting Tendency Criticism

The Subjective or Objective Reliability of the Gospels

What did this development mean for the Marcan hypothesis? From the perspective of its proponents it should have been a welcome development that the new method promised historical certainty for its achievement and a victory over Strauss as its ultimate result. The Tübingen scholars thus seemed to declare themselves brothers and helpers of the advocates of the Marcan hypothesis.

Yet there were some symptoms that caused suspicion. Firstly, it was not a friendly gesture when the new trend of Tendency Criticism resulting from Baur's approach designated everyone who had made an attempt to gain objective historical certainty as an "opponent of Strauss." The Tübingers averred that all such scholars had not progressed much further than the level of research reached before Strauss.[78] Furthermore, the adherents of the Tübingen school preferred the hypothesis of Griesbach whose conception of the second gospel was totally opposite to the Marcan hypothesis. Finally, the Tübingen school did not explicitly object to Strauss's rejection of the historical value of the gospels. According to von Hutten, the Tübingen school had even reduced the objective historical value of the gospels to one-fourth of their historical value in Strauss.[79]

For these various reasons it will be understood that the adherents of the Marcan hypothesis recognized enemies rather than friends in the new colleagues. Because of this development the Marcan hypothesis received a new challenge. In previous years the Marcan gospel had provided a shelter against the influence of the mythical conception of Strauss; the Marcan hypothesis would now attempt to test the strength of its weapons against the Tendency Criticism of the Tübingen school. This was, however, not to be achieved without fundamental sacrifices.

The Tübingen concept of history had gained too much ground for it to fail to penetrate the Marcan fortress. To some degree the Marcan hypothesis also had to assign an individual character to each of the gospels. But whatever dangers might arise in shaking their confidence in the reliability of the gospels, because of the subjective impact of the writers on their form and content, to them (that

---

[78]Baur, *Kritische Untersuchungen über die kanonischen Evangelien,* 63.
[79]Ulrich von Hutten, *Opera quae extant omnia* (Berlin, 1821–1827) xxxff.

is, adherents of the Marcan hypothesis) the Gospel of Mark would remain unscathed. It would remain the sheet anchor to which one had merely to cling in order to be safe when the calamity would reach a climax. This course of events will become evident when we pursue the further historical development of the Marcan hypothesis.

Heinrich Ewald's Militant Stance against the Tübingers (1850)

In the first place we encounter Heinrich Ewald as the spokesman for the Marcan hypothesis. He wrote about the "Origin and Essence of the Gospels" in three essays published in the *Yearbooks of Biblical Scholarship*[80] from 1848 until 1850. Simultaneously, in 1850, his book was published under the title *The First Three Gospels Translated and Interpreted.*[81] In this translation Ewald presented in concrete fashion his ideas about the composition of the writings in question by way of various letter types. He immediately disclosed how little sympathy the endeavor of the Tübingers had created among the proponents of the Marcan hypothesis.

A first acquaintance with Ewald in the area of Gospel criticism makes a peculiar impression upon the reader. In metaphoric language he speaks about the storms [of Gospel criticism] which had risen with force. Prior to the storm the sun [the Gospel] had become hazy and its light darkened until the power of the storm snatched away its veil restoring its free position and renewing its opportunity of giving light and warmth to the needy human heart. These attempts were of temporary benefit, however. Malicious people had created clouds of dust causing new darkness on earth and shrouding the face of the sun again. Satan himself seemed to have come down like the adversary of Job in biblical times, but in this case as an omen of future glory and better days. In the deepest need rescue would be near; Ewald could see its dawn already at the horizon.

When translated into prose this metaphor signified approximately the following. For centuries the Christians had not clearly known their Lord until Gospel criticism attempted to shed new light. It could do this without harm and succeeded in clarifying the faith. The apprehension of some anxious Christians for the sake of their Lord was, indeed, unfounded. "Had Christ not been present in former days, and is he not more than the four canonical gospels including all the Apocrypha?"[82]

---

[80]Heinrich Ewald, "Ursprung und Wesen der Evangelien," *Jahrbücher der biblischen Wissenschaft* 1 (Göttingen, 1848): 113-54; 2 (1849): 180-224; 3 (1850): 140-77.

[81]Heinrich Ewald, *Die drei ersten Evangelien übersetzt und erklärt,* 2 vols. (Göttingen: Vandenhoeck & Ruprecht, 1850).

[82]Ewald, *JBW* 1:114.

But as for the doubt of the scholars of the Tübingen school, of those perfidious philosophers who manifested a mean spirit and failed to appreciate the origin and essence of the Gospel—that kind of doubt should not be tolerated. The Tübingen school was, indeed, like Satan coming to earth, but then not in order to test the devout Job but rather as a curse on a sinful generation; if no rescue were coming the disaster would be immense.[83] Ewald continued, "For a thousand reasons it is now urgently needed that everyone perceive clearly what the real content of the gospels is and in what manner they came into being."[84] "It is high time that Christ should appear among us as being resurrected for the second time."[85] "If German scholarship will cause still more damage than it has already, and if it is not to become a mockery everywhere, then it is high time that a correct view of the Gospel come to light."[86]

With these words, by which he announced the occasion and the purpose of his writings, Ewald clearly indicated the point of view he had taken in connection with Gospel criticism. He did not fear any danger from criticism itself; as long as it remained within the limits acceptable to him it would not harm the faith of Christians. His deadly enemies were the Tübingers; against them all his efforts were to be directed. We will not ask for the cause of this hatred but only investigate why Ewald found in Mark an effective weapon for his confrontation and with what justification he made use of this weapon.

Ewald's Marcan Hypothesis

Here we touch upon the question to what degree Ewald can be called a proponent of the Marcan hypothesis. According to him the development of gospel literature reached its culmination in eight stages. Document after document came into being, while each succeeding document always incorporated the preceding writings, until this process came to a completion in our canon of four gospels. It would seem, therefore, that Ewald's system would allow no place for such a simple approach as the Marcan hypothesis.

Yet it appears, after further investigation, that this complex theory is nothing else than a variation on the same theme. Let us merely pay attention to the place the three Synoptics occupy in that process. The first attempt [in recording the gospel events] endeavored to portray the most glorious moments of the history of Christ, such as his baptism, his sojourn in the desert, the transfiguration, and also some simple but significant sayings of Jesus within their situational context,

---

[83]Ewald, *Die drei ersten Evangelien,* vi.
[84]Ibid., v.
[85]Ibid., vi.
[86]Ewald, *JBW* 1:115.

as they occur in Luke's travelogue. A second author collected the sayings of Jesus into a document that, since Schleiermacher, has born the name "Logia." Both writings were used in equal measure by a third author named Mark.

To these three sources another writer added a fourth document, "the book of higher history," which was a redaction of the oldest document featuring the most glorious moments in Jesus' life. It included the more detailed account of the temptations and some scenes from the passion of Jesus, which were adopted by Matthew and Luke.

After this followed our first gospel as a lake merging these various streams. In addition to the previous streams three more currents were formed, although they still remain to be identified. From these six tributaries emerged the canonical Gospel of Luke as a second lake alongside Matthew.

This general survey is sufficient to recognize the Marcan hypothesis clearly in this complex system. Also according to Ewald, Luke and Matthew did not know one another, but both adopted the Gospel of Mark, even though there were other links between each of them and Mark. These other sources were, however, of little importance to him. The "book of higher history" is nothing else than a means to explain the very detailed account of the temptations which could not have been derived from Mark.

The three documents that supposedly originated later than Matthew are that part of Luke that could not be explained by the previous documents. Because of the difference in the content and form, these remaining materials were divided by Ewald into three components—a contention to which one is entitled within the context of the Marcan hypothesis.

The only objection one could have at this point is the assertion that Mark used sources. However, this assertion disappears when we ascertain how Ewald dealt with the issue of the Gospel of Mark, when he states, "although in chronological sequence only a third document, because it has used two previous sources, it is yet to be considered basically the first original work and an entirely new creation."[87]

Ewald's Assessment of the Gospel of Mark

Ewald was of the opinion that Mark had a uniquely original character. The points he adduced as evidences were exactly the same as those advanced by the proponents of the Marcan hypothesis. The graphic imagery in Mark pointed to an author who had the materials in their most original form available. Nowhere is found to the same degree "this loveliness of fresh flowers, this pure vigorous

---

[87]Ibid., 2:203.

vitality of the materials."[88] They correspond strikingly to the tradition concerning Mark found in Papias. The Galilean content refers to Peter, the lack of chronological data indicates a "beginning" effort, the absence of the stories about the early years of Christ and the insertion of Aramaic words point to an early date as well. In sum, for Ewald the Gospel of Mark had exactly the same value as it had for each advocate of the Marcan hypothesis.

Furthermore we find in him what we discovered among earlier advocates of the hypothesis. The Mark which is incorporated in Matthew, which was also a source for Luke and which was referred to by Papias, is our Marcan Gospel, but at the same time not our canonical Mark. The Sermon on the Mount, the centurion of Capernaum, the closing chapter, and various characteristics have disappeared, while other features have been inserted or modified.

Those deviations from the original Mark, however, have not caused Ewald to ascribe them to a redactor. Therefore he did not elevate the third original document in the literature of the gospels to an Ur-Mark. These variations were, on the contrary, additional proofs that the second gospel had a very early place of honor among the first Christians. It was read and copied frequently. Our Mark is nothing else than such a copy.[89]

Ewald is therefore an advocate of the Marcan hypothesis. The more disdain he developed for Tendency Criticism, the more zealously he performed his role as challenger of the Tübingen theologians. This aversion must be regarded as the major explanation for this theory of the gospels.

It was not sufficient to conclude that Mark reached back to Peter and Matthew to the Logia, and that both thereby had their warrant of credibility. Nothing was to remain that could be claimed by the Tendency critics as a trait of the author's personality. In particular Luke, who was for Baur the most unique author of the Synoptics, was to be demoted. One could ascribe to Luke only a few minor remarks which he had inserted into his literary composition for the sake of clarification.

On the other hand, Ewald was not inclined to support an absolute belief in the content of the gospels. We have noticed above how he acknowledged the existence of real darkness in Christian interpretation and how he expected help only from the critical approach.

---

[88]Ibid., 204.
[89]Ibid., 208.

The Impact of Tendency Criticism on Ewald

While Ewald did not retreat one inch in respect to the Tübingers, yet he did not achieve much gain for the opposing party. The historical credibility of the Gospels was not helped by his lengthy exposition of the problems in gospel literature that had to be overcome. These problems were supposedly due to Jesus' sudden appearance and disappearance after the resurrection; they were related to his incomprehensible loftiness which leads to misunderstanding; they resulted also from the scattered recollections that had to cause wrong associations.

The historical credibility of the gospels was not helped either by Ewald's call for an appropriate reverence[90] in the presentation of the various gospel stories. If Jesus were to rise again, but not through the critical interpretation of the Scriptures, why would Ewald shrink back from the consequences? He did encourage his readers to honor Jesus by accepting the biographical stories the authors had preserved for us; he repeatedly assured his readers that "generally" the sequence of events could not have been unknown; he also defended the portrayals of the lofty moments in Jesus' history as having been inspired by faith and not by the stirrings of poetry as had been averred; he pleaded for a faith aroused by Jesus himself in which he implied that the most devout description of history is the most authentic.

The credibility of the gospels was not enhanced, however, by Ewald's apologies for the style and composition of the authors. The author loses confidence in the so-called literary resurrection of Jesus when Ewald argued that the search for harmony was a literary endeavor, when this needed a "felicitous inventiveness and imagination" to portray the loftiness in correct imagery, and when he asserted that such attempts are ventures by which one becomes "increasingly bold."

The tension between a critical evaluation and a faithful acceptance occasions an apologetic approach rather than a polemic. The authors of our gospels are supposedly safeguarded against intentional invention by assigning a written source to even the scantiest statement of information. The authors cannot be blamed for their mutual conflict and their recalcitrance against any further form of harmonization. They were not prejudiced, but simply had to contend with the circumstances in which they found themselves.

But where is objective historical certainty to be found in such a state of affairs? For Ewald it is primarily in the Gospel of Mark, which is such a "pure archetype among the early Evangelists."[91] The Marcan Gospel demonstrates by its simple sequence "genuine and pure originality." According to Ewald everyone will have to turn to this gospel if he wants to obtain an accurate portrayal of

---

[90]Ibid., 1:126.
[91]Ibid., 2:184.

Jesus' life and ministry. In this evaluation we hear clearly the keynote of the Marcan hypothesis, which is similarly the note to which each aspect of Ewald's theory is tuned in. Mark is for him the foundation on which everything else is constructed, the root by which the gospel literature reaches back to historical reality.

Limitations of Heinrich Ewald's Approach

Through Ewald the Marcan hypothesis came in touch with Tendency criticism for the first time in history. This affords us an occasion to observe the degree to which it could resist the attack of its adversary. Ewald did not recognize any personal theological inclinations in any of the Gospels, but he rather accepted a degree of arbitrariness by the various authors. For him the Gospels were works of art in which the sequence and form of the stories, even the selection of the materials, were entirely the fruit of the talent and the imagination of the authors.

This conception of the nature of the Gospels was henceforth firmly established in Gospel criticism, and even the Marcan hypothesis could not exist without it. But the recognition of theological influences and of personal inclinations because of historical circumstances were not yet accepted.

On the question of whether Ewald really has advanced strong arguments in defense of his viewpoint and for his assertion of an early date for the second gospel, we have to reply in the negative. He restricted himself to the common arguments which we will learn to appreciate later, but he applied these in a manner that had validity only for himself. His ambivalence in the defense of the historical character of the gospel was not convincing.

Ewald's passionate aversion toward his opponents and the arbitrariness by which he qualified some parts of the gospels as sources were not likely to inspire much confidence in his criticism. His high evaluation of Mark cannot be tested by any criterion. It merely was closely connected with the image Ewald had personally adopted of Jesus' nature and ministry. He first accepted arbitrarily a historical potentiality, after which he retrieved from this gospel the evidence of its presumed historical reality. In sum, we cannot say that the Marcan hypothesis was very much indebted to Ewald.

Chapter 2

The Development
of the Marcan Hypothesis
in France

The Ur-Mark Hypothesis according to Eduard Reuss (1860)

The Marcan Hypothesis Analyzed by Reuss

An entirely different impression is made by the composed, honest, and systematic labor of Eduard W. E. Reuss who was a worthy advocate of the Marcan hypothesis over a long period of time. If immutability of conviction and persistence in painstaking investigation could be called a criterion for the accuracy of his conviction, then certainly the issues of Mark's priority and origin could long be considered settled by this scholar.

Already in the first edition of his *History of the Sacred Scriptures of the New Testament,*[1] which appeared in 1842, Reuss indicated clearly the direction his studies were going to take. He already had declared himself by that time an advocate of the Marcan hypothesis. Even though in later editions he disclosed modifications at many points, his views remained basically unchanged as far as the form of his Marcan hypothesis is concerned. The editions of 1853, 1860, and 1864 show continued research by his more elaborate listings of literature.

In more detail and for French-speaking scholars only, Reuss dealt with this issue in four articles published in the journal of Timothée Colani under the title "Comparative studies on the first three gospels from the viewpoint of their common origin and their mutual dependence."[2] At the end of the last article he sum-

---

[1]Eduard W. E. Reuss, *Die Geschichte der heiligen Schriften Neuen Testaments* (Halle: C. A. Schwetschke und Sohn, 1842) x, 278. [ET post-Meijboom: *History of the Sacred Scriptures of the New Testament,* 2 vols., trans. from 5th rev. and enl. ed. by Edward L. Houghton (Edinburgh: T. & T. Clark; Boston: Houghton, Mifflin, and Co., 1884).]
[2]Eduard W. E. Reuss, "Études comparatives sur les trois premiers évangiles au point de vue de leurs rapports d'origine et de dépendance mutuelle," ed. Timothée Colani, *Revue de théologie et de philosophie chrétienne*10 (1855): 65-83; 11 (1856): 163-88; 15

marized his conclusion as follows: Luke is the only gospel that has been handed down to us in its original form. The sources of this gospel were (1) the oral tradition used in chaps. 9:51–18:14 and chaps. 22–24; (2) a document by Mark, the follower of Peter, for chaps. 4:31–9:50 and chaps. 18:15–21:38; and (3) some unknown sources employed for chaps. 1–4:30, 5:1-11, 6:20–7:50, and 19:1-27. According to Reuss, Matthew was not known to Luke.

The Gospel of Mark contained in its original form chaps. 1:21–13:37 with or without chaps. 6:45–8:26, which were sections that remained unknown to Luke. In a redaction Mark, or an unknown redactor, added the tradition of the passion account, namely, chaps. 14:1–16:8, and perhaps also the transition formulas in order to connect the various sections.

Matthew originally wrote a collection of "Words of the Lord," a document that remained unknown to Mark and Luke. Using the redaction of Mark and new sources for chaps. 1–4, 8:5-13, 9:27-38, 11:2-30, and 17:24-27, the evangelist Matthew wrote the first of our canonical gospels.

After this the first twenty verses of Mark were added by a copyist who was familiar with Matthew and Luke. Finally a last redactor added the disputed conclusion of Mark, chap. 16:9-20, from readings in Luke, John, and the book of Acts.

Reuss's Concept of an Ur-Mark

Generally speaking, the exposition above concerning the origin and mutual relationship of the gospels has remained the conception of Reuss, although some details were added in his second edition. Just one modification deserves attention, namely, his judgement about the meaning of Papias's testimony. In the first edition Reuss could easily forego his doubt about the identity of the document referred to by Papias with our canonical Gospel of Mark. In 1853 this doubt had been intensified considerably so that this identity, although still possible, was already called dubious. In his third edition the verdict by Reuss was: The Ur-Mark differs clearly from canonical Mark.[3]

This change of viewpoint is closely connected with other modifications in the conception of the mutual relationship of the gospels. In his first edition Reuss affirmed that our canonical Gospel of Mark was beyond doubt the source for Matthew and Luke. In the second edition he began calling this affirmation a "daring" assumption.[4] Finally, in his third edition Reuss expressed his conviction

(1857): 1-32; ["Nouvelles Études comparatives sur . . . "] *Nouvelle revue de théologie* (Deuxième série) 2 (1858): 15-72.
[3]Reuss, *Die Geschichte der Heiligen Schriften Neuen Testaments,* 3rd ed. (1860) §187.
[4]Ibid., 2nd ed. (1853) §191.

that our canonical Gospel of Mark contained several later additions which did not become known to Matthew and Luke. At first only the pericopes 1:1-13 and 16:9-20 were considered from a later redactor; then the transition formulas and "perhaps" the passion narratives were declared of later origin; finally, "with certainty" the passion narratives and probably also chap. 1:14-20 were considered of later date.

Of course, such a curtailment of our canonical Mark had to change the probability to certainty that Papias spoke of an Ur-Mark rather than of our present Gospel of Mark. This gradual change of conviction in Reuss is of peculiar significance for the history of the Marcan hypothesis. There is a certain limit that cannot be surpassed when one eliminates pericopes from a document. The borderline cannot be indicated. Each exegete has to follow his own intuition as his criterion in such a situation. As soon as the eliminated passages become too numerous, they cannot be called insertions anymore, but should rather be qualified as the original text.

As soon as such a gradual shift of content has reached its critical point the identity of the document changes as well. We noticed how Wilke could still call his Ur-Gospel Mark because the additions, by which it became our canonical gospel, were of little significance. In the same manner Reuss initially applied the testimony of Papias to our canonical Mark, because this gospel did not lose its originality by the mere absence of an introduction and a conclusion. But when he gradually began to refer to a complete redaction of the original Mark, the canonical gospel could not anymore be considered the same work as the original gospel. The concept of an Ur-Mark and simultaneously a modified understanding of Papias's report had thereby been necessitated.

Reuss's Criterion for Marcan Priority

The observations concerning the original text of Mark will be of importance for our final evaluation of the Marcan hypothesis. In pursuing the objective of the hypothesis itself the issue of an alleged Ur-Mark is rather irrelevant. Whatever position a proponent of the Marcan hypothesis takes in this matter, the Gospel of Mark [in original or in canonical form], is for him the oldest example of the gospel narrative. It remains for him the source from which a large part of the origin of the other Synoptics must be explained. The probability of Marcan priority was already given with the criteria used by Reuss, who in his investigation mainly focussed on the form and the length of the narratives.

Reuss accused his predecessors of not using external historical data in attempting to find a solution for the origin and the interrelatedness of the Synoptics. He reproached them for simply using the data in the gospels themselves. Reuss, however, has not adequately made up for their neglect by taking into account only a few external historical data, namely, Papias's testimony and a few other historical documents from which the origin of the gospels was to be explained. Consequently, the historical school did not receive in Reuss a strong champion for their cause.

Conversely, Reuss rather adopted some of the conclusions of the Tübingen school. He did accept the existence of different factions during the apostolic era. He recognized the possibility of their influence on the understanding of Jesus' words and on the character of the writings themselves. He even declared bluntly that the history of the Gospel to the Hebrews was connected with the theological opinions of those days.[5] Reuss also conceded that a Judaic point of view was prevailing in the document of the Logia.[6] Finally, he developed the idea that there were various diverging trends in the tradition which were harmonized by Luke.[7]

But he could not accept the notion that these circumstances would determine, to a considerable degree, the content and the form of the gospels. He could not concede that the authors themselves might be held responsible for the potential damage inflicted upon the credibility of their account. He still considered Mark far removed from professing theological concerns;[8] he felt the historical dependability of tradition could clearly be perceived in Matthew;[9] and he remained of the opinion that Luke gathered his historical materials without secondary intentions in mind.[10]

For Reuss the entire endeavor of the Tübingers went somewhat against the grain. Their point of view seemed excessive and incorrect to him when the objective of exegesis was merely a matter of resolving purely literary issues.[11] Their attempts were to be counted with so many previous and unsuccessful efforts over which history had already pronounced its verdict.

From the viewpoint of the proponents of the Marcan hypothesis it made no sense to claim a shorter document dependent on a more extensive original. This school developed the maxim that "when two gospels are mutually dependent the earliest date must be attributed to the shorter one."[12] From this presupposition it was therefore impossible to understand a Matthean priority. Why would Mark

---

[5]Ibid., 4th ed. (1864) §198. This edition will be used from now on.
[6]Ibid., §186.
[7]Ibid., §§205, 209.
[8]Ibid., §190.
[9]Ibid., §194.
[10]Ibid., §209, further developed in Eduard W. E. Reuss, *Histoire de la théologie chrétienne au siècle apostolique* [*A history of Christian theology in the apostolic age*], 2 vols. (Strasbourg and Paris: Treuffel & Wurtz, 1852) 2:344-65.
[11]Reuss, *Geschichte*, §§174, 185.
[12]Reuss, "Études comparatives," *RThPh* 10:76.

leave out the speeches he found in Matthew and why would he eliminate the introductory narratives found in Matthew as well as in Luke? Their quantitative maxim was also the ground for the opinion that Luke did not know the Gospel of Matthew, because he otherwise would have quoted it more extensively.

The "Comparative Studies" of the Synoptics by Reuss

With this quantitative argument the case for Mark's early age had been more than half decided. But Reuss did not want to consider his thesis as proven before a careful and detailed investigation entitled him to the same conclusion. It appears to me that the method of investigation itself reinforced his conviction concerning a Marcan priority. In his "Comparative Studies" the reader can trace his method in detail. It may be true that a scholar intent on publication should arrange the procedure of investigation in the most gradual manner for the benefit of his readers. Yet I am of the opinion that the argument of Reuss reflected merely the development of his own thought.

His research involved the presentation of a complete picture of the development of gospel history. In the various editions of his *History of the Sacred Scriptures* Reuss traced this development, beginning with recollections of the eyewitnesses and continuing with the tradition and the first recordings in our Synoptic gospels. In his "Studies," however, he followed the opposite direction. In these articles his starting point is the Gospel of Luke.

The study of Luke's relation to Mark leads to the recognition of an older source agreeing with Mark being the source for both. The comparison of Luke and Matthew gives occasion for mentioning the Logia document. Furthermore, the investigation of the relation of Mark to the first gospel leads to an outcome similar to the study of the relation between Mark and Luke. Finally, the Logia and the older source of Mark are found to be united in the composition of Matthew.

Starting from the gospels as they are, Reuss has ascended to their very origins. To me it does not seem accidental that the study of Luke was used as the starting point in developing the relation of Luke to both the other gospels. In the first edition of the *History* Mark is mentioned more emphatically as the source of Luke rather than as the source of Matthew. Here exists, however, a one-sidedness which could not remain without harmful consequences.

Reuss begins by pointing out that the followers of Griesbach proved the use Mark makes of the two other Synoptics from the sequence of its materials and from its blended text.[13] In another connection Reuss conceded that this method

---

[13]Ibid., 64ff.

[of comparing the various texts] was "apparently carried out with good reason."[14] Later, however, he discarded this comparative method as unworthy of a gospel writer and consequently ignored the respective phenomena of the Marcan text.

Leaving aside Mark's unique relationship to *both* Matthew and Luke, Reuss compared the total Gospel of Mark with Luke alone. The consequences of such an approach are immediately noticeable. By comparing only two gospels at a time while leaving out of consideration the text of the third, important materials are eliminated which are needed for a complete picture. Because Mark alternately agrees with one or both of the other gospels, it can just as easily be demonstrated that there exists a close affinity between Mark and Luke as between Mark and Matthew. With such an approach the chance to determine the affinity between Luke and Matthew becomes increasingly smaller.

In the comparison of Luke with Mark, Reuss noticed a great degree of similarity since they consistently agree in sequence where Matthew deviated. It also became evident that in the differences Mark and Luke have between each other, the reason could be accounted for in Luke while it remained inexplicable in Mark. Luke, for instance, omitted several sections (e.g., the selection of the four apostles, the anointment, Jesus' ministry in Nazareth), because he replaced these with other similar narratives. It could hardly be maintained, according to Reuss, that Mark would have eliminated these for the sake of his own less-beautiful readings.

On the basis of the great similarity covering mainly the first half of the gospel and in view of some other considerations, Reuss drew the conclusion that Mark has the highest claim to originality. After this conclusion it was not difficult anymore to accept the later origin of the passion narratives, and also of the stories recorded between the feeding of the five thousand and the confession of Peter. If it were not for the similarities in the first half of each of these gospels the additional passages in Mark would have created great difficulties for Reuss. Now he felt free to elevate Mark as the source for the Gospel of Luke.

When subsequently the relation of Matthew to Mark is investigated the agreement between these two strikes the eye as well. As proof of their great harmony, reference is made to the deviations in Luke in similar fashion as was done in the first comparison with respect to Matthew. In comparing the parallel omissions in Mark and Matthew the most extensive omission is considered as evidence of the most original document. The different sequence of narratives in Matthew must have been caused for internal reasons only, and therefore was of no difficulty for Reuss.

In conclusion, a comparison of the text of these two gospels leads again to the recognition of the originality of Mark. Since the agreement included here also

---

[14]Reuss, *Geschichte,* §189.

the passion narratives, the Marcan source of Matthew appeared to have been more complete than than of Luke.

Thus the double comparison leads, according to the position of Reuss, by necessity to the Marcan hypothesis. By comparing one gospel at a time with Mark a different conclusion had been obtained than perhaps would have been achieved in a simultaneous study of the three gospels.

The procedure of Reuss did not demonstrate that the agreement of Mark with the two other Synoptics takes place alternately.[15] This would not show in a process of single comparisons. For instance, Reuss deemed it improbable that Mark would have preferred the selection of the four apostles to the miraculous catch of fishes, or the anointing to the parallel narrative in Luke. But the possibility that Matthew could have been the source for these narratives in Mark was hardly, or not at all taken into consideration by Reuss.

When finally the relation of Luke to Matthew is established, the common elements of all three gospels are neglected because Mark is considered the common source.[16] The same deviating narratives that raised no doubts in Luke's use of Mark[17] are now important in proving that Luke was not acquaintanted with Matthew.[18]

If the procedure of an investigation always influences its conclusion, this is even more true in the case of Gospel criticism. As long as the criterion of evaluation for the major part is taken from the gospels themselves, it is obvious that different hypotheses can achieve the same degree of probability. The numerous hypotheses of the past have proven this point. Equally, the outcome will be different when a different gospel is used as the starting point.

Reuss had already preempted his proof of Luke's independence from Matthew by beginning with Luke's relationship to Mark. By contemplating the agreement of Mark with each of the parallel gospels individually, Reuss made himself immune from the impression he would have received from contemplating the mutual relationship of all the Synoptics simultaneously.

An Appraisal of the Consistent Literary Method of Reuss

Reuss continued to present further details resulting from his comparative text studies.[19] The data provided are largely matters that must fall in line with the

---

[15]See 152-53, below.
[16]Reuss, "Études comparatives," *RThPh* 15:23.
[17]Reuss, "Études comparatives," *RThPh* 11:175ff.
[18]Reuss, "Études comparatives," *RThPh* 15:19.
[19]Reuss, "Études comparatives," *RThPh* 11:181; see also *Nouvelle revue de théologie* (Deuxiéme sèrie) 2 (1858): 19ff.

basic conclusions reached before. Certain data do not provide additional evidence. For instance, the question whether an inaccuracy in Mark has been corrected by Matthew or whether it is the consequence of a less-careful redaction or misunderstanding cannot be resolved. Only when dealing with major issues can a decision be made. In each issue the judgement about dubious points will be in keeping with the view of the gospels that has been adopted already on the basis of the interpretation of other phenomena.

The proponents of various hypotheses will decide differently on the question, for instance, whether remarks of an archeological nature have been inserted or omitted, or whether the Aramaic words of Jesus resulted from an urge for concreteness or from historical recollection. This does not mean that truth cannot be gained on the basis of internal evidence alone.

Certainly there are places where the text of Matthew in comparison with the text of Mark clearly reflects a later date. But it is undeniable that Reuss has taken his case sometimes too lightly in dealing with the various points at issue. That the story of Jesus' walking on the water in Mark would be the most original version has no high degree of probability; it is equally unlikely that Mark's account of the death of John the Baptist is to be preferred above that of Matthew.

When Mark in 8:14 presents the disciples taking along just one loaf of bread, it must rather be conceived as an effort to make viable the breaking of the bread and its multiplication by Jesus; also the misunderstanding of the disciples should claim the attention of the reader. This interpretation seems more like a redaction than the parallel passage in Matthew 16:5, where in Reuss's opinion, Matthew wants to indicate by his words "they had forgotten to bring any bread," how little value that one loaf of bread was for Jesus.

The strength of the approach of Reuss is his strictly literary method in dealing with the issue of the gospel parallels. The literary approach plus his concentration on the sequence of the narratives represent his contribution as well as his limitation. The additional arguments from further details are not capable of supplying the missing evidence in his major approach.

The Impact of Eduard Reuss on French Scholarship

The work of Reuss was widely accepted by other scholars. In general it can be stated that in France the influence of Reuss caused the balance to tip in the direction of the Marcan hypothesis. Timothée Colani, the editor of the journal who published his articles, became one of his followers.[20] Among the supporters

---

[20]Timothée Colani, *Jésus-Christ et les croyances messianiques de son temps* (Strasbourg, 1864) 50.

of Reuss was also Edmond Scherer with whom we will deal later on. Joseph Ernest Renan included in his preface a brief commendation of Mark without granting it much influence in his *Life of Jesus*.[21] Albert Réville's well-known book was reviewed enthusiastically by Dardier.[22] Michel Nicolas wrote some essays on the same issue at a later date. Yet there was little difference between the results of the various scholars and the achievement of Reuss.

This symptom is not unusual. Whatever research could be done concerning Mark had been achieved already; the state of affairs was not such that one was at liberty to create more hypotheses. The matter with Mark was soon like the understanding of the Gospel of John. The character of this gospel is so distinctive that one cannot long be in doubt concerning the various possibilities. The decision about the authenticity or inauthenticity of the fourth gospel cannot be dependent anymore on the discovery of new premises.

In the present state of research it is considered a professional duty of the theologian to accept the current idea about the Gospel of John. A similar professional stance is expected concerning the Marcan issue. The answer to the question of whether or not Mark is the first in the series of the Synoptic gospels was given with such a resoluteness that no room was left for the potential discovery of new grounds.

Because of the dispassionate and in a certain sense impartial study by Reuss the Marcan hypothesis was considered the accurate position by many scholars. His arguments were valid for all those who endorsed in Gospel criticism the same position as Reuss. He and his followers were not inclined to acknowledge any influence of the personal circumstances of the authors of the gospels on the determination of the form and content of their narratives in the sense proposed by the Tübingers. What still remained to be achieved by the proponents of the Marcan hypothesis was taking note of the remaining problems in order to assess and overcome these by adjustments in the structure of their hypothesis.

Questions by Edmond Scherer Concerning the Luke-Mark Relation

We see a sample of this in the article by Edmond Scherer under the title "Some observations about the agreements of the first three gospels."[23] Despite the importance he attached to the work of Reuss, some objections remained which the Strasbourg professor had not been able to answer. However much Scherer agreed with Reuss that Mark was the source of Luke, he could not find

---

[21]Joseph Ernest Renan, *La Vie de Jésus* (Paris: Michel Lévy Frères, 1862) 562ff.

[22]In *Nouvelle revue de théologie* (Deuxième série) 10:272-88.

[23]Edmond H. A. Scherer, "Quelques observations sur les rapports des trois premiers évangiles," *Nouvelle revue de théologie* (Deuxième série) 8 (1861): 292-307.

any valid reasons why Luke would have omitted such major portions from his Marcan source, or why he merely adopted them in modified form. Also it could not very well be explained why there were still deviations in the sections where otherwise there was such close agreement in the sequence of materials, for instance, the visit of the relatives of Jesus and the accusation of a covenant with the devil: these narratives occur together in Mark 3:20-35 but appear in Luke in three different locations, namely, in 8:19-21, 11:14-23, and 12:10.

Furthermore, it is a surprising fact that the peculiarities of style characteristic of the second gospel have hardly been used by the two other gospel writers. The unity of style is so profound in Mark that it must seem highly improbable to accept a gradual development of the Marcan Gospel in the manner Reuss had to maintain for the sake of his synoptic theory. Even if the transition formulas are set aside, this unity of style still remains strikingly present in the remaining text.

These observations had almost caused Scherer to view all these stylistic elements as the imprint of a copyist of the original document. This would imply that the Ur-Mark would have been a much simpler document than Reuss had proposed. It would have been no more than a disorderly collection of notations used in various copies of different length.

According to Scherer, this would eminently explain the deviations in Matthew and Luke; it would have given a reason for the absence of Mark's peculiar style in those writings; it would have allowed for the more original readings both Matthew and Luke have over against Mark; and it would also have explained the unevenness in the use of their source by Matthew as well as by Luke.

This adaptation of the Marcan hypothesis would have satisfied Scherer perhaps more, if only he could have been convinced of the accuracy of his conjecture. Soon he felt it to be a "critic's fantasy,"[24] and what remained was the following conclusion: "The relation between Luke and Mark can only be explained when one accepts that the former has used the latter; yet there remains a difference between both that cannot be harmonized with this supposition." The question remains "in what way a solution to this contradiction can be found."

Questions by Scherer Concerning the Matthew-Mark Relation

Also, concerning the relation of Matthew to Mark, questions remained to be answered. Reuss had explained[25] the difference in sequence of the materials in Matthew from its internal structure, which supposedly was a demonstration of Jesus' ever-widening circle of ministry and of the increasing doubt and resistance to his message. This explanation did not satisfy Scherer, because it seemed to

---

[24]Ibid., 299.
[25]Reuss, *Nouvelle revue,* 2:36.

apply only to the first part of this gospel. He considered it more likely that the internal structure of both gospels conditioned by the different views of each of the authors resulted in the different arrangement of the same narratives.

According to Scherer, the gospels are organized serially around the following topics: the beginning of Jesus' ministry, the healings, and the teachings followed by the major miracles. It could happen, however, that a certain paragraph was considered by one author from a didactic angle, while the other author focussed on its miraculous content. Also, in case of two or three narratives in sequence, one author might arrange these according to the emphasis in the first narrative, while the other author might categorize these on the basis of the second or third story. However ingenious this conjecture, the question concerning the cause of the different sequence in Matthew was certainly not resolved any more convincingly than the conjecture it wanted to replace.

The question of sequence continued to plague the adherents of the Marcan hypothesis. It remained unclear in Reuss why an original gospel that was delineated so vaguely and that allowed so much freedom of arrangement to each of the other two Synoptics, caused the particular documents we have today. Scherer suggested the outline of the first two gospels as original. They certainly can claim a series of stories in common, but this commonality is definitely not inherent to the theological content of these gospels. Already in the application of this approach Scherer was at a loss when he had to explain why Mark's story of the raising of Jairus's daughter was relocated in Matthew.

The Proto-Mark Hypothesis

The Critical Studies by Albert Réville

The Marcan hypothesis received a new adaptation by Albert Réville whose work received an award from the Society for the Humanities in the Hague, Netherlands. It was entitled *Critical Studies on the Gospel of Matthew.*[26] I would do an injustice to Réville if I did not specifically indicate that there is hardly a trace of dependence on the theologian Eduard Reuss.[27] It is all the more striking how the Marcan hypothesis, to a certain extent and from a certain standpoint, is presented as a natural outcome of the mutual relationship of the gospels themselves. The different expressions of this hypothesis seem to be no more than the results of the more or less intelligent observations of particularities in the gospels.

---

[26]Albert Réville, *Études critiques sur l'Évangile selon St. Matthieu* (Leiden: D. Noothoven van Goor, 1862) xxiii, 346.
[27]Ibid., xviii.

Réville projected a considerably divergent conception concerning the Ur-Mark document. It involved the historical situation of this document as well as its length and the way it was used by Matthew. He agreed with Reuss that little can be achieved by using only canonical Mark for the explanation of the synoptic problem. We owe to Réville the current name of "Proto-Mark" for the document preceding Mark. The delineations drawn by both scholars of the older document are far from identical, however.

While Reuss attempted to limit the size of the original document as much as possible, Réville extended it even beyond the scope of the canonical Gospel of Mark. His opinion was that the few features which, dispersed throughout Mark, are of later origin,[28] and the few transition formulas, which occasionally take the place of a loose connection,[29] would suggest a gospel not much different from our present Gospel of Mark.[30] The only significant difference would be that the canonical Mark has omitted the following stories from the Proto-Mark which are still recorded in Matthew. They include the story of the Roman officer at Capernaum, the messengers sent by John the Baptist, Jesus' appearance in Galilee, and perhaps the indecisive followers of Jesus, which sections can be found in Matthew 8:5-10, 13; 11:2-6; 28:9-10, 16-20; and 8:19- 20.[31]

This divergence from Reuss is certainly not completely accidental. The text of canonical Mark has too many additional materials that can hardly be explained as coming from tradition. In the same manner the text of Matthew has sections not included in Proto-Mark or in the Logia that equally cannot be explained from tradition. Also the reference to other sources in Luke's prologue cannot adequately serve to explain the presence of these additional materials in Mark and Matthew. At this juncture, however, it is of more importance for us to pursue the question of how Réville arrived at his concept of Proto-Mark and whether we would be led to the same conclusion.

Arguments by Réville for a Proto-Mark

After giving a detailed demonstration of the close relationship between the first two gospels[32] Réville offers three ways of explaining this. Either Mark has used Matthew, or Matthew derived his material from Mark, or both had access to the same source. In order to reach a conclusion, Réville argued that the first two positions are not conceivable, because both Mark and Matthew alternately

---

[28]Ibid., 139ff.
[29]Ibid., 329ff.
[30]Ibid., 151.
[31]Ibid., 171ff.
[32]Ibid., 127.

have the prerogative of being the original text. As soon as this fact has been established only the third option remains and one has to decide for a common source in order to explain the agreement between both gospels.[33] However clear-cut this conclusion may seem, it does appear somewhat premature to me. There should at least be two additional options, namely, either our Matthew has known Mark although not in its present form, or our Mark has known Matthew but then equally in an earlier condition. In order to make a choice between these three options in an objective manner a new criterion of evaluation should be used.

Réville had already made up his mind, however, and it was this mind-set which caused him to overlook the two other conceivable options. He wrote: "We consider it almost redundant to call to the attention of the reader how much easier the solution of our problem has become through previous research." In their context[34] these words signify that with the recognition of writings which preceded the canonical gospels a possibility has been opened up which offers a way out of the contradictions in which one gets entangled with the investigation of the mutual relationships of the gospels. After recognition of the Logia document as a source for Matthew, whatever else remains to be explained should be derived from a similar source [and not from one of the gospels in an earlier stage].

The study concerning the Logia had given Réville the idea that common sources might constitute the connection between our gospels. It became plausible then to make further use of this discovery as well [and to suggest the existence of a document called Proto-Mark]. Even if this second source may be considered a Marcan Gospel at an earlier stage, this identity must be considered more or less incidental, especially since it is questionable for Réville whether the relation of Proto-Mark to the author of the second gospel can be described as the relation of source to writer.

Similarly it is certainly not accidental that the possibility of Mark's knowledge of an earlier stage of Matthew has been left out. Consequently, the thought of later additions to Matthew does not come to mind either since the greater extension of its earlier stage would still make it prohibitive that Mark could have used such a gospel. "A priori it must be considered likely in any case that the shortest gospel has preceded the longer gospel."[35] According to Réville, it is equally inconceivable for writers to "reject consciously an earlier narrative."[36] The main purpose in the composition of a gospel is allegedly "to recount the story of the Lord and to preserve the respective facts from oblivion."[37]

---

[33]Ibid., 142.
[34]Ibid., 115ff.
[35]Ibid., 128.
[36]Ibid., 116.
[37]Ibid., 128.

Mark is considered earlier also because of its vivid imagery and its love for particulars which are evidences of its affinity to an eyewitness.[38] The way in which the naiveté of the disciples and the effect of Jesus' miraculous power is portrayed points to an early date as well.[39] In other words, the theological position of the Gospel of Mark points to an early stage of development.

In sum, where Réville operated under such assumptions it was only natural that in the study of particulars and in the comparison of text parallels everything in Matthew turned out to be of later date than the text of Mark. This equally meant a negative answer to the question of Mark's use of the first gospel as a source.

Réville's Critical Norm for Identical Narratives

I reject even more the critical rule Réville formulated as a basis for the study of identical narratives.

> The irrefutable thesis is that, when two narratives agree in general, the most obscure and contradictory account betrays the closest familiarity with the narrated facts. After a certain lapse of time objections had to be raised from a theological or pragmatic point of view. The relation of the original to the corrected narrative becomes then that of text to paraphrase, of the unclear passage to its interpretation, of the reading to the gloss, of the prolix enumeration to its resumé—in any case the obscure passage is the oldest and cannot be held to have been derived from the clear passage.[40]

The crucial point is hidden in the words "in any case." We are dealing here with a rule in the abstract, and any abstract possibility must remain a mere possibility. Whenever this rule is being considered, it will depend on the nature of the specific case whether such possibility is historically correct.

For instance, there is certainly nothing more paradoxical than Jesus' answer to Peter's question concerning the value of self-denial for the disciples. The text in Mark states that everyone

> who has left house or brothers or sisters or mother or father or children or lands, for my sake and for the gospel, . . . will receive a hundredfold now in this time, houses and brothers and sisters and mothers and children and lands, with persecutions, and in the age to come eternal life.[41]

---

[38]Ibid., 129, 138.
[39]Ibid., 134, 136.
[40]Ibid., 129ff.
[41]Mark 10:28-31; cf. Matt 19:27-30; Luke 18:28-30; see Réville, *Études critiques* 132.

The peculiar nature of this promise, together with the addition "for the sake of the gospel" and the limitation "with persecutions," is ample evidence of the fact that this passage in Mark represents a later version of the gospel account. [The simpler version in Mt.19:27-30 appears to be earlier.]

It is true that "E'lo-i, E'lo-i," as the exclamation of Jesus is quoted in Mark 15:34, renders it more difficult to explain the crude misunderstanding of those words among the bystanders than the words "Eli, Eli" in Matthew.[42] Yet it is definitely to be supposed that in the original version of the narrative the citation from Psalm 22, "Eli, Eli," was the reading causing misunderstanding among the bystanders.

Also, the historical notation in Mark 2:26, "when Abiathar was high priest," as an indication of the time when David was to have asked for the shewbreads, is certainly subject to objection. But whether these words therefore qualify Mark as the oldest informant remains doubtful.[43] [If these examples demonstrate that obscurity is not necessarily an indicator of originality, we may assume that Réville's ground rule has its limitations.] Applying this rule to appropriate cases will, indeed, restrict considerably the number of places, which might suggest the priority of Mark to Matthew.

An Appraisal of Albert Réville's Synoptic Studies

First, the question should be raised whether Réville has demonstrated conclusively that there has been a Proto-Mark which was used in the composition of the canonical gospels. The answer must be that the assumption of the existence of a common source, Proto-Mark, has only relative value. The identification of this source with the Gospel of Mark in an earlier stage was caused in part by his hesitancy to consider it a Proto-Matthew. One reason for this hesitancy was the general acceptance of the Logia as a source for Matthew; a second reason was Réville's notion that the brevity, the imagery and the theological character of these Logia in Mark testify to its earlier date. With the validity of this last surmise stands or falls the convincing power of Réville's argument. If upon later consideration his thesis turns out to be incorrect, the results of comparative text studies alone cannot sustain the concept of a Proto-Mark either.

Ingenious, indeed, was an additional reason which Réville discovered for the diverging sequence of materials in the first two gospels. It was connected with the manner by which the redactor of Matthew supposedly made use of his

---

[42]Mark 15:34; Matt 27:45; see Réville, *Études critiques* 133.
[43]Réville, *Études critiques* 131.

sources. This redactor gave the Logia a prominent place, according to Réville, so that the second source had to adjust its sequence to the Logia's sequence of materials. Here we find a third explanation since that offered by Reuss for the different arrangement of materials in Matthew! With keen perception it is pointed out[44] how the division and contents of the Logia document provide the reason why an inversion of the pericopes of Mark by Matthew has taken place.

Properly speaking one would expect this deliberation to be superfluous with Réville's conception of Matthew's use of the second gospel. He could have provided a simpler explanation by assuming that Matthew only knew Mark insofar as he was still alive in his memory. Observations of various kinds might have been used as proof for this assumption.[45] The difference in style, the little impact of Mark's literary characteristics on Matthew, the deviating form of the narratives by way of abbreviation, inversion, contraction, omission, and the alteration of the narratives to a point beyond recognition; all these could have led to the conclusion that recollection was the only point of contact between these gospels.

I do not want to raise the question to what degree these very discrepancies argue against a dependence of Matthew on Mark.[46] This would involve the same arguments raised against J. L. Hug and even against the Tradition hypothesis in its form of the oral Gospel hypothesis. I also do not want to investigate whether the argument that our canonical Mark was unknown to Matthew[47] would not weaken the plea for a common source, for the existence of a so-called Proto-Mark. But I would like to ask whether or not too much speculative imagination has been employed to explain the different sequence of materials in the first two gospels.

Can the opinion really be upheld that Matthew would have overlooked only the peculiar traits of Mark, but not the internal coherence of this gospel? Even if this assumption could be accepted, it still would be of little value. These arguments can only be of significance when the early date for Mark has been investigated on other grounds, and when its claim for such recognition has been firmly established. As long as this is not the case, the work of Réville can only be considered a modification of the ideas of Reuss and Scherer. He is a magnificent example of what ingenuity is able to achieve in Gospel criticism.

---

[44]Ibid., 196ff.
[45]Ibid., 150ff.
[46]Ibid., 118ff.
[47]Ibid., 138.

Critique of the Marcan Hypothesis by Michel Nicolas (1864)

Finally Michel Nicolas should be mentioned in the series of French authors. He combined two articles previously published in the *German Review,*[48] into an essay in his *Critical Studies on the New Testament*[49] on the status of the discussion of the synoptic problem. In the history of the Marcan hypothesis the work of Nicolas is a significant symptom enabling us to make an evaluation of the state of health of this hypothesis. Nicolas professed himself to be a proponent of the theory developed by Reuss and Réville, but far from wholeheartedly.

Although the history of Gospel criticism had not yielded better options, considerable problems remained for the Marcan hypothesis, according to Nicolas. In spite of his inclination to acknowledge a Logia document in explaining the origin of the gospels,[50] he continued questioning whether Papias did not refer to our canonical Gospel of Matthew instead of to the Logia.[51] Thus only with great difficulty could Nicholas agree with a Marcan hypothesis [based on a Logia source]. This was partly because he, even more than his predecessors, attributed decisive importance to the length of the gospels in explaining their mutual relationship. [According to this principle it would be unusual for Mark to abbreviate the Logia.] In contrast to Nicolas, other proponents of the Marcan hypothesis could allow a certain liberty to the writers of the New Testament in omitting certain narratives, for whatever reason.

Nicolas could not tolerate such freedom as the following case may illustrate. The section of Mark 6:45–8:26 is missing in Luke and was, also according to Reuss, not present in his source. The section was, however, known to Matthew because he has it almost in its entirety. [Thus Matthew must have used a more extensive source than Luke had.] Matthew did omit, however the stories of the deaf and dumb man and of the blind man mentioned in Mark 7:32-37 and 8:22-26. This omission did not cause any problems for either Reuss or Réville, because they could find acceptable reasons for the elimination of these stories. For Nicolas, however, this omission was sufficient ground to reject the presence of those stories in the original source. Because of this, he had to find another source for these stories, which made his Marcan hypothesis more complicated.

---

[48]French title: *Revue Germanique.*
[49]Michel Nicolas, *Études critiques sur la Bible, Nouveau Testament* (Paris: Michel Levy Frères, 1864) xix, 429.
[50]Ibid., 93.
[51]Ibid., 120ff.

Critique of the Proto-Mark Hypothesis by Michel Nicolas

This complexity was compounded because Nicolas seemed confused by the vague idea of a Proto-Mark. For the same reason as Reuss and Réville he saw in the unusual agreement in sequence, content, and vocabulary, evidences that Matthew had known Luke as well as Mark. Like Reuss and Réville, Nicolas was led to believe that the original Mark differed from our present gospel on the basis of its literary characteristics and its expressions of later date. Réville had resorted to the Mark of Papias because of his need for a common source, which then required him to analyze the relation of this common source to our canonical Mark. Nicolas, however, approached this issue from the opposite direction. He started from the canonical Mark, which he considered a source of Matthew, and proceeded to a Proto-Mark because of the irregularities he found in Matthew.

This procedure did not come about without difficulty, which became manifest from the manner in which he discussed the passion narratives and the section of Mark 6:45–8:26. Both portions are common to Matthew and Mark, but with deviations in both gospels which make it difficult to recognize either one of them as a source for the other.

Nicolas viewed both gospels therefore as different adaptations of common sources, which were not to be identified with Proto-Mark. For the remaining parts of these gospels, however, Nicolas did recognize this so-called Proto-Mark as a common source.[52] This discussion should demonstrate that for Nicolas the concept of Proto-Mark had not yet acquired a fixed form.

A similar vacillation can be observed in his discussion concerning the relationship between the document mentioned in Papias and our second gospel. According to Nicolas, the consistent testimony of Papias for the authenticity of the canonical Gospel of Mark should prevent us from reading in the same Papias a testimony for a totally different document. It can be well understood that Nicolas directed his criticism against Baur and Schwegler for accepting an earlier Marcan document, but his reproach should also have included Schleiermacher and Credner. The reason for his criticism was that Schleiermacher and Credner had removed themselves so far from canonical Mark, that a mere redactor obtained the right to the title of Mark.

Nicolas, however, wanted to retain this name for the author rather than for the redactor. The relation between Proto-Mark and canonical Mark must have been such that the transition of one into the other supposedly escaped the attention of the church. The redaction did involve, according to Nicolas, the organization of materials, because Papias referred to a disorderly notation of facts and not to an orderly gospel. The church must therefore have overlooked a

---

[52]Ibid., 86ff.

considerable difference! What remains of the evidence of the close relationship of Mark with each of the two other Synoptic Gospels? Why did Nicolas complain in another connection that the Marcan hypothesis did not adequately explain the difference between Mark and Luke, and the different sequence in Matthew?[53] [Would not the original Mark permit one to expect any variation if it was simply a disorderly notation of facts?]

An Appraisal of the Contribution by Michel Nicolas

In sum, all the ambivalent statements concerning a Proto-Mark made by the various defenders of the Marcan hypothesis seem to have merged in Nicolas. Nowhere can one get hold of him. Various possibilities ranging from an unorganized document to an almost canonical gospel emerge and disappear as circumstances may require. This vagueness and lack of conviction concerning the Proto-Mark is the cause of Nicolas's desire to adopt a separate source for the passion narratives, and another source for the section of Mark 6:45–8:26.

Finally, Nicolas suggested a third source outside of Proto-Mark for the stories of the deaf and dumb man and of the blind man. He judged rightly that these stories would not serve as a recommendation of the Marcan hypothesis.[54] This lack of conviction is also the reason why Nicolas, with all the respect he cherished for the hypothesis, comes across as one who will desert its banners on the first possible occasion.

---

[53]Ibid., 117ff.
[54]Ibid., 110.

Chapter 3

Sixteen Years
of Consolidation
in Germany (1850–1866)

The Affirmation of the Marcan Hypothesis
by Orthodox Theologians

General Concurrence with the Marcan Hypothesis

We will now have to turn our attention from France back to Germany. The historical development led us from Ewald to Reuss. The great agreement in the pattern of the Marcan hypothesis among the French scholars was the reason for pursuing their development up to the present time. At this time we have to ascertain how, beginning with Ewald, a new current of conviction flowed through German scholarship.

Ewald did not set the tone for further investigation in the same manner as Reuss did for the French exegetes. Yet what we find in Ewald will be encountered among his successors, namely, (a) the awareness of the value of the Marcan hypothesis in the battle against the skepticism of the Tübingers, (b) the application of the testimony of Papias to our canonical Mark, with the added possibility that our present Mark is not the original text anymore, and (c) the assertion that the second gospel finds its place in gospel history between the Logia and the canonical gospel of Matthew.

During the first ten years after Ewald no new investigations in support of the hypothesis were introduced, but rather only attempts presenting proofs for the clear conclusions that the history of criticism had already revealed. Weisse was right when he wrote that the recognition of the early date of Mark by so many scholars, who independently from one another had come to similar results, could not be due to accident and arbitrariness.[1] But we should also not lose sight of the

---

[1]Christian Hermann Weisse, *Die Evangelienfrage in ihrem gegenwärtigen Stadium* (Leipzig: Breitkopf und Härtel, 1856) 90.

fact that the relative necessity of this concurrence among so many theologians was largely a result of the reaction against Strauss and the Tübingers.

The words of Heinrich Thiersch could serve as a motto for the Marcan hypothesis:

> The Ur-Gospel, which has been searched for by so many scholars, we possess in our canon. It is qualified by the history of its origin and by its internal quality to serve as a strong wall in the defense of sacred history against all attacks of the Mythological hypothesis.[2]

Weisse expressed himself more philosophically when he called the position taken by him and his sympathizers the consequence of a "spiritual requirement of the best and most healthy kind."[3] To find in history a subject that answers to the requisites of his Christian faith was for him a need of the soul that had been wounded by Strauss and Baur. The recognition of credible sources in Mark and Matthew provided an excellent gratification for this need. The way Weisse made use of these sources in drawing the image of Christ has been observed above in the treatment of his *Gospel History*. At this time it is of relevance to indicate the keynote with which to a large degree the proponents of the Marcan hypothesis were in harmony.

The reason Weisse turned the attention of the readers to the concurrence of so many scholars was because he wanted to derive from this concurrence the conclusion that the hypothesis championed by him had its reason for being. The cited work, *The Question Concerning the Gospels Updated,* was written by him as a supplement to his main work and at the same time as a commendation of his exposition of the relationship of the gospels.

Ewald's proposal of a similar conception of the gospels was one more reason Weisse rejoiced in enumerating the number of supporters. Strengthened by the view of his friends, Weisse soon forgot all the misery brought upon him by Bruno Bauer who had abused his hypothesis. The priority of Mark had found an increasing number of advocates, even a Tübinger, [Albrecht Ritschl], had been won for this position. Weisse's *Gospel History* therefore could not yet be considered obsolete. Only a few modifications, which his conception had undergone over the years, needed to be brought to the attention of the readers.

A second scholar who was equally indebted to Ewald wrote a booklet about the same subject, which he dedicated to the theological faculty of Zürich. In 1858 he participated in the jubilee of his alma mater, the University of Zürich. His study bore the title *The Quest of the Gospels in General and the Johannine*

---

[2]Heinrich W. J. Thiersch, *Die Kirche im apostolischen Zeitalter und die Entstehung der neutestamentlichen Schriften* (Frankfurt a. M., [1]1852; [2]1858) 104.

[3]Weisse, *Die Evangelienfrage,* 90.

Question in Particular.[4] It was as if Titus Tobler—for thus he identified himself later—wanted to celebrate the triumph of the hypothesis at the occasion of the twenty-fifth anniversary of the Zürich academy. He considered himself a champion of the Marcan hypothesis also by asserting that "after Ewald's conclusive exposition" it should no more be considered a "hypothesis."[5]

The Marcan hypothesis had, indeed, reached such a stage that it could contemplate writing its own history and demonstrating its emblem of nobility to German scholarship. Looking back after the fact, however, we can perceive that to a considerable degree its success was connected with a certain religious need among its proponents. Moreover, as I mention before, the burgeoning success of the Marcan hypothesis must be attributed to the intricate relation between the gospels as a result of the history of their origin.

Papias's Testimony Applied to Canonical Mark

A new and not to be underestimated reinforcement of the recognition of the priority of Mark came from Heinrich Thiersch and especially from Heinrich A. W. Meyer whose widely used commentaries were able to disseminate the ideas of the Marcan hypothesis in numerous minds. Since the third edition of his exegetical handbook, of which the volumes on Matthew appeared in 1853 and Mark in 1856, Meyer shared his changing opinions on the origin and the mutual relationship of these gospels in his introductions. Also for him the current proofs for the originality of Mark were valid. Meyer only objected to the assertion that Papias would have referred to an Ur-Mark. Meyer's interpretation of the reference in Eusebius did not give him any reason to assume a precanonical Mark. He therefore did not share Ewald's idea concerning lost documents, not so much because this would conflict with his interpretation of Papias's words, as that for him the origins of Matthew and Luke could be explained without the use of an Ur-Mark.

For Meyer's exegesis the proofs for secondary elements in the text of Mark were increasingly inconclusive. The Logia document provided a satisfactory explanation for the less original expressions in Mark.

[This second wave of popularity of the Marcan hypothesis during the 1850s involved the text of our present Mark.][6] Previously the concentration had been an earlier form of Mark, designated either as Ur-Mark or as Proto-Mark. During the second period of the consolidation of the Marcan hypothesis the acceptance

---

[4]Titus Tobler, *Die Evangelienfrage im allgemeinen und die Johannesfrage insbesondere* (Zürich, 1858).

[5]Ibid., 10.

[6]See 65, above.

of an earlier form of Mark did not necessarily lead to the adoption of a Proto-Mark as we find illustrated once again in Weisse and Tobler.

After Tobler had attempted to establish the priority of Mark, by which he meant our canonical Mark, he deemed it probable that the present text is not complete and that certain pericopes have been lost. Tobler listed the following missing sections: the account of the Adulterous Woman, the conclusion of Mark, the Sermon on the Mount, the Roman officer of Capernaum, and a more detailed Temptation account. The cause of these omissions were, however, not to be attributed to a redaction but rather to the frequent use made of this gospel.

Imperceptibly some one might have removed some of these pericopes, or theological reasons might have been present in the case of the adulterous woman. Also certain parts of this gospel might have become superfluous after their adoption by Matthew or Luke, such as the Sermon on the Mount. [Thus we still have the original document, even though incomplete.]

Equally, upon the example of Ewald, Weisse took the liberty to consider such pericopes as Matt 3:7-12; 4:3-10 and sections from chaps. 5–7; 8:5-10; 11:2-19; 12:22, 27, 28, and 30 as originating from Mark, even though these portions are not found there any more.[7] The motivation compelling Weisse to do so was his opinion that the respective pericopes could not have found a place in a document called the Logia, which in the strict sense of the word was not gospel history.[8]

To suppose a new source was too hazardous, especially since Ewald already had pointed to the possibility that Mark had been transmitted to us in a mutilated form. Even if this explanation seemed somewhat arbitrary to Weisse, he consoled himself with the idea that a complete second gospel was out of the question in any case, because of the general recognition of its inauthentic conclusion.[9]

That indeed such a precanonical document does not have to be considered a Proto-Mark, is illustrated also in the case of Ewald. Because of the wealth of Christian literature during its very early beginnings, Ewald proposed the possibility of an earlier gospel by Mark "preceding the last redaction or rather abbreviation which it underwent not long before its adoption in the canon."[10] To what degree this earlier gospel was related to the document mentioned by Papias was not stated by Ewald. In general it can be maintained that the concept of a Proto-Mark originated through a certain interpretation of the testimony by Papias, while

---

[7]Weisse, *Die Evangelienfrage,* 88ff., 155ff.

[8]See Weisse, *Die evangelische Geschichte: Kritisch und philosophisch bearbeitet,* 2 vols. (Leipzig: Breitkopf und Härtel, 1838).

[9]Ibid., 165.

[10]Heinrich Georg August Ewald, *Geschichte Christus und seiner Zeit* [*History of Christ and His Times*], vol. 5 of *Geschichte des Volkes Israel* (Göttingen: Vandenhoeck & Ruprecht, 1855) ix.

conversely a precanonical Ur-Mark resulted from the criticism of the gospels themselves.

The Logia as a Direct Source for Mark

The third point of emphasis during the period of consolidation of the Marcan hypothesis was the recognition of the use of the Logia by Mark. This thesis by Ewald,[11] judged incorrect by Weisse[12] and considered less important by Tobler,[13] found a defender in Meyer.[14] It was for the latter a means to explain the less original expressions in Mark, although this means was not always adequate. The possibility that Matthew had "again rejected"[15] the expansion of tradition, or that he had "restored"[16] the original order, shows that discrepancies did not go unnoticed by Meyer. He was led to the Logia as a solution because of his observation that there are clusters of sayings by Jesus in Mark as well in both other Synoptic Gospels. For Meyer these sayings could conveniently be explained from the collection of sayings existing already prior to Mark.

The Suggestion of a Proto-Matthew by Bernhard Weiss (1861)

This brings us to a new approach to the question of the Marcan hypothesis. In the journal *Studies and Critiques,* in 1861, the Königsberg professor Bernhard Weiss wrote two articles under the title "On the History of the Origin of the Three Synoptic Gospels."[17] The evidences of later origin in Mark, which some scholars in France initially had attempted to explain away, led to the acceptance of a Proto-Mark. These evidences of later origin were connected with the elaborations and traces of interdependence of Matthew and Luke, and were supported by Schleiermacher's interpretation of the Papias account concerning the Logia. Proto-Mark was supposedly used by Matthew as well as Luke, and in various

---

[11]Ewald, "Ursprung und Wesen der Evangelien," *Jahrbücher der biblischen Wissenschaft* 2 (1849): 204.

[12]Weisse, *Die Evangelienfrage,* 144.

[13]Tobler, *Die Evangelienfrage,* 25.

[14]Heinrich August Wilhelm Meyer, *Kritisch exegetisches Handbuch über das Evangelium des Matthäus,* 3rd ed. of *Kritisch-exegetischer Kommentar über das Neue Testament* 1/1 (Göttingen: Vandenhoeck & Ruprecht, 1853) 33.

[15]Heinrich A. W. Meyer, *Kritisch exegetisches Handbuch über die Evangelien Markus und Lukas,* 3rd ed. of *Kritisch-exegetischer Kommentar über das Neue Testament* 1/2 (Göttingen: Vandenhoeck & Ruprecht, 1855) 135.

[16]Ibid., 136.

[17]Bernhard Weiss, "Zur Entstehungsgeschichte der drei synoptischen Evangelien," *Theologische Studien und Kritiken* 34 (1861): 73.

places they had enriched this source with their own elucidations and additions. Since it was considered an established fact that Matthew did not know Luke and vice versa, there had to be a common source for similar passages.

Now also the case presented itself that, in addition to the passages which were only common to Matthew and Luke, there were some sections unique for Matthew or for Luke only or sections from the alleged common source that were adopted by one gospel and not by the other. Such variations could give rise to different descriptions of the common source as it also happened in actuality. The inevitability of this was inherent in the word "Logia" used by Papias for a document that was supposed to contain only words of Jesus, and therefore did not provide a way to explain the narration of events.

In Germany, Ewald had therefore accepted the existence of sources prior to the time of Mark including the Logia as one among many documents. As was mentioned above, Ewald's assumption was based on the wealth of early Christian literature. The observation of clusters of sayings also in the second gospel provided additional support for this assumption. For Meyer this conception was decisive enough to disqualify the whole concept of a Proto-Mark, and to associate with the common source the places where Mark in comparison with Matthew was less original.

Bernhard Weiss continued in this direction. A careful study of Mark caused him to discover such a unity in the style of this gospel that he considered it as one indivisible unit. According to Weiss the Gospel of Mark had received this consistent character from an independent author, even though he may have used some sources. Because of this unity, the canonical gospel of Mark could not possibly be a redaction of an earlier shorter or deviating form of Mark. Furthermore, it appeared unnecessary to Weiss to assume that the Logia would have contained nothing but sayings and speeches. By adding numerous pericopes this source developed under his hand into an extensive Proto-Matthew. Included were, of course, those narratives which had previously been derived from a Proto-Mark document.

The Originality of Both Matthew and Mark

It stands to reason that this conception of the origin of the gospels was the fruit of a thorough study of details. Weiss noted places where Matthew was the least original, which was true as well for Mark in other places. At times both situations coincided in one common paragraph; often where Mark showed himself dependent on the speeches in Matthew, the latter was dependent on Mark for its introductions or conclusions; even within the speeches themselves traces of dependence on Mark could be found. Frequently the case was so complicated that no solution seemed possible. These observations led to the supposition that

Matthew and Mark must have used a common source, the former somewhat more exactly, the latter more freely. Furthermore, Weiss concluded that the redaction by the author of the second gospel was known to the author of the first gospel during the process of his writing.

As soon as the theory of a common source was deemed acceptable it greatly discouraged the search for evidences of mutual dependence. In Weiss at least, such evidences often meant very little. This is particularly connected with the notion that the descriptive unity of Mark betrays great originality. The implication was that the loose coherence and the indistinctness of Matthew needed a writing similar to Mark for its explanation.

This point was the limit beyond which Weiss could not go; he had reached the boundaries of the Marcan hypothesis and the entrance into hostile territory. The accurate and careful research in the second gospel had caused Weiss to reject the concept of a Proto-Mark. A wider view of the Logia document had given him the means to provide an acceptable explanation for all the symptoms that elsewhere had occasioned the assumption of a Proto-Mark.

The final outcome of the endeavor by Weiss was a shift in the common documentary background of the Synoptics and consequently a transformation of its character and name. The argument based on the brevity of Mark had thereby lost its cogency. Had Weiss added a slight modification in the value of Mark's graphic imagery, and had he adopted a somewhat wider conception of the Proto-Matthew and of the Gospel of Matthew in general, he would have changed allegiance and would have deserted to the camp of his adversaries.

The Culmination of the Marcan Hypothesis— Heinrich Julius Holtzmann

Holtzmann's Eclecticism (1863)

Above we were dealing with a scholar in whom the Marcan hypothesis attempted to break away from the pattern set by Ewald. Bernhard Weiss had undertaken the research of the gospels with a greater measure of independence than had seemed possible among the adherents of the Marcan hypothesis thus far. With this achievement he had paved the way for Heinrich Julius Holtzmann who performed his investigations on a much wider scale, independently from any scholar. His publication in the 1860s became widely known. It bore the title *The Synoptic Gospels, Their Origin and Their Historical Character.*[18] Because of its

---

[18]Heinrich Julius Holtzmann, *Die synoptischen Evangelien. Ihr Ursprung und geschichtlicher Charakter* (Leipzig: W. Engelmann, 1863) xvi, 514. [In his 5th ed. of *Krit-*

detailed treatment and its comprehensive content it may be considered an achievement of the most intensive effort. In this study the Marcan hypothesis gathers all its wisdom, but at the same time betrays all its weakness as well. What Wilke attempted from his standpoint has been achieved by Holtzmann from the viewpoint of academic scholarship with equal conscientiousness. A somewhat extensive evaluation of his book should be appropriate at this place.

Let us first of all look for the major argument that Holtzmann presents as a justification of his hypothesis. Repeatedly he points to the fact that his conclusion is not the outcome of data extraneous to the gospels, but entirely the result of internal criticism.[19] That is exactly what we could hope for when we take into consideration how easily exegesis can be prejudiced by those external and seemingly compelling reasons. However, if we ask what makes the tree grow which yields such precious fruit, we are continually rebuffed by Holtzmann and finally we find ourselves outside of his book with a reference to contemporary scholarship.

Holtzmann's fourth chapter, entitled "Test Cases,"[20] opens with a declaration that all the phenomena that will come under discussion will be welcome as confirmations of the results of recent research. In other words, these test cases are not needed as data that have to be evaluated before a final conclusion can be reached. Indeed, a summary of the status of research is given on page 167. In proceeding further we find in paragraph ten a "proof of existence"[21] of a second source. In delineating this source Holtzmann considers it sufficient to simply refer to the remaining obscure portions that cannot be associated with the major source. Thus, the second source is contingent upon an original document which he calls "source A" in paragraph 5. Sound methodology, however, does not require another name, but rather a justification for the existence of such a source. With this kind of reasoning we are simply referred to the present stage of development of Gospel criticism.

Does the contemporary stage of research actually provide a justification for a hypothesis? Holtzmann proceeds to point out that neither the Oral Tradition hypothesis, nor the Ur-Gospel hypothesis, nor the Utilization hypothesis may be considered an ultimate solution to the problem. For him, however, each of the three hypotheses has contributed to the contemporary solution. Holtzmann suggests a combination of the valid elements from each of these theories. He continues by asserting that the present accumulation of insights constrains us to be

---

isch exegetisches Handbuch über das Evangelium des Matthäus (1864) viii, Meyer predicted Holtzmann's book would contribute to the victory of the two-source theory.]

[19]Ibid., 359, 243.

[20]German: "Proben."

[21]German: "Nachweis der Existenz."

selective in the variety of potential constructs of gospel history. Such a selective approach should be adjusted to the latest insights of contemporary scholarship. According to Holtzmann, the general opinion of almost all scholars is that the interrelatedness of the Synoptic Gospels points to a common documentary source enlarged with a certain measure of tradition.

Imperceptibly the conviction of a scholar has replaced the lessons from history which still have to be considered. All scholars do, indeed, agree that the present form of the gospels is not the only and original one. It is also commonly agreed that the source of textual concurrence is to be found partly behind the canonical gospels, but the emergence of this commonality is less clear. To point to a common source, to an Ur-Gospel with a canonical title, can only be done after Griesbach's hypothesis has been declared "untenable."[22] From that moment on, however, one looses the right to recognize such an Ur-Gospel as "the only certain result" that has emerged from the lesson of history. This right is forfeited especially since Griesbach's hypothesis also attempted to compose "a summary of the valid elements of most of the accepted hypotheses."[23]

Thus the lesson that Holtzmann draws from history he first has projected onto its data. When he calls his Ur-Gospel "A" in order not to prejudice its character by giving it some other name,[24] it looks, indeed, as if a purely internal criticism must and will provide "A" with a more articulate form and name. But as soon as Holtzmann proceeds to this articulation on the following page, he drops all pretext. We discover that he concentrates precisely on the Marcan hypothesis. As the result of internal criticism he presents nothing more than his conviction of the existence of an original writing in the form of an Ur-Mark. The directions of history are to him apparently no more than a predilection aroused by a certain trend in Gospel criticism.

In sum, Holtzmann has attached himself to the Marcan hypothesis for extrinsic reasons and attempts now to present it as a necessary consequence of Gospel criticism. He intimates that this is the resolve in which all critical scholarship has acquiesced. So great is his sympathy for this hypothesis that the entire description of Gospel criticism is organized around the development of the Marcan hypothesis. The agreement or disagreement with a major or a minor point of the Marcan hypothesis becomes the criterion by which a positive or negative verdict is pronounced in each instance over the entire effort of the various New Testament scholars.

---

[22]Holtzmann, *Die synoptischen Evangelien,* 66.
[23]Ibid., 65.
[24]Ibid., 66.

The Two-Source Theory of Holtzmann

Thus Holtzmann has declared himself in advance as a proponent of the Marcan hypothesis. To the question regarding the cause of this predilection he gives us no uncertain answer. It is not just a retrospective and grateful overview of accomplished research when he testifies to the inestimable blessings of this investigation.[25] This has also made it possible for him to draw a historical portrayal of Jesus that can be accepted by a critical mind. Already on the first page of his book Holtzmann can hardly suppress his desire to reach this objective. The real issue behind this quest is the possibility of a recognizable image of Christ without having to resort to apologetics, or without running the danger of losing one's claim to scholarship. As so often before, the Marcan hypothesis again offered an exceptional means to satisfy this desire for historical certainty.

It is with the same desire in mind that Holtzmann points to the simplicity of his hypothesis. This consists, of course, not in the fact that he assumes only a few writings preceding our gospels—paragraph eleven has demonstrated otherwise.[26] The simplicity consists in the conception that the sources are not interwoven in a complex manner and thereby not obstructing a potential discovery of the origin of the gospels and their historical background. Here is the salient point from which Holtzmann's book is developed; here is the code from which he derives the right to present the Marcan hypothesis as the most natural outcome in the world. For him the terminal point of the history of Gospel criticism is the Marcan hypothesis and the composition of an Ur-Mark its most logical sequel.

Thus Holtzmann, confident of his rightful cause, proceeds to construct his first source of the Synoptic Gospels. The repentance preaching of John the Baptist, the temptation story, the Sermon on the Mount, the story of the Roman officer of Capernaum and of the adulterous woman are taken from somewhere else in order to become part of the Ur-document. Intentionally or accidentally these narratives had been omitted by the canonical compiler of the second gospel. The narratives underwent a fate similar to that of the many other verses and smaller features which at present are lacking in our canonical Mark. Other traits of lesser value offer only a meager compensation for the omission of so much material.

Having identified the narratives originating from the first common source, there remain in Matthew and Luke extensive and incongruous portions which are to be assigned to the second source, namely to the well-known Logia document.

---

[25]Ibid., 168.
[26]Ibid., 157-68.

But while formerly the material of this document was retrieved from the content of Matthew, now it is derived by Holtzmann from the content of Luke. Based on a supposition that gospel writers in the compilation of their writings proceeded with a certain freedom, one does not need to focus only on their common elements in gathering the texts belonging to the common source. Holtzmann is of the opinion that what occurs in only one of the two gospels Matthew or Luke can also be assigned to the common source, as circumstances may require. Thus the most unrelated elements can now be placed together in the same source document. Such parables as the Unrighteous Judge and the Dishonest Steward, which heretofore have been considered typical of Luke, now find a place in the Logia document.

The Critical Procedure of Holtzmann

From these two major and other minor sources the origin of our gospels is explained—in the style of Wilke—with a commanding boldness. For Holtzmann there hardly remain any uncertainties. The entire work of the redactors can be followed text by text. Their secret thoughts, which they never suspected would ever come to light, have now come into the open. Thus it is learned that Matthew first intended to omit the account of the Divorce Notice, Mark 10:3-5. But after he had proceeded to Mark 10:10 he discovered the indispensability of the verses concerning the divorce; so he then decided to include those words after all, but now after verse 9.[27] The story of the Fig Tree (Mark 11:20-23) presents a similar case, where Matthew omitted the first part and then reversing his decision included the second part.[28] A similar incident caused the evangelist to relocate Mark 1:8 whereby he disrupted the original sequence, which can be retrieved from Matthew (see Matt 3:7-17).[29]

In order to understand why Luke repeatedly did the opposite of Matthew, namely, placed verses in an earlier context than his source, Holtzmann's conjecture is that Luke first read the various sections of the document at hand in order then to render the content somewhat freely. In sum, in reading Holtzmann's book the constant impression is that the uncertainty of the theologians with respect to the origin and the mutual relationship of the gospels is merely their own doing.

Yet Holtzmann's assertive procedure remains arbitrary as long as it lacks a verification justifying his own analysis of the gospels. One may assume that a case has been made when, in addition to the possibility, also the probability of

---

[27]Ibid., 196.
[28]Ibid., 198.
[29]Ibid., 68.

a certain development of the gospels has been shown. It will depend therefore on whether the "test cases" given in Holtzmann's fourth chapter really demonstrate this probability, even though Holtzmann does not deem this necessary any more. He advances two literary phenomena that, superficially considered, seem to provide conclusive evidence: the doublets and literary characteristics. When verses with the same content occur twice, the best explanation seems to be the use of two different sources. When furthermore the language and the vocabulary possess a dual character the issue may be considered conclusively resolved, at least to Holtzmann.

The Four Categories of Doublets

That some verses occur twice in one gospel had already been observed by scholars, who had used these duplications as evidence for the accuracy of the Marcan hypothesis and the related Logia theory. Weisse had been the first scholar to summarize these under the category of doublets and since that time these were given frequent attention by critics.

Subsequently, Holtzmann divided these doublets into four categories. There are some doublets, according to him, which already existed in source "A" in consequence of reiteration of the same sayings by Jesus himself. Secondly, there are doublets which came into being through the conflation of both sources. Thirdly, there are conflated doublets, which occur in one of the gospels only, that equally could have been employed by the other author had he not intentionally avoided these. Finally, there are doublets where the same sayings in one of the sources were used in two different contexts in the gospels.

It immediately creates the impression that these categories of doublets have been constructed on the basis of the supposedly proven Marcan hypothesis. The first category includes reiterated predictions of the imminent approach of the last things (Mark 9:1 and 13:30) and the two admonitions to humility (Mark 9:35 and 10:43-44). These illustrate such doublets as could have been present in an original document without necessarily indicating the use of two sources.

[The fourth category seems to yield most examples.] Several sayings in Matthew were, because of the composition of this gospel, adopted from a later place in one of the sources and used in an earlier context. Examples of these are sayings about giving offence (Matt 5:29,30; 18:8,9), about divorce (Matt 5:32; 19:9), about love for the little ones (Matt 10:40, 42; 18:5), and about the power of faith (Matt 17:20; 21:21). Other passages have been repeated from earlier places in the sources. Examples of these are the fate of the fruitless trees (Matt 3:10; 7:19), the relation of the quality of the fruit to the tree (Matt 7:16; 12:33), about the first and the last ones in the Kingdom (Matt 19:30; 20:16), about honor among men (Matt 6:1; 23:5), about true greatness (Matt 20:26; 23:11), about taking an oath (Matt 5:34; 23:22), and about mercy on Sodom in the Judgement day (Matt 10:15; 11:24).

When the second category only yields four doublets that have been derived from the use of two sources, it is clear from the entire organization into categories that ultimately the proof, which had to be rendered, is lacking in Holtzmann. These four doublets are about the relation of having and receiving (Mark 4:25; Matt 13:12; Luke 8:18 and Matt 25:29; Luke 19:26), about self-denial (Mark 8:34-35; Matt 16:24-25; Luke 9:23-24 and Matt 10:38-39; Luke 14:27, 33), about the reward of professing Christ and the consequences of denying him (Mark 8:38; Matt 16:27; Luke 9:26 and Matt 10:32-33; Luke 12:8-9), about the destiny of persecuted Christians (Mark 13:9-13; Matt 24:8-14; Luke 21:12-19 and Matt 10:17-22; Luke 12:11-12).

For the just-mentioned category, Holtzmann derived the conflation of sources only from those doublets that accidentally fall within the limits previously determined for each, namely, that occur in one gospel only. For those doublets that stay outside of this delimitation, or that occur in Mark itself, he has another explanation or apology. If the majority of these doublets do not require the assumption of the use of more than one source, certainly the minority of the cases Holtzmann presents as valid proofs are not cogent either. Furthermore, when one is not able to find in Mark the original reading of those verses that supposedly would have caused the emergence of the doublets, then only Matthew and Luke remain as possible sources for the doublets and an explanation for this phenomenon still needs to be found.

Literary Evidences for the Marcan Hypothesis

I would like to make a similar observation concerning Holtzmann's argument from the literary characteristics in the Synoptic gospels. After the studies of his predecessors in this area, Holtzmann yet considered his own labor not redundant since those scholars, in spite of their devoted study in this area, did not specifically use their insight for a solution of the synoptic problem.[30] Moreover, Holtzmann asserted, it will depend upon the conclusion of his research whether his proposed hypothesis may be called probable. With all diligence he set to work to articulate various literary phenomena. At first glance it seems remarkable that the uncommon form of the Mark-Logia hypothesis, as it came to be known in Holtzmann's studies, could be as cogently defended or even be proven from the aspect of the use of language in the Synoptics as Holtzmann leads the reader to believe.

---

[30]Ibid., 274.

Looking more closely, one soon discovers what has happened. The procedure of Holtzmann is similar to his discussion of the doublets. The evidence has been drawn from the presupposed proofs and again not without some partiality. Holtzmann points to the evangelists' selection of different words expressing the same thought as evidence that the various gospel writers have used a common source in a modified manner.[31] Holtzmann focuses attention (a) on simultaneous use of synonymous words, (b) on the difference in the names of persons, and (c) on the divergence in sentence construction, (d) on the alternate agreement of two evangelists in the sequence of words as well as in the use of clarifying words, and (e) on the difference in the form of expression, and finally (f) on the difference among all of the evangelists simultaneously.

Surveying these observations one can only conclude that this is an argumentation after the manner of Wilke, which in the present stage of scholarship should not be considered valid any more. The possibility that Matthew remained faithful to himself by omitting or avoiding expressions peculiar to Ur-Mark should not be accepted from a scholar like Holtzmann,[32] especially since his greatest grievance against the Griesbach hypothesis is the similar supposition that Mark has consistently avoided the peculiarities of his sources. If Holtzmann deems this unlikely for Mark, [why would he consider it acceptable for Matthew?].[33]

What ultimately is left of the difference in the vocabulary and style of both sources can be perceived by the following complexities: (a) the authors Matthew and Luke have supposedly transferred their own peculiarities to their sources; but (b) reciprocally they also have experienced the impact of both sources so that the peculiarities of these sources are reflected in Matthew and Luke as well, even in passages where they were not dependent on their sources. Finally (c) there remained a neutral territory occasioned by the fact that the evangelists sometimes made an indiscriminate use of their sources. When in that neutral territory the authors allegedly even have improved upon their sources, then the distinctive meaning of language has almost faded out.

For an evaluation of Holtzmann's literary approach we should take into consideration first, to what degree any difference in style and vocabulary is caused automatically by the variety of content in the parts assigned to Mark and the Logia. We also should take note how strange Holtzmann's remarks are which ultimately have to demonstrate the independence of Matthew[34] and Luke[35] from

---

[31]Ibid., 275ff.
[32]Ibid., 297, 300.
[33]Ibid., 294.
[34]Ibid., 301.
[35]Ibid., 331.

the style of Mark. After these considerations there remains little justification for ascribing Matthew's favorite expressions "the Son of David" and "the Christ"[36] as well as Luke's concept "apostles" to an Ur-Mark.[37] From a wider perspective there equally is little justification for Holtzmann's deriving from source "A" the long list of expressions arranged by Zeller[38] indicating the characteristic concepts for Matthew and Luke which also appear in Mark.[39] There is no basis for the determination that the first two authors have selected these expressions from an Ur-Mark.

Holtzmann's Use of External Historical Criticism

We do not find in Holtzmann the remaining common arguments for Marcan priority based on Mark's brevity and literary imagery. The brevity could hardly be maintained as an argument, since he had to include in his Marcan hypothesis the supposition that considerable portions of a common source had intentionally been omitted by the the redactors.[40] The omission of the speeches by Mark is considered natural for an author who wanted to become a pioneer for a new kind of literature, a narrative approach in contradistinction to the already existing collection of sayings. [Consequently Holtzmann could not make use of the argument for Marcan priority based on Mark as the shortest gospel]. Although, incidentally, Holtzmann does refer to the imagery and to the wealth of details as evidence of an original portrayal of events.[41]

Holtzmann points particularly to the natural unity and order in Mark, in a manner as if this would indicate a neater originality in comparison with the other authors whose inaccuracies could hardly be from an eyewitness.[42] The imagery of Mark's gospel is, in Holtzmann's opinion, a unique evidence confirming the tradition concerning that Gospel, which otherwise can claim little credibility on its own merits.[43]

Here we are touching a delicate question. The justification of Holtzmann's opinion concerning the manner in which historically the Marcan Gospel came into being did not come easily to him. What the tradition states about the

---

[36]Ibid., 276.

[37]Ibid., 277.

[38]Eduard Zeller, "Studien zur neutestamentlichen Theologie. 4. Vergleichende Übersicht über den Wörtervorrath der sämmtlichen neutestamentlichen Schriftsteller," *Theologische Jahrbücher* (Tübingen, 1843): 443-543, esp. 528.

[39]Holtzmann, *Die synoptischen Evangelien*, 351.

[40]Ibid., 116.

[41]Ibid., 115, 449.

[42]Ibid., 65, 121, 431.

[43]Ibid., 369.

interpreter of Peter "may very well be true." That John Mark was considered the author of the original Gospel "is quite possible."[44] But to seek an apostolic source for the little material added to the original sources by an editor is deemed superfluous by Holtzmann.[45]

Papias may have known the common-source document of the gospels,[46] but did he also know the canonical Gospel of Mark? Did he know both other gospels, which were at that time already half a century old?[47] What was the relationship between both original sources? Whence the incidental agreement in the mentioning of the Sermon on the Mount?[48] About all these points Holtzmann either speaks in a doubtful tone or not at all, which certainly does not enhance his position.

From Holtzmann's standpoint it is not possible to speak more positively about such historical questions. On all sides the Tübingen quest has commanded his respect, even though he seems to stand his ground courageously. Holtzmann has not quite been able to keep out the Tübingen concept of history. Also for him the gospels are not detached from the conflicting parties during the early church. The historical credibility of the gospels is rather relative to him, since the intention of the authors was ultimately not purely historical in nature.[49]

Yet Holtzmann does not want to use the modern conception of the situation of the early church as a foregone conclusion in Gospel criticism.[50] It is always a gratifying notion to him to determine the value of the writings according to their original date,[51] without taking their content into consideration.[52] Then, after the investigation of their origin and their mutual relationship, he pronounces the verdict over their credibility.[53] Still this apparent indifference about the outcome of historical criticism must not be overestimated. Holtzmann does not fail to attach a high evaluation to those parts whose origin remained unknown to him.[54] On the other hand, he also discovers, in an original document such as Mark, traces of the effect of pious imagination.[55]

The incomplete results obtained by this ambivalent approach is not unwel-

---

[44]Ibid., 373.
[45]Ibid., 369.
[46]Ibid., 370.
[47]Ibid., 412.
[48]Ibid., 385.
[49]Ibid., 66.
[50]Ibid., 57.
[51]Ibid., 401.
[52]Ibid., 497-514.
[53]Ibid., 419.
[54]Ibid., 422ff.
[55]Ibid., 446.

come to Holtzmann. For him this approximate outcome provides sufficient guarantee of the historical character of the major portion of the content of the gospels, while at the same time it leaves adequate room for an explanation of that which transcends the realm of his historical faith. This vacillating approach is also the reason why Holtzmann undauntedly seized upon the Marcan hypothesis, although he did not without trepidation approach the environment of Peter.

An Appraisal of Holtzmann's Contribution

With all the detailed accuracy with which he treated his subject and in spite of all the diligent study he devoted to his book, Holtzmann must nonetheless be accused of arbitrariness. I do not assert that his entire study is saturated with statements to the effect that the Mark's text itself should be held the most original, or that priority should be denied to the texts of Matthew and Luke. These are exegetical issues that will be discussed in part three of this thesis. I do maintain, however, that Holtzmann, by the structure of his book, betrayed what was going on in his own mind.

From beginning to end he posited the Marcan hypothesis as a proven fact, in order then on the other hand to act as if he was providing a conclusive argument. By this circular reasoning Holtzmann revealed how his entire study was nothing else than a commendation of the hypothesis to himself. [In other words, the Marcan hypothesis has forced itself upon him quite independently of his own research.] When so much scholarship and so much accuracy cannot succeed better in convincing him and others of the validity of the Marcan hypothesis, then certainly its case is still in suspense.

The One-Source Theory of Karl Heinrich Weizäcker (ca. 1865)

With good reason it can be predicted that Holtzmann's work will remain influential for the advocates of the Marcan hypothesis in Germany during the next several years, something which for Ewald's work was much less likely because of the complex nature of his solution of the gospel issue.

Since the publication of Holtzmann's voluminous work, German scholarship has yielded only a variation on the same theme by Karl Heinrich Weizsäcker. This theologian claims the right to posit an Ur-Mark, which is basically a return to the Ur-Gospel hypothesis in the form it had in Wilke.[56] Weizsäcker starts from the presupposed mutual nonacquaintance of Matthew and Luke, and assumes the

---

[56]Karl Heinrich von Weizsäcker, *Untersuchungen über die evangelische Geschichte, ihre Quellen und den Gang ihrer Entwicklung* (Gotha: R. Besser, 1864) xvi, 580.

unfamiliarity of both with the canonical Gospel of Mark. Observing the brevity of Mark and the little original character of Matthew, Weizsäcker felt prompted to reject the Griesbach hypothesis. In his critical comparison of the first three gospels Weizsäcker is directed to an Ur-Gospel, which must serve to explain the common elements in all three of the Synoptic gospels. Of course, this document can be found in its most original form, only in our canonical Mark. The difference which exists between the Ur-Gospel of Holtzmann and that of Weizsäcker consists mainly in the fact, that the latter finds no reason to suppose that portions have been omitted by the canonical editor.

Weizsäcker has a somewhat different conception of the second main source that yielded materials for the composition of the gospels. According to his idea this second (Logia) source did not originally include the following materials: the address against those who accused Jesus of a covenant with the devil, the parable of the growing grain, and the parable of the mustard seed.[57] Weizsäcker ascribes the imagery, the explanatory remarks, and the Aramaic expressions in Mark largely to a redactor, because they are not found in the other gospels.[58]

Thus we obtain an Ur-Mark that fulfills all the requirements of being a document explaining the agreement in form and content of the Synoptic gospels. This Ur-Mark has little value as a source of history,[59] nor does it correspond to the description of Papias. The quote from Papias by Eusebius proves merely that the tradition did not consider the second gospel as a mere excerpt but as a full document.[60] In sum, for Weizsäcker the Ur-Mark is the common source explaining the agreement and difference in form and content of the Synoptic writers, who did not know one another in their canonical form.

The implication of Weizsäcker's hypothesis is an unusual interpretation of Matthew. When he discovers obscurities in that gospel they are for him direct evidences of a later origin than Mark. For instance, in dealing with the pericope concerning the demon that possessed the Gerasene, he observes that Matthew does not identify this demon by the name "Legion." Consequently, the large number of perishing swine loses its explanation. When Jesus calls the death of the officer's daughter a "sleep," one has to be an adherent of the Marcan hypothesis to discern in these words an attempt to leave the crowds in ignorance regarding the miracle to be performed. Furthermore, Weizsäcker characterizes Matthew's description as erroneous because he does not explicitly distinguish the crowd from the three confidants,[61] as is indicated in Mark. Similar inferences are

---

[57]Ibid., 46ff.
[58]Ibid., 63.
[59]Ibid., 127.
[60]Ibid., 30, 118.
[61]Ibid., 54.

drawn frequently in Weizsäcker, but to dwell longer on his work seems redundant.

The Situation of the Synoptic Discussion in 1866

The Typological Interpretation of Gustav Volkmar

With the discussion of Weizsäcker we have approached the present era in the history of the Marcan hypothesis. It has spread so widely that [Johann] Gerhard [Wilhelm] Uhlhorn could present the Marcan hypothesis as a proven position in his recent review of the status of the discussion.[62]

Before returning to our starting point, that is, the definition of the hypothesis, one more observation needs to be made. During the days when Mark offered a safe haven from the danger of mythic belief, Bruno Bauer transplanted the "false Tübingen approach" into the sphere of the defenders of the Marcan hypothesis. His allegiance to the Marcan hypothesis surpassed all previous evils. Something similar has happened in the latter half of the history of the hypothesis. It is remarkable that one of the most extreme adherents of the Tendency criticism of the Tübingen school, namely, the influential theologian Gustav Volkmar, would embrace Marcan priority.

The natural unity of Mark had been for Bauer the occasion to join the ranks of the Marcan priorists. The same discovery induced Volkmar to take this position. In his work *The Religion of Jesus,* he describes the second gospel as a Christian epic, a polemic essay from a Pauline standpoint protesting against sensual contemplations.[63] I do not intend to pursue Volkmar's description in detail. It will suffice simply to point out that Volkmar discovers too much meaning in the plain stories of Mark. His division and analysis of the epic portrayal is too farfetched and too subtle, which may be demonstrated by a few examples.

For Volkmar, the purpose of the gospel is portraying the glory of true Christianity, in particular in Christ's ministry and in his suffering. Because of this purpose, the gospel is naturally divided into two parts, each of which individually comprises four subdivisions. The effect of the ministry is revealed in four stages: first, in general; second, as elevated above Judaism; then as a power against all impediments; and finally as a universal religion. Secondly, the suffering of Christ reveals the glory of Christianity also in four stages, namely, (a) in the way to

---

[62]In *Zeitschrift für historische Theologie* 1, ed. Niedner (1866): 86.
[63]Gustav Volkmar, *Die Religion Jesu und ihre erste Entwicklung nach dem gegenwärtigen Stande der Wissenschaft* (Leipzig: Brockhaus, 1857) 215-63.

suffering, (b) in conflict, (c) in suffering itself, and finally (d) by entering into glory.

Anything that does fit this division of the effect of the gospels must be subsumed with some stretch of the imagination under the categories set up by Volkmar. For example, the universal character of Christianity is portrayed by the stories in Mark 6–8, namely, in the unbelief of the inhabitants of Nazareth as a type of the unbelief of the Jewish people; in the mission of the twelve who must feel themselves at home anywhere in the world; in the feeding of the five thousand, which still leaves food for the twelve tribes; in Jesus crossing the sea of Galilee, as Paul at Troas [crossed over to Macedonia] in his missionary endeavor; in the healing of all the sick in the area of Gennesaret; in the purity of heart which is available to all; in the raising of the daughter of the Syrophoenician woman and in the healings in the Decapolis; in the second feeding of the multitudes after which Israel asks again for signs; in the hardness of heart of Israel, which by the mouth of the disciples does not understand a simple warning against the Pharisees; finally, the universality of Christianity is portrayed in the Blind Man of Bethsaida, who illustrates the gradual acquiring of correct insight into the universal character of Christianity.

Irrespective of the question whether such a typological interpretation is correct, it will be difficult to assign the stories under the same categories as has Volkmar. Additionally, narratives occurring in the section supposedly emphasizing the elevation of Christianity above Judaism could with equal justification be categorized under the heading of the universal character of Christianity. [There is further the problem that the gospel does not heed Volkmar's sequence of categories.] Already in the beginning of Mark, the fourth and final category, namely, the universality of Christianity, was revealed by Jesus' departure from Capernaum and his refusal to return. In this case, Volkmar explains that the universality had become known publicly and fits therefore in the first category concerning the effect of Christianity in general.

The references to universality are thus not limited to the section of Mark 6–8. Within the compass of these three chapters even Volkmar found stories that do not fit this particular category. The entire history of the beheading of John the Baptist in Mark 6 is called an episode Mark inserts by way of an interlude. Similarly the return of the disciples followed by their sailing to a desolate place makes for a beautiful connection between the preceding section and the feeding of the four thousand, but none of these narratives in Mark 6 fits the category of universality.

Assessment of Volkmar's Value for the Marcan Hypothesis

What holds true for these three chapters of Mark can be applied to the interpretation of the total gospel, which Volkmar claims to be a well-ordered epic. Grave objections remain even if one accepts the viability of such a typological interpretation. Yet all of this is presented with a self-confidence as if there were no problems involved. In the same confident manner Volkmar depicts the subsequent history of original primitive Christianity. His popular poetic style is fascinating but thereby all the more dangerous. Upon closer observation, however, his exaggeration is unmistakably clear.

Adolf Hilgenfeld uses Volkmar's book as an illustration of the dangerous consequences of the Marcan hypothesis. This much is certain: we are dealing here with a very peculiar form of this hypothesis. From a Tübingen point of view it is perhaps the only possible form, but its true advocates can hardly welcome Volkmar as their brother. Just like Bauer's *Critique of Gospel History*, Volkmar's *Religion of Jesus* has the potential of bringing the Marcan hypothesis into disrepute for the second time.

Although the Tübingers could reconcile themselves, to a certain degree, to the Marcan hypothesis, they persisted stubbornly in opposing the acceptance of a Proto-Mark. For instance, when Bruno Bauer considered the canonical Gospel of Mark to be somewhat different from its antecedent, he called it merely a case of text mutilation. Even though Volkmar had considered an earlier document for some time, he later showed himself less and less inclined to accept a Proto-Mark.

In his *Religion of Jesus*[64] Volkmar considered Mark's discussion concerning the coming of Elijah (Mark 9:12-13) initially a thoughtless shift [from a future advent of Elijah to a past event in the person of John the Baptist]. In his first publication, Volkmar considered verses 9:35, 38-40 as well as 16:8-14, 17-18 as improper insertions. In a later publication,[65] however, Volkmar had changed his mind, finding no reason anymore to seek any redactional changes in the present text of Mark. For the alleged shift of interpretation in Mark 9 he acquiesced to Hitzig's explanation [attributing the confusion concerning the coming of Elijah to the disciples themselves].[66]

Albrecht Ritschl's Valuation of Canonical Mark

Ritschl is an even more outspoken opponent of the concept of a Proto-Mark. In justifying his conception of the Gospels in his study on *The Old Catholic*

---

[64]Ibid., 204ff.
[65]Gustav Volkmar, *Die geschichtstreue Theologie* (Leipzig: Brockhaus, 1860) 81ff.
[66]See 28ff., above.

Church, Ritschl contributed an article in the *Tübingen Yearbooks* about the state of synoptic research.[67] He observed that the Marcan hypothesis thus far seemed to depend on the arbitrary acceptance of interpolations and redactions of the Gospel of Mark. He concluded that in that case it would be better to abandon the hypothesis altogether, since it cancels itself out by these very interpolations.[68] Ritschl is nonetheless of the opinion that he can demonstrate the need for a Marcan hypothesis but without any redactional changes in Mark. His article served mainly as a reminder to his readers that one should be guided by the total tendency of the gospels when considering particular issues.

As an example of this certainly commendable method Ritschl made three observations. [His first observation concerns disruptions of the sequence of Mark's account by Matthew.] In the Gospel of Mark the discovery of Jesus as Messiah by his contemporaries seems to Ritschl only a gradual recognition of Jesus' dignity. When Matthew already in the beginning of his gospel portrays the welcome of Jesus as Son of David and yet summons secrecy, it demonstrates that the sequence of Mark has been disrupted. A similar disruption occurs in the case of Jesus' surprise concerning the confession of Peter.

[A second observation concerns inversions of the sequence in Mark by Matthew.] When Matthew calls the disciples "the salt of the earth" and "the light of the world" in the beginning of his gospel, he creates an inversion of the development in Mark. Matthew begins with a high profile of the disciples and then continues to show their limitations by having them ask later for an explanation of the parables or for a place of honor in the Kingdom.

Ritschl noted that Mark begins with a low profile of the disciples and continues portraying them in steady development. The recognition of these arguments as evidences for an early date for Mark is entirely related to the critics concept of order and of the theological nature of Mark. We will discuss the theological aspects of Mark later. The third argument by Ritschl for the accuracy of the Marcan hypothesis should now be discussed in more detail.

The Hebraic Quotes in Matthew
as an Argument for the Marcan Hypothesis

Ritschl observed that references to the Old Testament in the first gospel are partly derived from the Septuagint, namely, when they are inherently related to the context of his narrative. On the other hand, the references which reflect the

---

[67]Albrecht Ritschl, *Die Entstehung der altkatholischen Kirche* (Bonn, 1850); and "Über den Gegenwärtigen Stand der Kritik der synoptischen Evangelien," *Theologische Jahrbücher* 10 (1851): 480-538.
[68]"Über den Gegenwärtigen Stand," ibid., 511ff.

ideas of the writer himself are derived from the Hebraic text of the Old Testament. In discussing the exceptions to this rule Ritschl raises the question[69] whether it would be likely that Mark could have used Matthew as his source for the narratives avoiding all references to the Hebraic text. The sequel to this question was that references the author of the second gospel could not ignore were relayed to his introduction. Ritschl continues to question whether it would not be more natural that the exceptions to the rule by Matthew refer to his dependence on Mark! For Ritschl the answer is in the affirmative, [especially since these Hebraic references are directly related to Matthew himself].

This linguistic analysis seems rather conclusive when Matthew does indeed quote the contextual references from the Septuagint and his editorial references from the original Hebraic text. In the main part of his gospel, Matthew, indeed, deviates from this rule in contexts that agree with Mark, who has transferred these references to his introduction. At first sight Ritschl's analysis would confirm his position.

The contextual as well as the editorial rule is ignored, however, at least once by Matthew, which leads one to question Ritschl's proposition. The words from Malachi 3:1, which in Matt 11:10 are [said to be] quoted by Jesus, are from a Greek translation deviating from the Septuagint, although some acquaintance with the Septuagint is involved in this passage. In the same manner some influence of the Hebraic text can be detected in several contextual references. The words "and not" (καὶ οὐ) in Matt 9:13 and 12:7 show Hebraic origin. The reference in Matt 26:31 and the sequence in Matt 19:18 and 22:37 also demonstrate Hebraic influence. [Therefore it cannot be maintained that contextual references are consistently derived from the Septuagint.]

On the other hand, the words of Isaiah 40:3 have been derived from the Septuagint, although they occur in an editorial reference by the author (Matt 3:3). Similarly, influence of the Septuagint can be detected in phrases that are genuinely Matthean, such as Matt 27:35, which reminds the reader of Ps 22:2. Generally the linguistic use of the Septuagint influenced the form of several gospel narratives in Matthew, [which weakens the argument concerning the Hebraic orientation of the editorial references].

The multiplicity of exceptions makes it difficult to apply Ritschl's rule consistently. Moreover, the diffusion of both kinds of references disqualify this method of analysis for providing a conclusive argument. When the three wise men indicate the birthplace of the new king with an appeal to Micah, introduced by the words "for so it is written" (Matt 2:5), or when Jesus associates his custom of speaking in parables with the prophet Isaiah whose prophecy "with them is fulfulled," we merely encounter stylistic variations [rather than transitions

---

[69]Ibid., 522.

from contextual to editorial references].

These examples demonstrate that such a distinction cannot clearly be upheld. Passages such as Matt 21:42 and 26:31 are not following Ritschl's Rule for contextual references either. The more examples we give, the greater becomes the objection against strictly defined rules. Because of these exceptions, an observation by Ritschl that only Matt 11:10 and Matt 3:3 were deviations from the customary pattern followed by Matthew loses much of its cogency and certainly cannot serve as proof for Matthew's dependence upon Mark.

An Appraisal of Albrecht Ritschl's Analysis

When the references in Matthew show acquaintance with the Hebraic as well with the Septuagint text, while Mark has only references to the Septuagint, a strong argument for the originality of Mark would be posed. It would, indeed, be hard to imagine that Mark would have scrupulously avoided Hebraic references. But is it relevant asking the question this way? In the first place Mark does not "avoid" Hebraic references consistently. His parallels to Matt 3:3; 19:18; 22:37; and 26:31 show traces of his acquaintance with the original Hebrew text. Moreover the word for "marry" (ἐπιγαμβρεύσει) occurring in Matt 22:24 and lacking in its parallel (Mark 12:19), cannot be construed as a case of avoidance since the missing word is not in the original Hebrew text (Deut. 25:5) but rather appears as a general term used in the narrative of Gen. 38:8.

On the other hand, there are omissions in Mark in the sometimes literal references to the Septuagint by Matthew (Matt 1:23; 2:6; 21:16). All this should demonstrate that a conclusion concerning the dependence or originality of a document should not be based on different types of references but rather on theological content. The narratives using the references should first be compared. After this, further linguistic analysis might be appropriate and could even reverse the original conclusion if, indeed, unusual language patterns occur.

The procedure of Ritschl becomes quite suspect when he calls attention to mere formal differences of references that are of equal content. I do not want to mention the scant differences in the use of pronouns and articles. I also see no point in discussing passages such as Mark 7:10; 10:7-8; 10:19; 15:34, where both evangelists alternately agree more closely with the Septuagint. These differences cannot be very significant, because we may assume that the authors as well as their copyists knew the references by heart and could easily modify any quote.

Of more importance are the deviations in four places in the Gospel of Mark, namely, Mark 4:12; 10:19; 12:19; and 12:30, [where Matthew seems to have the original reading]. (a) The subjunctive in Mark 4:12 is said to originate from the indicative used in Matt 13:13; (b) the sequence in Mark 10:19[70] represents a change from Matt 19:18, and consistently the negative construction with οὐ has replaced the Matthean use of μή; (c) Mark 12:19 changes the construction of Matt 22:24 considerably; (d) finally, the dative which is governed in Matt 22:37 by the preposition ἐν is used in Mark 12:30 as a genitive following the preposition ἐξ; furthermore, the words "and with all your strength" have been added in Mark 12:30; and, remarkably, every change in these verses in Mark is paralleled exactly by Luke. When these four major deviations in Mark have been subjected to closer scrutiny, Ritschl's whole argument concerning the Old Testament references loses its cogency. We may justifiably doubt the relevance of any of these data.

Dutch Supporters of the Marcan Hypothesis

Up to this point we have discussed the most important German and French works that have contributed to the Marcan hypothesis. The Marcan hypothesis has gained prevalence also in the Netherlands, and most likely will enjoy this position for a considerable time.

Already in 1858 Professor Prins referred to the studies of Reuss in a manner that betrayed his predilection for this hypothesis.[71] When afterwards the award-winning study of Albert Réville gained public attention, it became increasingly fashionable to use the Marcan hypothesis. W. H. van de Sande Bakhuyzen spoke about the great achievements of New Testament criticism gained by the Marcan hypothesis in particular.[72] Dr. M. A. N. Rovers confidently declared that the originality of the Gospel of Mark had been demonstrated on solid grounds.[73]

In various dissertations the hypothesis served as a basis for research. Dr. Lambrechts deliberately attempted to explain the difference between the second gospel and Luke using the Marcan hypothesis as his point of departure.[74] When

---

[70]See [Friedrich Karl] Albert Schwegler's explanation of this changed sequence in his *Das nachapostolische Zeitalter in den Hauptmomenten seiner Entwicklung* [*The Post-apostolic Age in the High Points of Its Development*] (Tübingen: L. F. Fues, 1846) 473.

[71]*Godgeleerde Bijdragen* (1858): 812.

[72]*Godgeleerde Bijdragen* (1865): 468.

[73]M. A. N. Rovers, *De synoptische Evangeliën* (N.p., n.d.) xi.

[74]Thus I would interpret the purpose of his work, although the title of his study indicates a completely opposite intention. The title of his dissertation is "An exegetical-theological study in which the diversity of messages and narrations indicates Luke's use of Mark's text." The author used the "Benützungs [Utilization] hypothesis" which rejects any original text in Matthew as well as a Proto-Mark. This, however, does not explain the issue that Luke's source had no passion story. The author also does not mind accepting some verses in Mark from another source. Verses 9:39, 41; 10:24, 46; and 11:16 are de-

referring to texts from the Synoptic Gospels it has become customary to do this from the text according to Mark.

Finally, the Marcan hypothesis will benefit by the support of Professor [J. H.] Scholten who in his work about the Gospel of John promised a future exposition of this theory.[75] He already used this hypothesis as a basis for his comparison of the historical nature of John with that of the Synoptics. As everywhere else, so also in the Netherlands the Marcan hypothesis is enjoying a dominating position.

Concluding Delineations of the Marcan Hypothesis

The Anti-Tübingen Reactionary Group

We will now return to the point where we began. We have pursued the history of the Marcan hypothesis in its various forms. In doing so we have had an opportunity to answer the question of its essence and its purpose. Its definition can briefly be formulated as follows. *The Marcan hypothesis believes that the second gospel is the oldest gospel, even though it may be a gospel with dubious delineations. It is yet considered the source for Matthew and Luke.* This broad definition allows room for everyone in some way associated with this theory.

Within the scope of this definition we can distinguish three different groups. The oldest and most antiquated group based its hypothesis only upon the brevity of Mark. To this group belonged the scholars who worked during the time before Strauss. The second group embraces the men who under the influence of the Enlightenment belonged to the extreme left, or to the "ultra's" [who based their theory on the natural unity of the Gospel of Mark]. Finally there were those who found support in the Marcan hypothesis in their battle against Strauss and Baur.

If I am not mistaken, the last group should, properly speaking, be called its genuine advocate. We have observed how Weisse called his discovery a completely new approach and how everyone attempted to dissociate himself from

---

rived from another source, according to Dr. Lambrechts. One notices again how a Proto-Mark is not the same as an earlier form of the Marcan text; see 161-80 in Johannes Lambrechts, *Specimen exegetico-theologicum qua e sermonis narrationisque diversitate Marcum et Lucam hunc illius textu usum esse colligitur* (Lugduni Batavorum, 1863).

[75][Scholten's subsequent monograph was *Das älteste Evangelium: kritische Untersuchung der Zusammensetzung, des wechselseitigen Verhältnisses, des geschichtlichen Werths und des Ursprungs der Evangelien nach Matthäus und Marcus,* Aus dem Holländischen mit Genehmigung des Verfassers übersetzt von Ernst Rud (Elberfeld: R. L. Friedrichs, 1869). —ed.]

any connection with Bruno Bauer, [a major spokesman for the second group]. Even though the proponents of the Marcan hypothesis rejoiced in the conversion of Ritschl [from the Tübingen school to their camp], they were far from enthusiastic about the joining of their ranks by Volkmar. [The third group has clearly a sense of identity and a common adversary.] It is, therefore, the third group to which in particular I have to address myself. Such a focus is even more crucial since every argument used in favor of the hypothesis has found its best articulation within this group of scholars.

The form of the hypothesis as it occurs in this group will naturally need to be identifiable by additional qualities. In the first place we notice that in the history of the past thirty years two periods can be distinguished, separated by the activities of F. C. Baur. The common challenge (from Tübingen) was first Strauss's mythical conception of New Testament history, while (later) with Baur it became the issue of Tendency criticism. In neither period could the adherents of the Marcan hypothesis maintain their stand without adjustments. A certain compromise, a giving and taking, was necessary in both periods. But to this end Mark provided excellent services both by its origin as well as by its character. In Mark's Gospel the New Testament touched historical reality and in it also theological expression had its beginning.

The qualities that the proponents maintained concerning the originality of Mark were diverse in nature. [The three major qualities were the following.] (1) Mark is the shortest gospel and thereby testifies to its early date over against the other Synoptics. (2) Mark possesses a graphic literary imagery that can only be explained as having originated from an eyewitness. (3) Mark's self-consistency gives him considerable advantage over the inconsistencies of Matthew. This last aspect was especially of great influence on the evaluation of Mark's particular features.

Variety among the Proponents of the Marcan Hypothesis

But in spite of Mark's advantageous qualities, problems remained for advocates of the Marcan hypothesis. In Matthew there are passages that in comparison with Mark's text show a more original character. This phenomenon was explained in two ways. First, the Marcan document to which Papias refers could have been a document other than our second gospel, namely, a Proto-Mark which was used by Matthew. Secondly, if Papias referred to our canonical Gospel of Mark, we can refer to the clear traces of an editor in that gospel. Since the conclusion of the canonical Gospel of Mark is inauthentic, the critic is justified in assuming the influence of interpolation at other places.

Aspects that might lead one to suspect Matthew is the oldest gospel do not create major difficulties for proponents of the Marcan hypothesis. Additionally, there are significant phenomena to be considered beyond the typical arguments based on the brevity of Mark and the graphic unity of its text. [Among these phenomena are the following:] There are places where Matthew undoubtedly has a later text; Matthew employs diverging linguistic sources, while Mark remains self-consistent; there are reiterations in Matthew that are mentioned only once in Mark; finally, Matthew uses two kinds of references to the Old Testament, while Mark agrees with only one. All of these points place Mark [for the advocates of the Marcan hypothesis] in the position of being beyond any doubt the oldest gospel.

The form of the hypothesis is, however, not the same among all its proponents. It is conditioned by the degree a particular argument is being emphasized. If the testimony of Papias is the major principle of argumentation, the hypothesis obtains definite historical character. If one approaches the issue from the agreement and difference in the form of similar narratives, the discussion obtains a literary character. If aversion to claims for the historical nature of the gospels becomes the driving force, the hypothesis gains a more theological nature.

These distinctions also determine the place the various forms of the hypothesis occupy in the history of Gospel criticism. The Ur-Gospel hypothesis as well as the Utilization hypothesis are generally considered antiquated theories. The Marcan hypothesis has gained a place of honor among the "Combination hypotheses." Yet Wilke and Holtzmann are close to an Ur-Gospel hypothesis in their position; Meyer, Weiss, and Lambrechts are closely associated with the former Utilization hypothesis. Lambrechts and Tobler even defend openly their acceptance of the Utilization theory. Thus there remains considerable variety within the embrace of the adherents to the Marcan hypothesis!

The Major Theses of the Marcan Hypothesis

The hypothesis presents itself today with much self-confidence. It has assumed a place of authority in almost all universities. When it looks back on its past it can rejoice over its speedy victory. It sends its commentaries and writings in all directions. It has begun to gather and disseminate the fruits it considers it has produced for historical research. Holtzmann formulated the meaning of the expression "Son of Man" from the Gospel of Mark.[76] Schenkel developed from Mark a complete life of Jesus.[77] In sum, everywhere the adherents of the hypothesis are strongly convinced of their justifiable position and of the virtue of their cause.

---

[76]*Zeitschrift für wissenschaftliche Theologie* (1865): 212.
[77]Daniel Schenkel, *Das Charakterbild Jesu, ein biblischer Versuch* (Wiesbaden: C. W. Kreidel's Verlag, 1864) 288.

Yet, Strauss could not see anything else than the "swindle of the century"[78] in this theory, and Hilgenfeld reiterated incessantly the Roman adage "I am of the opinion that Carthage should be destroyed!" [applying this to an annihilation of the Marcan hypothesis]. A peculiar situation, indeed! On both sides equal decisiveness, and on both sides an equally strong language. The explanation of this phenomenon is that the issue is considered to have been settled. No new research of details is undertaken anymore; no surprising new light is being shed over certain crucial texts; no as-yet-undiscovered historical evidence is wanted to tip the scales in one direction or to the other!

The research of many years has caused the same dilemma for Mark as it has for the Gospel of John. "Who is not for me is against me!" says the gospel. The priority of Mark is either accepted or rejected, just as the authenticity of the Gospel of John is either recognized or rejected with equal decisiveness. This does not mean there is no place for a variety of opinion. As there are still different ideas concerning the date of origin of the fourth gospel, so too there are also different approaches to the relation between Mark and Luke or Mark and Matthew. But in general both the question of the relationship of Mark to the other Synoptic Gospels and Mark's value as source for historical research, are considered settled issues.

This conclusion has been reached by motivations extraneous to the Gospels themselves. The answer to this question is directly connected with the acceptance or rejection of two theses, namely, the brevity of a gospel proving its early date, and secondly, the imagery of Mark betraying its association with an eyewitness. A third thesis might be added referring to the inauthenticity of the longer ending of Mark, that thereby allows for the assumption of further interpolations or omissions. [This third thesis opens the debate concerning a potential and more concise Ur-Mark or a more elaborate Proto-Mark.]

The impact of these three theses upon the assessment of details and problems is incalculable! When we consider how every hypothesis has been able to justify itself with exegetical statements, it is not too audacious to assert that the real cause for the various positions must be located in these theses themselves. In traversing the history of the Marcan hypothesis we have observed that many scholars found the strength of their argument in their conviction concerning

---

[78]David Friedrich Strauss, *Der Christus des Glaubens und der Jesus der Geschichte. Eine Kritik des Schleiermacher'schen Lebens Jesu* (Berlin: Franz Duncker, 1865) 54. [As recently translated, Strauss said, "this whole orientation (theory of Marcan priority) remains for me passing humbug—like 'futurist music' (Wagner) or the agitation against smallpox vaccination." In Strauss, *The Christ of Faith and the Jesus of History. A Critique of Schleiermacher's Life of Jesus,* trans. and ed. by Leander E. Keck, Lives of Jesus Series (Philadelphia: Fortress Press, 1977) 47n58.]

the accuracy of one or more of the above-mentioned theses. Their theory would collapse if these theses were removed from them.

We will therefore have to test first of all these theses and their implications. If they turn out to be untenable, we will have to confront the gospels in an impartial manner, in order to discover whether there are phenomena that can be interpreted differently depending upon one's own critical presuppositions. In the history presented above we have already discussed the arguments of lesser importance. These will gain significance only after the major issues have been settled. The lesser arguments do not as such contribute to the probability of the Marcan hypothesis. If the same has to be said about the major arguments, then the case for the Marcan hypothesis remains at best precarious. If also strong objections arise from impartial study of the gospels, the Marcan hypothesis will have lost its reason for being.

When we finally deal with the points that allegedly argue for a late date for Matthew, we will have to evaluate these independently from the ideas concerning brevity and imagery. If the objections against either a late date for Matthew or a late date for Mark are compared on an equal basis, we will see in which direction the balance moves. [Thus, after having discussed in more detail the three main theses of the Marcan hypothesis we will elaborate on the lesser arguments, which are of theological and exegetical nature. In conclusion we will assess the linguistic characteristics in both Matthew and Mark in order to approach the issue of priority on an objective basis.] An answer to the last question will be the final objective for this research project.

Part Two

Critique
of the Marcan Hypothesis

Chapter 4

The Three Theses
of the Marcan Hypothesis

Thesis One
The Brevity of Mark

The Gospel of Mark is relatively brief in comparison to the other two Synoptic Gospels. For this reason it may claim an earlier date than the other two much-more-extensive documents.

Such is the thesis we find in various forms among the advocates of the Marcan Hypothesis. On first impression this conclusion seems quite plausible. This thesis is based, however, on the premise that the purpose of the evangelists was to preserve as many reports as possible about Jesus' life and work; in other words, they intended to be as complete as possible in their historiography.

May we really assume such an objective for the evangelists? First of all, we should place ourselves in the circumstances under which the Gospels came into being. [From the recorded parables and admonitions we gain the impression of a certain spiritual regression.] The parable of the Foolish Virgins reflects the growing carelessness of some Christians caused by the delay of the Lord's return (Matt 25:1-13). Another parable intimates that the servants appointed to manage the household considered themselves relieved from responsibility (Matt 24:48-51).

Consequently, the vigilance of the early Christians occasionally waned and the delay of reward blunted the incentive to a life of moral obedience (Matt 25:14-30). Even though faith on earth might have decreased (Luke 18:8), the awareness was still alive that the current era would soon be replaced by a new age. From the exhortation in Luke 21:28, "Look up and raise your heads," we may infer that some early Christians looked forward to the redemption with heads down. The evangelists, however, still expected a return of the Lord in the near future. [The cause of missions must have been of minor importance to the authors of the gospels.] They did not seem concerned whether the nations would gather around the Lord's table, or whether they would receive accurate or inaccurate knowledge of the life of the Lord of the Christians. It certainly was not the objective of the evangelists to collect the scattered traditions for posterity.

The Relation of Faith and History in the Gospels

Did the evangelists really have a purely historical perspective in mind when they wrote for their contemporaries?

Let us consider the objective of their writings. The Christians had long since changed their focus of attention from the territory of Palestine to the clouds of heaven from where the Son of Man was to return. The prophet of Nazareth had, in their understanding, already become a heavenly ruler. Even though the glorified image of Christ was still portrayed with some historical features, the traits of exaltation predominated and the light of the risen Christ was jubilantly proclaimed. This glorious light conversely illuminated the story about Jesus as he lived and worked in Palestine. Lofty designations, such as the "Son of Man on the clouds," the "Son of God," the "Savior of the World," adorned the man of Nazareth. The image of the risen Christ was inadvertently superimposed upon the historical Jesus.

Not only were the evangelists no longer in a position to perceive Jesus in purely historical terms, their readers did not expect them to do so either. When people in antiquity consulted history they seldom were interested in mere factual data, but rather in the message and meaning of history. History was their moral teacher and the object of theological contemplations. This must likewise have been the case with their testimony concerning Christ, who for the Christians was the principal content of their religious convictions. Those features had to be presented which would enhance the image of the living Christ.

The readers of the gospels did not assume a conflict between the data of history and their religious conceptions. The purpose of the evangelists, therefore, could not simply have been a description of the historical Jesus; they rather intended to portray an image of Christ that agreed with their convictions. The work of the evangelists was thus not historical but rather theological in nature.

This explains why the portrayals of Jesus differed: they were conditioned by the perspective under which their subject was viewed. Sometimes Christ was depicted as the fulfiller of the prophecies to Israel, at other times he was portrayed as the gentle shepherd tending the deserted sheep and bearing their diseases. He was depicted as the quiet servant whose words were not resounding in the streets, as well as the Savior of the world, whose advent created joy and provided redemption to the oppressed and the afflicted. Finally, Jesus was seen as the rescuer of the perishing, as the miracle worker who could overcome any power or resistance and who was admired by thousands of followers.

One additional aspect should be mentioned. As soon as the image of Christ had permeated the inner life of the devout mind, it influenced all the ideas and convictions of its spiritual nature. The implications of Christ for religious life, for mankind, and for the history of the world had provided points of reflection which were considered of crucial importance. It was altogether natural that the early Christians expected divine counsel in all circumstances and miraculous solutions for all their difficulties.

The faithful looked for a wide range of directives from their Christ. Sometimes they cried in despondency that their fervent prayers concerning the consummation of earthly life remained unanswered; on other occasions the Christians aimed at conformity with the world to the neglect of the concerns for the future, while other groups felt the urge to break all ties with unrighteous Mammon.

Certain groups were not sure whom they could accept as brothers and friends, who were to be considered true sons of the Kingdom. Some believers were puzzled about the validity of the old Law in the new Kingdom, while others pondered over the conditions for entrance into the Kingdom. All these questions were addressed by the early Christians directly to Christ [and are reflected in our Scriptures].

There were also people who in their search for the essence of Christianity even considered heretical concepts, and became oblivious to the internal peace in the churches. There was even partisanship and schism. Issues of the day divided the members. The more vehement these disturbances became the more decisively the authority of Christ had to be upheld.

Christ was the center of all thoughts and conceptions; he was interwoven in all expressions of faith; and to him every idea was related. Thus the diversity of all these people led to gospels of different character, conditioned by circumstances, time and place, and by the disposition of their readers. Of course, the point of view of the authors and their distinctive convictions also contributed to the style and content of their gospels.

The Historical Setting of the Gospels

We can even go a step further. The concern of the evangelists was not only closely related to doctrinal issues but also to the moral applications for their own day. From the content of the gospels we must conclude that these were written for the purpose of admonition. The portrayal of Christ was meant to be like a mirror reflecting his normative image to the contemporaries of the evangelists. The gospels were to expose the defects of the times in which they were written.

The authors of the gospels wanted to cast the light of Christ on daily concerns and their gospels were meant as directives for change in action and thought. This intention is clear to a lesser or greater degree in each evangelist, irrespective of his emphasis on either doctrine or practice. The portrayal of Christ was the medium by which the author attempted to get his personal convictions across to the reader. This personal intention is one more reason for the distinctive character of each of the gospels.

The early Church Fathers considered the essence and purpose of the gospels in a similar manner. They gave equal attention to the variety in the fourfold gospel message as to its unity expressed in such diverse forms. The church saw the apostolic gospels symbolized in the four creatures of Revelation or in the four streams of Paradise. It indicates that the church fathers were genuinely aware of the unique character of each individual gospel.

It is of significance that the church never wholeheartedly endorsed the effort to harmonize the four gospels into one. The gospel harmonies were only used in smaller circles, and were associated with movements that never became popular in the church at large.

The grounds for accepting the four gospels in the canon were similar to the grounds for rejecting other gospels. These grounds were primarily doctrinal in nature. The acceptance of the canonical gospels may not always have been based on conscientious study of the consistent doctrinal nature of the documents as a whole: sometimes a single passage of great doctrinal import may have determined the value of the complete document. None of this alters the fact that for the Christians of the first century our distinctions between data of history and issues of faith did not exist. Matters of faith and doctrine were of first importance for the early Christians, while historical detail was considered of secondary importance.

We should heed the testimony of the church and interpret the gospels in the way the evangelists intended them to be read. The particular character of each of the gospels emerged from their unique subject and purpose; their variety was caused by the intellectual level and viewpoint of the authors as well as by the time and place of their composition.

The Provenance of the Gospels

At this point the question must be raised concerning the impact of the above-mentioned circumstances upon the form and content of the gospels. To answer this question we must ascertain the nature and the structure of the sources available to the authors. We will not try to distinguish between written and oral sources at this time.

There were first of all recollections from the life of Jesus: the general development of events, some of his journeys, his sojourn in particular places, and unusual incidents in his life. Especially the striking expressions and impressive speeches had been retained in the memory of the disciples. These recollections were not sufficient in variety or comprehensiveness to provide a complete outline in which all later topics could be included. They provided only enough information to serve as a backdrop [for the message of the evangelist to his readers].

They described the situation of Jesus' ministry in such a manner that the readers would have an authentic impression of his earthly life. Apart from this, each evangelist was free to arrange the scenario of his gospel proper to his purpose.

New stories originated from vague recollections, from studies of the Scripture or from various scriptural associations. Later situations were projected back into the times of Jesus or influenced the reporting of incidents in his day. We may assume that to a certain degree such projections of ideas took place unconsciously. The abundant life evoked by the new movement, by the ministry of the apostles, but especially by the brief but powerful manifestation of their Lord, was a fountainhead of myths and legends flowing forth in great variety.

But the more the authors were removed from the time and place of the original events of history, the more they were challenged to critical reflection and a clear presentation of events. They had to replace the vague notions and unconscious projections [by more specific data]. What later the Church asserted about the Apostolic Fathers, namely, that theological intentions could hardly be separated from historical facts, was equally valid for the witnesses mentioned in the gospels themselves. The mind of Christ had pervaded all of life. What else would a dynamic principle of life be if it could not offer comfort and support in the most difficult circumstances? The early Christians quite naturally associated the truths emerging from later situations with the teachings of Jesus himself.

Life-styles were proclaimed by presenting Jesus as an example. The preachers did not anticipate any accusation of dishonesty in this respect. The situations creating the greatest difficulties for the churches had the strongest impact upon the formation of the gospel narratives and their precepts. This was especially true in the case of the impelling issue raised so emphatically by the ministry of the apostle Paul, namely, the relation of the Jews to the Gentiles and their common accountability to the Law and the Gospel. How much variety in life-style did emerge from this issue alone? The relation of Jew and Gentile could be viewed from several moral perspectives and the doctrinal issues could be approached from many different angles.

Also the role of personalities came into play. The apostle Paul had been a source of offense to many Christians, although others considered him a man of great spiritual authority. The other apostles were likewise subjected to similar conflicting evaluations. Peter especially played a dominant role. All these attendant circumstances could not help influencing the form and content of the gospel narratives.

Test Cases from the Gospels

The above-described conception of the origin and value of the gospel accounts is not merely an arbitrary hypothesis. It is amply confirmed by the literature of the first centuries. Also within the confines of the gospels we are reminded repeatedly of this state of affairs. A few examples [concerning the issue of the gentiles] may serve to demonstrate this.

Whoever reads the story of the Canaanite woman in Matt 15:21-28 will very likely ask the question, Why this persistent refusal to help after that humble plea by the woman? One might suggest that Jesus wanted to test her faith. This could be inferred from Jesus' commendation of her great faith before he proceeded to her healing. Other aspects of this story, however, speak against such an interpretation. When the disciples were annoyed by her shouting, Jesus answered, [seemingly out of context], that he was only sent to the lost sheep of Israel. His reply was directed towards the disciples and not to the woman. This implies, however, that his refusal [to help a Gentile woman] is not presented as an occasional test of faith for this woman but rather as a statement of principle for the disciples.

One would have to make the assumption, therefore, that Jesus allowed himself to be persuaded by the perseverance of the woman. But it is not likely that Jesus was more narrow-minded than the disciples who urged him, "Do what she asks (ἀπόλυσον αὐτήν) and be rid of her!"

Thus neither the testing of faith nor the hesitant giving in to a persistent woman seem to be tenable interpretations of Jesus' refusal to help. The essence of the story points rather to the original idea that Christianity was meant solely for the Jews. Furthermore, the story conveys that this original approach was to be modified at the insistence of the gentiles. They, too, wanted to share in the messianic blessings even though in a subordinate role.[1]

Even more explicit is the story in Luke 7:36-50 urging us to a similar interpretation. When Jesus allowed himself the homage of a sinful woman, Simon the Pharisee began to doubt Jesus' role as a prophet. Jesus then demonstrated by the parable of the debtors that the person who is forgiven most will have the greatest love. Accordingly, Simon's doubting was unfounded. The woman proved by her great love that much had been forgiven to her, so she could not be considered a sinner anymore. But Jesus went further than this [in his application]. He explicitly compared the veneration of the woman with the hospitality of his host. It turned out that a lesser degree of love was received from the Pharisee.

There are two unusual elements in this story. In the first place, there is the question of when and by whom the sins of the woman were forgiven. [There is no record of her being forgiven.] In the city the woman was merely known as a sinner. Jesus simply assured her in Simon's home of the forgiveness of her sins. Secondly there is something unusual in the reasoning that forgiveness and

---

[1]David Friedrich Strauss, *Das Leben Jesu, kritisch bearbeitet,* 2 vols., 3rd ed. rev. (Tübingen: Osiander, 1838–1839) 220.

love are interrelated and that love should follow forgiveness. There is no better explanation for this than the supposition that the woman represented the Gentiles rejected by Israel.

The whole story seems nothing else than an explication of the Pauline concept that in Christ Jew and Gentile are one. The story illustrates that the Gentiles because of their faith had overtaken the Jews who were held back by their self-righteousness. In the new age Gentile Christians are as far ahead of the Jews as they once were behind.[2]

Conclusion and Challenge of Thesis One

Thus all kinds of considerations, viewpoints, and situations gave meaning to the various stories. These perspectives became concrete and were reflected in the narratives of the Christ event. These stories plus additional recollections by eyewitnesses spread all over the church and became the building blocks available to the evangelists in the composition of their writings. This also explains why, with such a state of affairs, the size and content of the documents came out so differently. Even if various authors used the same source, or if one author was familiar with the work of another author, or if all authors drew from tradition, their gospels had to turn out differently.

One can be sure that the authors could not deem all source materials equally suitable for their objective. Their work was not simply a careful compiling of data. The use of sources was only a means to achieve the portrayal of Christ that the author of a particular gospel had in mind.

Not every story would contribute to a particular conception of the greatness of Christ. Only such words were acceptable from Christ as contained salutory truths and provided necessary directives [for a concrete historical situation]. Not every circle of readers was in need of the same admonitions and doctrinal teachings. In the selection of their materials, the authors were guided in their work by local and temporal concerns. Neither considerations for sequence nor scrupulous attention to the content of their sources was their ultimate motive for inclusion of source materials. On the contrary, the more imposing the approach of the new document and the more particular its objective, the more independent the author was in the use of his sources.

Something else should be considered. The historical criticism of the nineteenth century has succeeded in discovering the origin and characteristics of

---

[2]This interpretation seems to me the most acceptable because of the use of the perfect tense for the verb form "forgiven" (ἀφέωνται); also because of its agreement with other narratives, namely, Jesus' rejection in Nazareth and the calling of the four disciples. These stories deal with the same issue, even though they show considerable variants.

a major part of gospel history; its delicate touch has revealed the theological purport of the various stories. That theological touch must, however, have been infinitely more delicate in the days of the evangelists themselves when the stories received their particular form. As a rule the evangelists were led in their selection of materials by the obvious intention expressed in the text. It is quite plausible, however, that they also would reject certain materials for fear that some insignificant features might create misunderstanding.

One single word or one ambivalent expression could be a reason for the author to omit a certain account. Furthermore, it is quite likely that certain appropriate sections might not find a place in the new document either. Because of editorial shifts and changes in the text certain source materials might appear out of context or redundant to the author.

Our conclusions with regard to the subject matter and its objective, as well as concerning the sources and the composition by the evangelists, have decisive implications. All these considerations run counter to the position that the gospel that has the least amount of material should of necessity be the earliest document. When the proponents of the Marcan Hypothesis place a special emphasis upon this thesis, they start out from an incorrect conception of the situation in the first centuries and its impact upon the formation of the gospels.

But this judgement is pronounced too soon, because it is still the crucial point of our research. The advocates of the Marcan Hypothesis could never concur with this analysis of history that is so contrary to their view of gospel history. They reach a similar negative verdict about the historical approach of their opponents, [the adherents of the Tübingen school]. When some of the proponents of the Marcan Hypothesis accept the Tübingen theory of history in general, they do not integrate that theory [of theological motivation by the authors in their composition of the gospels].

Here is the first criterion external to the gospels by which its critic must decide whether or not he should, of necessity, attribute priority to the Gospel of Mark in relation to the other Synoptics. With the validity that one attaches to the brevity of a gospel for determining its age, stands or falls a decisive consideration in favor of the Marcan Hypothesis!

Thesis Two
The Literary Imagery of Mark

A second argument for the priority of Mark is the following. The proponents of the Marcan Hypothesis assert that

the second evangelist exhibits a vivid imagery in his style and depictions, [thus suggesting an eyewitness account].

The observation concerning the literary imagery as such is certainly valid. The evangelist Mark has been widely applauded for his style by many New Testament scholars, irrespective of their conception of gospel history. There is less unanimity, however, regarding what conclusions are to be drawn from this characteristic of Mark.

Opinions are divided especially in determining the relation of Mark to the two other Synoptics on the basis of style. Even within the circle of adherents of the Marcan Hypothesis, different conclusions are drawn. For some text critics the vivid imagery in the second gospel demonstrates that its content was not derived from written sources. Others are of the opinion that the style indicates the author was in close touch with eyewitnesses. All adherents of the Marcan Hypothesis agree, however, that Mark, who seems so accurate and is so picturesque in the narration of his stories, thereby testifies to his greater originality. Over against the much simpler parallels in the other Synoptics, with their inexactness and sometimes conflicting statements, Mark seems to be the earliest and most original document.

The argument from style plays a dominating role in the history of the Marcan Hypothesis equal to the argument based on the shorter text. Before we can respond to the second argument we have to delineate the issue which now is to be discussed.

Literary Imagery and Historical Credibility

It appears to us that the imagery and vivid presentation in Mark are discussed in an abstract sense. For in fact style offers no proof for or against the historical nature and the credibility of a document. A book presented as a novel in its title does not need to be inferior in descriptive value in comparison with a historical study. The history of literature points to a long series of works that speak about death and eternity in the most vivid style and yet lack historical detail. [Graphic imagery and historical documentation are not necessarily identical.]

But the credibility of the Gospel of Mark as historical source is not really the issue in our discussion. Our research focuses primarily on the interrelatedness of the Gospels. This objective limits the area in which we need to move. We have to take note of the phenomena that characterize the second gospel only to the degree that they give this gospel its peculiar character [in view of the other two Synoptics]. The special characteristics, such as a vivid style, are of such nature that they appear to be derived neither from written sources nor from apostolic tradition. Because of the relative insignificance of these two possibilities as sources for the literary characteristics of an author, neither needs to be discussed.

Two other possibilities remain. These characteristics must have originated (a) from the memory of eyewitnesses or (b) from the imaginative style of the author. If the style points to an eyewitness account it could be a strong argument for an early date for the Gospel of Mark. The other two Synoptic Gospels are, indeed, much simpler in style and less specific in description. On the other hand if the imagery is due to the creative imagination of the author, objections might be raised against the total Marcan Hypothesis [and argue rather for Mark as the last of the Synoptics]. Careful studies of the nature of its imagery and style will, therefore, be the only means to determine whether the Gospel of Mark reflects an early eyewitness account or the literary quality of the author.

One more remark may be permitted. My description of the point of difference between the positions is in agreement with the way I have meant to determine the essence of the Marcan Hypothesis, namely, as a search for the historical validity of the gospels. On the theological left we encounter the Tübingen scholar Gustav Volkmar, who would not have been ready to accept the true advocates of the Marcan Hypothesis because of his own view of history. For him the picturesque details and the minute yet balanced narratives speak of a Christian novel. Thus the most ancient gospel document was born completely from the creative imagination of a poet.

But for the true proponents of the Marcan Hypothesis, this is not a tenable view. The proponents of the Marcan Hypothesis fear that if they gave up the historical nature of Mark's picturesque imagery, they would thereby surrender the originality of the total Marcan Gospel. [The contextual history of the Tübingers conflicts with the documentary concept of history.]

Grammatical and Stylistic Peculiarities in Mark

I will now attempt to portray in outline form the imagery of Mark. Difficulties arise, however, when one wants to delineate the phenomena that are to be a part of this portrayal. The imagery is related, on the one hand, to linguistic characteristics. On the other hand, it is connected with doctrine, and especially with Christology. Moreover, the total symmetry in the presentation of the gospel contributes considerably to its literary clarity. This last point will be discussed under the topic of the unity of Mark.

With a study of Mark from a linguistic point of view one must deal with grammatical as well as stylistic features. The latter include words the author uses only once (or rarely), as well as his favorite expressions. But when among his favorite expressions words such as εὐθέως [εὐθύς] (at once) and πάλιν (again), ἔρχεσθαι (to come) and ἤρξατο (he began) play a major role, we notice that issues of style and grammar are interwoven. The gospel as a whole is given a vivid and narrative character by the repeated use of the present tense and the historical imperfect, by diminutives, by double negatives and tautologies, by questions and answers, especially in direct discourse.

Whoever wants to have a clear presentation of the character of Mark and wants to feel the difference that exists in this respect between Mark and the other gospels should read the following episodes: the description of the beheading of John the Baptist (6:17-29); the demonic possession of the Gerasene (5:1-20); the symptoms of the epileptic (9:14-29); the discussion resulting from the touch by the woman with a flow of blood (5:25-34); or the response of the disciples to the suggestion by Jesus to feed the 5,000 (6:34-44).

For an adequate evaluation of these passages one should equally compare the general description of Jesus' activity in Mark 1:35-39; 3:7-12; and 6:54-56 with their parallels. Whoever has read these and similar portions from the Gospel of Mark will discover the nature of his style, and cannot help noticing its uniqueness.

Historical, Personal, and Geographical Details

Already in these examples, the style not only influenced the form of the narrative but also its content. The material in Mark, in comparison with Matthew and Luke, is enriched by numerous specific details. Mark knows the exact words accompanying the performance of Jesus' miracles. The little daughter of Jairus was raised up as soon as she heard the words of Jesus, "Talitha Cumi" (5:41). After the word "Ephphatha" the ears of the deaf man were opened (7:34), and following the words "Peace! Be still!" the storm was stilled (4:39).

There is a certain specificity in references to the persons present (including their names) and also in the listing of geographical locations (1:9, 20, 29; 2:14; 3:6, 17, 22, 32, etc.). Thus Mark mentions, for instance, Bartimaeus as the name of the blind man healed at Jericho (10:46), and Alexander and Rufus as the sons of Simon of Cyrene (15:21). Usually Mark knows exactly the place where the story has taken place, "on the sea shore" or "on the way" or "at home." Mark even indicates the specific location where Jesus was sleeping when the storm almost caused the boat to sink: "He was in the stern asleep on the cushion" (4:38). When the deaf mute was healed he was set apart from the crowd (7:33), the blind man was even "led out of the village" (8:23).

Even numbers are given with precision in Mark's Gospel. There were 2,000 swine that drowned in the sea (5:13); the cock, which was to bring Peter to repentance, crowed twice (14:30); the disciples went out two by two casting out demons and preaching the gospel (6:37); the crowd could be fed for an amount of 200 denarii (3:38)—the same crowd, which in groups of fifty and a hundred, ate from the miraculous bread (6:40).

Minute Details of Moods and Impressions

We have observed the nature of Mark's imagery. But we need to develop a yet more focussed presentation of it. Mark takes great pains in describing psychological details related to Jesus—of the impressions he makes on the crowd, of his speaking, of his thought, of his gestures, and also of the depth of his emotions.

Let us merely mention Mark's portrayal of the crowds. After the healing of Peter's mother-in-law in Capernaum, at nightfall, the crowds gathered around Jesus with all their sick and demon-possessed persons, so that the whole town was thronged outside the door of Peter's home (1:33). When Jesus had left the town, and a leper had been healed outside of town, Jesus could not return openly to Capernaum and he had to remain outside in the country (1:45). It is no wonder that the crowd gathered again (2:2) after Jesus had managed to return and the news about this had spread.

Soon the crowd became a terrifying throng and Jesus was forced to take care that a boat was available (3:9). That concern was not out of place: moments later the boat served as a place of refuge (4:2). Even at home Jesus had no rest. He could not even eat a bite of bread because of the throng of people (3:20); when the disciples returned from their mission, they would like to rest and eat, but again the crowd did not allow this. The disciples evaded the turmoil and went by boat to a deserted place—to no avail, for people came from the surrounding cities and (having kept the boat in view) were already gathered at the spot where the boat landed (6:31-33).

We can see that every detail is minutely recorded in contrast with the vague description of the crowds that we find in Matthew. We also observe that same precise detail elsewhere, [for example,] in Mark's description of Jesus' journeys.

In the Gospel of Luke Jesus refused the request of the crowd at Capernaum to stay with them with a general reference to his mission to other cities, "I was sent for this purpose." According to Luke, the mission of Christ prohibited him from staying (Luke 4:43).

In Mark we find the same situation with a different and negative response by Jesus (Mark 1:38). Jesus had just left the town through the gate and the disciples mentioned the desire of the crowd to see him. Jesus, however, shared his intention to preach elsewhere, "for that is why I came out." Jesus did not want to go back on his decision.

There is something unclear about the story of Jesus' walking on the sea in Matthew. The reader does not know whether the focus of the story is on the walking on the water, on the stilling of the storm, or on the response of Peter (Matt 14:25-33). This is different in the Gospel of Mark. The disciples had been fighting the storm from the evening until the fourth watch of the night and yet had not been able to reach the other side of the lake. Jesus had observed them from a mountain near the shore. When he wanted to get across the lake Jesus intended to overtake them and to go ahead of his disciples to the shore. Their anxious cries, however, caused Jesus to change his mind [causing him to still the storm] (Mark 6:47-52).

Another example [of comparison between Mark and one of the other Synoptics:] Matthew 16:1-12 shares two pericopes involving the Pharisees after Jesus had gone to the area of Magadan. Matthew reports first their question for a sign with his customary introduction of the speakers and concluding with a departure of Jesus.

Matthew's second account deals with the leaven of the Pharisees. The misunderstanding of the disciples is explained by the preceding verse (Matt 16:5) by the statement that the disciples had forgotten to bring any bread in coming across the lake.

We should not ask for the occasion of this crossing of the lake; it should definitely not be associated with the preceding verse referring to Jesus' departure (Matt 16:4). The evangelist Mark, however, does take this liberty. By doing so his preceding pericope is given a peculiar meaning. According to Mark, Jesus had landed in Dalmanutha (Matthew: Magadan). The Pharisees came to him with the request for a sign, which disturbed Jesus deeply. "Why does this generation seek a sign? . . . No sign shall be given to this generation!" (Mark 8:12) The reference to a sign is emphatically stated twice. Thus Jesus reacted vehemently and his reaction is underscored by his getting into the boat and departing for the other side of the lake.

Mark's minute descriptions create new impressions, which brings us to another peculiarity of this author. The question for a sign by the Pharisees elicited a deep sigh from Jesus (8:12). This is not the only time that Mark refers to expressions of emotions. In his gospel Jesus "loved" the rich young ruler (10:21) and he "embraced" the children (9:36; 10:16); he was "grieved" at the hardness of heart of the Jews (3:5) and before healing the deaf man he "sighed," looking up to heaven (7:34). According to Mark, Jesus looked at his opponents "with anger" when they criticized him for healing on the sabbath day (3:5), and he was "indignant" when the disciples attempted to keep the children away from him (10:14).

It is quite appropriate within this context when Mark describes Jesus as being "moved with pity" when he saw the leper; after having healed the man Jesus "sternly charged him, and sent him away at once" (1:43).[3] Such an unusual attitude is certainly not without meaning. Mark's portrayal of Jesus is imbued with deep emotions. [Mark conveys an attitude of concentration when he depicts]

---

[3]See the discussion of this passage in *Godgeleerde Bijdragen* (1866): 196ff.

Jesus as "looking around" on those who sat about him (3:34) or when Jesus, "seeing his disciples," rebuked Peter (8:33). [Mark creates a sense of suspense] when Jesus "looked around" [at everything going on in the temple before leaving for Bethany] (11:11). [In sum, the minute details of moods and impressions give a special character to the Gospel of Mark.]

Literary Imagery as a Clue to the Synoptic Problem

Mark's graphic portrayal is one of the clues whose value in determining the synoptic problem has to be assessed. I have selected striking examples on purpose, because Mark's literary character should be evaluated from its most prominent expressions. The reader may have noticed that Mark gave special attention to the miracle stories. It is in view of these accounts that the question must be asked whether such stories are the fruit of religious imagination or of historical recollection. One will understand right away that the answer to this question depends on circumstantial evidence.

Ewald discovered in the Gospel of Mark "the fragrance of fresh flowers, the pure abundant vigor of the sources." Strauss, on the other hand, cynically wanted to leave this observation to the "special insight" of the man [meaning Ewald] who saw in the Reverend F. Chr. Baur a reincarnation of the infamous C. F. Bahrdt of the preceding century and who considered the extremely intelligent Reimarus a "scatterbrain."[4]

The issue of the literary imagery in the Gospel of Mark is, therefore, a second external clue for determining whether or not this gospel shall be held as an original document of early date. If one cannot recognize a conscious literary effort in Mark's portrayal, or a sample of the author's creative imagination, then there remains nothing else than associating Mark as closely as possible with an eyewitness. Such graphic imagery could not possibly be the result of oral tradition or the composition from written sources. Vivid memory must in that case be the reason the author could refer to the sighs of concern and the gestures of Jesus. From the viewpoint of Mark as an eyewitness account, the parallels [in Matthew and Luke] must be referred to a later date.

However, if we cannot detect in the minuteness of Mark the characteristics of an eyewitness account, this literary imagery leads to a totally different conclusion. In this case we would disagree with Volkmar that a Christian epic could have been the origin of gospel literature from which the vague and incoherent style of Matthew would have developed at a later date. The contrast between the

---

[4]David Friedrich Strauss, *Das Leben Jesu für das deutsche Volke bearbeitet,* 2 vols. (Leipzig: F A. Brockhaus, 1864) 128. [Again, Strauss's second "Life of Jesus" (1864) is to be distinguished from his earlier "Life" (see n. 1 above).]

reverent reporting of Matthew and Luke and the dynamic narration by Mark would then point to a later era for the second gospel. Thus the graphic details in the Gospel of Mark could very well lead to a totally different conclusion from the one cherished by the proponents of the Marcan Hypothesis.

The Consistent Progression of Mark's Account

But I have not exhausted the subject of style. I must add the observation that the narration in Mark is also more developed than that in Matthew. This is due, in major part, to the continuous progression in Mark's recording of Jesus' history. [In Mark] the reader can follow the life of Jesus in all its details from his early ministry up to his death on the cross.

After the imprisonment of John the Baptist, Jesus went to Galilee to begin his proclamation. Along the lakeside he gathered his first disciples (1:16), and he entered Capernaum (1:21) where the synagogue and the door of Peter's house became the locations of his first miraculous acts. Early the next morning Jesus began his journey to the other Galilean towns (1:35). After some days of preaching (2:1) Jesus returned to his home in Capernaum (2:2). By the lake he encountered Levi in his tax office, which became the occasion for a meal with tax collectors (2:14-16).

We may assume that Mark in 2:23 refers to the first sabbath following that in 1:21 when Jesus began his public ministry in the synagogue at Capernaum. After this initial week the disciples supposedly broke the sabbath law by plucking heads of grain (2:23), and Jesus was accused of the same violation after having healed a man with a withered hand (3:1). Following this second sabbath in his ministry Jesus again visited the lakeside (3:7), climbed a mountain in order to appoint the twelve disciples (3:13), and returned to his home (3:19). Again he went to the lakeside (4:1); that evening he crossed the lake (4:35). After Jesus returned the next day, he would have remained near the lake (5:21) if Jairus had not requested his help. From Jairus's home (6:1) Jesus went to Nazareth where he preached on the sabbath.

From this time on Jesus was a wandering prophet (6:6), but he remained in the proximity of the lake. After the return of the disciples from their mission he went by boat to a solitary place (6:32). That place must have been across the lake (6:33), because Bethsaida to which they went afterwards (6:45) was situated on the west side in the land of Gennesaret (6:53). Soon after that they were again in a house (7:17), from where Jesus arose and went away to the region of Tyre and Sidon where he also entered a house (7:24). Then he returned via Sidon and the Decapolis to the eastern shore of the Lake of Galilee (7:31). After a brief stay in Dalmanutha (8:14) Jesus crossed the lake again to Bethsaida (8:22).

In the northern regions of the lake he taught and performed his miracles in villages (8:27), on a mountain (9:2), or in a house (9:28). Then he passed through Galilee (9:30) to reach his home in Capernaum for the fifth time, which completed his Galilean ministry. Arising from there Jesus began his mysterious (10:32) journey beyond the Jordan to Jerusalem (10:1). In the surroundings of the capital his movements can be followed with the same accuracy. Jesus entered the city, went to the temple that same evening, looked around briefly, and then went immediately to Bethany. During the following days Jesus went every morning to Jerusalem (11:12, 20) and on the day of the Passover he went in the evening (14:17). Then the Passion story takes its beginning.

On purpose I have traced the public ministry of Jesus as described in the second gospel. This demonstrates in the first place how descriptive Mark is in his details as well as in the progression of his whole account. It also shows how this author was of the opinion that Jesus' life could be encompassed within those strict delineations.

Mark could be criticized for his liberal use of houses into which Jesus could withdraw to be by himself, or to be with the disciples to give them more specific instruction. But when we notice that he speaks of the doors of those houses (1:33; 2:1) and that he makes use of verbs like "to rise" and "to go out" (1:35) in order to create a transition to the following episode,[5] we discover that Mark was quite conscious of the literary liberty he took. In spite of these literary devices, however, he does not lose the progression of his narrative.[6]

One might want to assert that Mark does not present a continuous progression since there are loose connections in the second chapter. In this case the reader overlooks the fact that the attendance in the synagogue of 3:1 refers by means of πάλιν ("again") to the visit in 1:21. Also the walk along the lakeside in 4:1 refers to similar walks in 2:13 and 1:16 by means of the same adverb πάλιν. The progression of Mark's account is unmistakably continuous in spite of the possibility that one could assume other events were in the author's mind. By analogy one should therefore refrain from assuming deletions at other locations such as events which occurred in the land of Gennesaret (6:53), the Decapolis (7:31), and in Galilee (9:30). In such cases one might suppose the author wanted the reader to insert the unmentioned facts from Jesus' life. [Such

---

[5]In Greek, ἀναστὰς ἐξῆλθεν καὶ ἀπῆλθεν; see also 2:13 ἐξῆλθεν; 6:1 καὶ ἐξῆλθεν ἐκεῖθεν; 7:24 ἐκεῖθεν δὲ ἀναστὰς ἀπῆλθεν; 9:30 κἀκεῖθεν ἐξελθόντες; 10:1 καὶ ἐκεῖθεν ἀναστὰς ἔρχεται; 10:17 καὶ ἐκπορευομένου αὐτοῦ εἰς ὁδόν.

[6]In Matthew the meaning of the verb ἐξέρχεσθαι is mostly general "to go out" or "to go away"—cf. Matt 9:31; 11:7, 8, 9; 13:3, 49; 15:21, 22; 18:28, etc., and perhaps also 14:14. The only time before the entry into Jerusalem this verb is used in a literal sense for the movements of Jesus is in 13:1. Here, however, is added ἀπὸ τῆς οἰκίας. In Mark the reverse takes place. There we always find an antecedent to which the prefix ἐξ is related. This is mostly a house, or the name of a town, e.g., ἐκ τῶν ὁρίων Τύρου (7:31). So certainly also Mark 6:34 as a parallel to Matt 14:14.

insertions would, however, disrupt the train of thought of the evangelist.]

Across a wide field of occurrences Mark has drawn clear lines that are meant to delineate the image of Jesus as a sober but concrete and complete personality. This confronts us again with the alternative: either this modest sketch is the descriptive equivalent of a seemingly rich life, or this gospel is the product of religious art. In the latter case it would mean an art that has far outdistanced the historical actuality. For me the choice in this alternative is not very difficult.

The graphic description of Mark cannot have preceded in time the vague and legendary character of Matthew. The wealth of all kinds of materials could not have allowed such a drawing in clear delineations during the first generation. No outline could have been equivalent to the historical actuality. The author who first gathered materials for his picture of Jesus must have been conscious of the fact that he presented an incomplete [and as yet unbalanced] account of the events of his day. Such awareness we should find reflected also in the form of his document. [Since Mark does not show such awareness he most likely was not among the first evangelists.]

The Narrative Approach of Matthew

Let us make a comparative study of the text of Matthew. Also in this gospel we find some clear demarcations. In Capernaum, Jesus went for the first time to the synagogue, after which he went into the house of Peter (8:5, 14). The healing of the two men in Gadara was preceded by the stilling of the storm and followed by the return across the lake (8:23, 28; 9:1). [There is a gradual succession of events:] the withdrawal into solitude, the feeding of the five thousand people, and the sailing to the other side of the lake (14:13, 25, 34). From this point one could draw about the same lines of development as in Mark: via the regions of Tyre and Sidon, the Lake of Galilee, Caesarea Philippi, and Capernaum, to Jerusalem.

But especially at the beginning of the gospel, where Mark is so precise we find Matthew presenting Jesus as a wandering prophet. Matthew does this so categorically that it is quite impossible to insert Mark's data into this general account. [According to Matthew,] Jesus was at the lake side immediately after his first public ministry (4:18). His change of domicile had already taken place (4:13ff.), which creates a gap in the narrative. There is no need any more to mention Jesus' initial mission from Capernaum. Matthew announces immediately,

> And he went about all Galilee, teaching in their synagogues and preaching the gospel of the kingdom and healing every disease and every infirmity among the people. (4:23)

And some chapters later we read,

And Jesus went about all the cities and villages, teaching in their synagogues and preaching the gospel of the kingdom, and healing every disease and every infirmity. (9:35)

When the "Mission of the Twelve" had been completed Matthew reports, "he went on from there to teach and preach in their cities" (11:1), although no sojourn of Jesus had been mentioned since the reference to Jesus' wandering ministry in 9:35. Again we read a few chapters later, "As they were gathering in Galilee . . . " (17:22).

One might assume that some detail has been provided in between those spaces created by the statements concerning Jesus' wandering ministry. On the basis of such an assumption the reader might want to pursue the transitions used by Matthew. He simply uses expressions like "then" (τότε, see 9:14; 12:22; 13:36; 15:1; 17:19) or "at that time" (ἐν ἐκείνῳ τῷ καιρῷ, see 11:25; 12:1; 14:1).

Matthew indicates the movement from one place to another by the words "from there" (ἐκεῖθεν), but the respective places cannot be identified. In 9:9 Matthew states, "Jesus passed on from there," which refers to the leaving behind of a whole city (9:1). The words in 11:1, "He went on from there," refer to the unknown location of the missionary address. The same words in 12:9 refer to the grainfields where the sabbath law had been broken. Similarly in 13:53 these words refer to the lakeside where the parables had been told to the crowds, unless one would take these as a reference to the house mentioned in 13:36. Later we will see that there is no antecedent for the "from there" in 14:13. In 15:21 the words "Jesus went away from there" refer to a departure from the whole region of Gennesaret (14:34). Similar words in chapter 15 give the appearance as if Tyre and Sidon (15:21) were on the way from Gennesaret (14:34) to the Lake of Galilee (15:29).

These simple transitions do not give much minute detail. A similar incoherence can be noticed in 13:1 where Jesus left a house he had not entered before. In 14:13 Jesus boarded a ship in search of a lonely place, while according to the context, he was still far from the lake, namely, in Nazareth (13:54). Because the crowds follow him on foot the "lonely place" must have been on the same side of the lake [namely the western shore]. Yet when Jesus and his disciples "had crossed over," according to 14:34, they arrived at the western shore of the lake. All of this is quite different from the evangelist Mark, who does not omit a single house in composing his narrative, and who reports the entering as well as the leaving of a city like Jericho.

For Matthew two days in the temple suffice [for recording the events]. On the first day he has Jesus declare the "robber's den" to be a house of prayer. Subsequently the children proclaim his glory as the "Son of David" because of his numerous messianic miracles (Matt 21:12-17). A second day is needed to describe Jesus' triumph over all hostile resistance (Matt 21:18-23:39). Mark, however, needs an additional day to set the stage for the events [described in Matthew]. A penetrating look around at everything going on in the temple is a prelude for all the significant events to follow (Mark 11:11).

Yet this peculiar character of the first gospel is quite natural. Whatever may have been caused by the use of sources or by [later] editors, Matthew's incoherent character should not surprise the reader. It is not hard to understand why the advocates of the Marcan Hypothesis would try to explain any ambiguity in the text of Matthew by resolving it in a comparison with Mark. That the sick people arrive late in the evening (Matt 8:16) must, according to these scholars, be explained by reference to the sabbath in Mark 1:21; when Matthew mentions that the relatives of Jesus stood "outside" (Matt 12:46), they connect this with the house mentioned in Mark 3:19 [because it happens to precede Mark's parallel statement about the relatives]. The "going abroad" after his ministry in Nazareth (Matt 14:13) is associated with Jesus' traveling around the villages of Galilee in Mark 6:6 [because this, too, took place after the ministry in Nazareth].

[The questions for the proponents of the Marcan Hypothesis are these:] Is it likely that a clearly outlined gospel could be the source for all gospel literature? Can the use of such a gospel as a source, for example, be the cause for the later unclarities in the other gospels? Could we conceive that (a) the nature of a recently emerging legend, (b) the wealth of materials, (c) the approach of the Matthean Gospel itself, all taken together, offer a far more conclusive explanation? Is not the apparent wealth of detailed information in Mark an argument against its association with an eyewitness report? The advocates of the Marcan Hypothesis would, of course, answer all these questions in the negative.

Thesis Three
The Redaction of the Canonical Gospel of Mark

Introduction

The preceding questions have already introduced us to the third point of our discussion. We noticed among the advocates of the Marcan Hypothesis an endeavor to disclaim the canonical text of Mark in order to discern behind it the evangelist, who would better satisfy the needs of many scholars. Weisse, indeed, did not yet see the need for an original Mark, and Heinrich Meyer and Bernhard Weiss looked for other ways to explain the later portions in the Gospel of Mark. Schleiermacher thought he could find a historical trace of that original gospel. It was like seeing the mast of a sunken ship at low tide: everyone joined in to get this ship afloat. The rescuers, however, did not find more than a flag and many bystanders could not accept the credibility of the wreckage. But we will concentrate on this beach scene later. At this time we should first question the right of taking the liberty to disclaim the canonical text of Mark.

The thesis the proponents of the Marcan Hypothesis adopted in this connection was the following.

> *The Gospel of Mark bears in its final chapter the proof that extraneous parts have been inserted. We do therefore have the right to assume similar insertions elsewhere.*

This seemingly simple thesis is actually confounding, because it asserts either too little or too much. It says too little in giving the impression that Mark alone would be subject to interpolation; the thesis says too much by implying that an inauthentic conclusion necessitates that one suspect other interpolations.

The assumption of potential insertions is a phenomenon resulting from research. From our studies of classical literature we have obtained the right, even the obligation, to assume this potentiality in researching such writings. We should use this literary phenomenon as any other literary device obtained by scholarly effort.

We do have to be open to the possibility of interpolations whether there are special indications of such or not. Even if there were not the slightest trace of suspicion concerning the authenticity of Mark's conclusion, we would still be obliged to analyze critically the text of Mark. Conversely, however, the apparent inauthentic conclusion of Mark 16:9-20 should not cause the reader to be especially suspicious concerning the remainder of Mark's text.

The Distinction between Ur-Mark and Canonical Mark

The devastating consequences of the thesis mentioned above can be demonstrated by comparison with the discussion of the Gospel of John in the history of criticism. Those consequences have come clearly to light especially within the circle of the sympathizers of the Marcan Hypothesis. Consider how its proponents have drawn lines of demarcation between the "first" and the "second" Mark, and how there are as many delineations as there are authors.

There is an enormous difference between the Ur-Mark of Reuss and the Ur-Mark of Weisse. Reuss constructed an Ur-Mark without an opening chapter, without passion narratives, without transitions, and without any structure. Weisse, in following Ewald, assumed an Ur-Mark beginning with the preaching of John the Baptist, continuing with the temptation story, the Sermon on the Mount, the Roman officer in Capernaum, and the speeches about John the Baptist, and concluding with other supposedly original sections. The positions of Reuss and Weisse are on each end of the spectrum, allowing many options in between. As these positions have been discussed in part one, above, I will not review them at this time. But I would like to make an observation using the history of criticism concerning the Gospel of John as example.

It is well known how Credner thought he could isolate grammatical interpolations from the Gospel of John; similarly Professor [J. H.] Scholten was of the opinion that dogmatic interpolations could be identified. Weisse considered the speeches as having been added by a redactor; and [Alexander] Schweizer assumedly detected the magic miracle stories as inserted by a later Galilean redactor. Renan considered the historical development of John the nucleus of this gospel, while Weizsäcker held the Christological approach as uniquely Johannine.

This listing of the various forms that the Johannine Ur-Gospel took by the analysis of its components led to the acknowledgement among scholars that the need for such distinctions was in the mind of the scholars rather than in the character of the gospel itself. This phenomenon creates the suspicion that, some time in the future, a similar judgement will be pronounced over the analyses of the Gospel of Mark. Both discussions are, however, not entirely parallel. The unity of John is more evident than the unity of Mark.

The Gospel of John has a unique character, while the Gospel of Mark is more on the level of the other two Synoptics. Also the variety of analyses of the Gospel of John were more divergent than the projections of an Ur-Mark, which had a greater degree of similarity. But the resemblance between some forms of the Ur-Mark is rather accidental and proceeds from a general similarity in the thought patterns of the theologians involved.

In the discussion concerning the Gospel of John the recognition of its authenticity was at stake. In the discussion of Mark the issue was rather its relation to the other Synoptic gospels. So it could happen that two scholars, on the basis of their view of the synoptic problem, felt the need for the Sermon on the Mount in their conception of the Ur-Mark, or that both scholars discarded a passion story for a similar reason. This does not, however, change the essence of the Marcan problem very much.

The proponents of the Marcan Hypothesis act arbitrarily whenever they take the initiative to isolate a separate Ur-Mark from the canonical Mark on the basis of external criticism. That arbitrariness avenges itself by a lack of agreement among these scholars. Every succeeding literary critic who is so audacious as to create an Ur-Mark will most likely occupy a new paragraph in the history of the analysis of the second gospel.

The Literary Unity of the Canonical Gospel of Mark

The prognosis of ever-new proposals concerning an Ur-Mark is not based merely on experience but also on the nature of the Gospel of Mark itself. This gospel does not permit an analysis into components; it even forbids this approach by its very structure. In the discussion of the literary imagery we observed that the author intended to present a continuous development by means of the inter-connections of the narratives. In the following paragraphs I want to go farther and demonstrate that this continuity was at no point interrupted.

In addition to the interconnection of the narratives there are everywhere indications of anticipation of a later development of the narrative, as well as references to earlier portions of the narrative. After Jesus had won his first four disciples (1:16-20) we are informed a few verses later that Jesus entered the house of Simon and Andrew, and that James and John joined them (1:29). When Jesus had gone into the boat at the beginning of the chapter (4:1) he was later taken along "in the boat, just as he was" (4:36). Already in the previous chapter Jesus had ordered the disciples to have a boat ready because of the crowds on the shore (3:9). [Thus Mark continually builds his story upon previous details.]

Jesus withdrew "with his disciples" in 3:7 in order "to call to him those whom he desired" in 3:13. He united them into a unified group of twelve and gave them power to cast out demons. He also gave them authority to proclaim the advent of the Kingdom (3:13, 14). Three chapters later the apostles actually went out and exercised their power over unclean spirits (6:7). The curse of the fig tree and the withering of this tree are reported on two separate occasions (11:12-14 and 20-26). The reaction to the first incident was, "And his disciples heard it" which anticipated the reaction on the next day, "Master, look!" After the Pharisees and the Herodians had devised a plot against Jesus in 3:6, they implemented their plans in 12:13. During the crucifixion darkness fell at the sixth hour, Jesus expired at the ninth hour (15:33,34), while the nailing to the cross had taken place at the third hour (15:25). Similar small traits are characteristic for Mark. They provide a certain cohesiveness by which this gospel receives an integrated literary unity.

This unique nature of Mark appears even more strongly in other literary aspects. I am not referring here to the basic tendency of Mark. We will discuss the observations of Hilgenfeld concerning [apocalyptic tendencies] at a later time. [I am rather referring to Mark's view of the disciples.] In the Gospel of Mark there is, namely, no trace of an increasing awareness by the disciples or by the crowds of their recognition of Jesus as the Christ. The theological implications of this approach must be considered later as well. At this time I want to focus on those features that give Mark's Gospel its singular character and its internal unity. It is, first of all, a persistent habit of the author to present the disciples in a paternalistic manner. In the case of the parable of the Sower, a mere question for explanation is already a reason for astonishment by Jesus. According to Mark 4:13 Jesus remarked, "Do you not understand this parable? How then will you understand all the parables?" In accordance with the assurance given in 4:11 that to them the secrets of the Kingdom had been given, the disciples received not only at this time but also on later occasions an explanation of every parable told by Jesus (4:34).

[Secondly, this paternalism often changes to a reproachful attitude towards the disciples.] When they were terrified by a storm Jesus addressed the disciples with the words, "Why are you afraid? Have you no faith?" (4:40). Jesus' words seemed of no avail, they were still filled with great fear when they asked with awe, "Who then is this, that even wind and sea obey him?" (4:41). A few chapters later we read again, "Then are you also without understanding?" (7:18).

The disciples had expressly declared that they did not understand what Jesus meant with the words, "What comes out of a man is what defiles him" (7:20). In the following chapter concerning the leaven of the Pharisees Jesus was once again astonished at their crude misunderstanding, "Do you not yet perceive or understand? Are your hearts hardened? Having eyes do you not see, and having ears do you not hear?" (8:17-18). With these last words the disciples were even placed on the same level as the crowds, [of which it was also stated that they were seeing but not perceiving and hearing but not understanding] (4:12).

In accordance with these statements quoted from Jesus, the evangelist repeatedly makes narrative observations along the same line. It was of no surprise to him that the disciples were terrified when they saw Jesus walking over the waves (6:50), "for they did not understand about the loaves, but their hearts were hardened" (6:52). The offer by Peter to build tabernacles was not anything unusual to the author, "for he did not know what to say, for they were exceedingly afraid" (9:6). It was equally normal to the evangelist that the disciples fell asleep in the garden of Gethsemane, "for their eyes were very heavy; and they did not know what to answer him" (14:40).

[Thirdly, the disciples are described as being totally unqualified for their future roles of leadership.] They were repeatedly a cause of dissatisfaction for the crowds (9:28; 10:13). They demonstrated an immature attitude in faith and personality. In response to Jesus' question of who had touched him, they simply pointed to the thronging crowd (5:31). Later the disciples ineptly calculated the expense for feeding five thousand people (7:37). Sometime afterwards they still had not learned anything when 4,000 people needed to be fed (8:4). Even after both of these miracles they kept complaining about the lack of bread (8:16). They did not grasp what was meant by "the rising from the dead" (9:10). The announcement of Jesus' suffering was an enigma to them (9:32), in spite of the fact that Jesus had conveyed this message "plainly" (8:32). At an earlier occasion the disciples did not dare to ask him any questions (9:32). No wonder that Jesus "was walking ahead of them" in going up to Jerusalem and that they "were amazed," and "those who followed him were afraid" (10:32). Such descriptions [of paternalism, reproach by Jesus, and the ineptitude of his disciples] are by design, and contribute greatly to the unique character of the Gospel of Mark.

By contrast, Jesus is consistently depicted in majestic grandeur. He remained the center of the thronging crowds, as we noticed above (107ff.). The throng became at one moment so intense that there was no way to answer Jesus' question, "Who has touched me?" (5:31). Even in Syria Jesus could hardly find a moment of rest (7:24). On the other hand Mark reports a continuous attempt by Jesus to keep his identity secret. On various occasions the command was given not to broadcast a miraculous event (1:44; 5:43; 7:36; 8:26, 30; 9:9). The only conclusion to be drawn from the paradox [between the popularity and the secretiveness of Jesus] is that we are here touching upon another peculiarity of the author of the second gospel.

A consistent Christological design can be discovered in the Gospel of Mark. With the exception of 13:32 Jesus is only by God himself designated to be the "Son of God" (1:11; 9:7); furthermore, [he is recognized as such] at least four times by unclean spirits (1:24; 3:11; 5:7; and by implication also in 1:34). Finally [the identity of Jesus is recognized] by the Roman centurion at the cross who saw that Jesus "cried out and breathed his last" (15:39).

The unusual point is that initially the assurance was given that the demons were not allowed to broadcast their recognition of Jesus as the Christ (1:25, "Be silent"; 1:34, "he would not permit the demons to speak, because they knew him"; and also 3:12, "he strictly ordered them not to make him known"). However, when the Gerasene man had been redeemed from the demons, he was told to proclaim the mercy he had received (5:19). This command indicated that at least with regard to the demons, secrecy was no longer required. Consequently, after this event no clairvoyant demons occur anymore.

Jesus was called Christ by the disciples for the first time in 8:29 by the profession of Peter. Also in this context the admonition was heard, "he charged them to tell no one about him" (8:30). After this event the titles "Christ" and the equivalent term "Son of Man" occur only a few times in Jesus' teaching of the disciples. Finally, a public statement was made in front of the high priest that he was the Christ, the Son of God, and the Son of Man (14:61-62). The title "Son of David" was used for the first time by the blind man Bartimaeus (10:47-48).

Soon after this the crowds adopted this name for their praise during the entry of Jerusalem, "Blessed is the Kingdom of our father David that is coming" (11:10). I must concede that the reference [to the term "Son of David"] could be purely accidental or it could have been caused by the use of certain source materials. However, the role the demons play in this gospel cannot be attributed to chance. This feature of the Gospel of Mark may be considered one of the indications of the internal unity of this gospel.

The above-mentioned aspects [of the dependence of the disciples, the specific Christological design, the initial secretiveness of Jesus, and of the clairvoyance of the demons], together with the literary imagery demonstrated earlier (110-11) are of significance for what later will be said about the theology of Mark. The fact that imagery and linguistic particularities blend together in Mark's Gospel will also need further discussion. When considering the Gospel of Mark from one angle one has to keep in mind the other aspects as well. This blending of characteristics confirms the impression of internal unity.

Dr. Réville attempted to prove that the Gospel of Matthew had been composed by one author on the basis of repeatedly occurring peculiarities of expression and word formation. If Réville could accept this argument for a gospel that has far more divergent elements than any of the other three canonical gospels, how much more likely is a literary proof for the internal unity of the Gospel of Mark!

The Style of the Canonical Gospel of Mark

But I have not even mentioned the peculiar style of Mark. Also in this respect one immediately detects its unique character. Mark's style is quite developed, but at the same time it is somewhat dull. The Gospel of Mark abounds in pleonasms, which appear by repeating the same idea in different expressions, or sometimes by adding the opposite idea, at other times by indicating that after a specific word or act the anticipated result actually took place. The direct question [by Jesus and others] provides a vivid element in the Gospel of Mark; also characteristic are the use of the direct quotes, the use of the present tense and the historical imperfect, of diminutives and of verb forms such as ἔρχεσθαι (to come), ἐπερωτᾶν (to ask), and ἤρξατο (came).

Except for the use of some Hebraic phrases, it is peculiar for Mark's grammar that he has a predilection for the finite verb, for the combination of a verb and its object derived from the same verb stem [cognate accusative or dative], and for the repetition of verbs from the same verb stem or from compounds of the same verb. Mark likes to repeat the noun instead of using a relative pronoun, he has a wealth of adverbs, an accumulation of negatives, and the elliptic use of ἵνα (that) and τί (which) as relative pronouns.

Finally, there are in Mark's vocabulary words that occur only once or very seldom, and Aramaic or Latin expressions are distributed throughout his gospel. In spite of all these and still other peculiarities,[7] the Gospel of Mark has a

---

[7]Examples and detailed expositions of Mark's peculiar literary character can be found in Karl A. Credner, *Einleitung in das neue Testament* 2 vols. (Halle: Verlag der Buchhandlung des Waisenhauses, 1836) 102ff.; Wilhelm Martin Leberecht De Wette, *Lehrbuch der historisch-kritischen Einleitung in die kanonischen Bücher des Neuen Testaments,* 6th ed. (Berlin: G. Reimer, 1860; [1]1826) 195; Heinrich Julius Holtzmann, *Die synoptischen*

consistent imaginative description of its stories and intentionally well-connected pericopes. All these characteristics contribute considerably to an internal unity that cannot be found to the same degree in the other two Synoptic gospels.

This internal unity leads of necessity to the conclusion that the complete gospel has been composed by one author. I do want to apply some caution, however. Specialized study of Mark's internal quality may lead to the recognition of its unity in conception and composition. Such specialization, however, should include the synoptic problem as a whole as well as the historical data from sources outside the second gospel. The observation of internal unity can therefore only point to the probability that the mind of one author has put his stamp on this gospel. An exception may be made for the conclusion of this gospel, which on the basis of internal and external argumentation appears to be from another hand. For the remainder of the Gospel of Mark, however, this internal unity would argue against the assumption of other insertions in this gospel.

Not without reason did I refer to the *probability* [of single authorship]. First of all it should be noted that the *improbability* of single authorship cannot be proven either. This conclusion alone is sufficient to teach us something about the practice of Gospel criticism. Some proponents of the Marcan Hypothesis identify the document mentioned in Papias with our canonical gospel. These scholars do not feel free to assume a lost document on the basis of Papias's testimony in order to explain the interrelationship of the gospels. This position forces these theologians to assume that a certain part of the present gospel was written by a later hand. They need this assumption in order to avoid the difficulties for the Marcan hypothesis that arise from the present text. Such literary critics act, however, in conflict with the probability of the origin of the Gospel of Mark, [which, because of its internal unity, points rather to single authorship].

One should, of course, not deny these scholars their freedom to approach this problem in their own particular way. We only may request, however, the fulfillment of one condition, namely, to be open to the probability of single authorship which, indeed, is more likely than the assumption of a composite gospel. The so-called proof that Mark was the basis for Matthew and Luke should also be discounted as a probability. My suggestion is not appropriate, however, since it concerns the issue of our discussion.

We can conclude that the theory of Marcan priority is tenable only if a certain amount of material is eliminated from the canonical Gospel of Mark, in

---

Evangelien: Ihr Ursprung und geschichtlicher Charakter (Leipzig: W. Engelmann, 1863) 280ff., 107, 415-16; Bernhard Weiss, "Zur Entstehungsgeschichte der drei synoptischen Evangelien," *Theologische Studien und Kritiken* 34 (1861): 646ff. [See also David Peabody, *Mark as Composer*, New Gospel Studies 1 (Macon GA: Mercer University Press, 1987) iii, 216. —ed.]

spite of all the probability to the contrary. History has taught us that this elimination of materials, however minutely carried out, has led to as many different results as there were viewpoints of authors. Both observations [with regard to the need for an earlier document as well as its composite authorship] can be added to the series of phenomena that create suspicion concerning the whole Marcan Hypothesis.

The fact that scholars had to assume improbable interpolations for the sake of explaining the priority of Mark in relation to the other two Synoptic Gospels is a sign of weakness. These scholars furthermore were forced to delineate an earlier Mark either wider than the canonical Gospel of Mark or narrower; and sometimes they applied a combination of both procedures. In spite of their reconstructions, these scholars did not obtain a usable text. They rather had to resort to the hypothesis of several more or less developed forms of that same document. Such considerations finally led to the confusion [concerning a composite Proto-Mark] expressed by Michel Nicolas (see above, 61-63). [Using an example from navigation we could compare] this concluding event in the history of the Marcan Hypothesis with the sending of distress signals by a ship on the open sea after it has sailed out with full sails.[8]

The Interpretation of the Testimony of Papias

The scholars mentioned in the preceding paragraphs were those proponents of the Marcan Hypothesis who followed Weisse in his interpretation of the quote from Papias by Eusebius. Because of this approach to the synoptic problem these theologians were led to believe in an earlier form of Mark. They hesitantly separated some verses from the canonical text of Mark on the basis of the twelve inauthentic last verses of this gospel. Those eliminated verses were attributed to a later interpolator, a fictitious editor for whose existence these scholars had no justification. The unified literary character of the Gospel of Mark should have convinced them otherwise. Instead, they were punished with a confusion of tongues.

We are facing a totally different question, however, when a particular scholar produces historical evidence for a lost document. Such an approach would be similar to Schleiermacher's discovery of the Logia. The conclusion that the literary character of the Gospel of Mark does not contain extraneous elements from another source can still allow for the assertion that the canonical Gospel of Mark would be a conscious and independent redaction of an earlier similar work.

---

[8][In Holland, in 1866, Meijboom's readers would especially appreciate the irony and humor of this nautical anomaly. —ed.]

On the other hand, the contention that Mark is not a redaction from an earlier original document [that is, proto-Mark] will depend upon two points. In the first place it has to be ascertained whether the other sources, from which Mark supposedly has drawn his material, are known. In that case he should have done so to such a degree that there remained no place for an original document from his own hand. I am referring here, of course, to the question whether the Gospels of Matthew and Luke individually or collectively should be recognized as sources for the Gospel of Mark.

But since the priority of Mark is the point of discussion I cannot make use of this argument. Also the opinion of [Karl Reinhold] Köstlin has to be set aside for later discussion. This author adopted an earlier writing by Mark in addition to the Gospels of Matthew and Luke as sources for the canonical Gospel of Mark.

There is a second requirement to be met for a clear proof that the second gospel has not been redacted from an earlier Marcan document. This is the argument for a Proto-Mark on the basis of valid historical evidence. As soon as that earlier document has been identified [by way of historical research], it will not be difficult anymore to assume the same name for both documents. However, the assumption that this first Marcan document would be related to the canonical second gospel will never get beyond a mere supposition.

The argument for a Proto-Mark as an original document should be based, however, on actual external proofs. This means in our case, one will have to decide on the basis of historical research whether the testimony of Papias refers to a document other than our canonical Gospel of Mark.

The question [about the intention of Papias] does not have an easy answer. The history of the interpretation of the Papias quotation by Eusebius casts considerable suspicion on the whole argument.[9] There is literally not one word in those seven lines in Eusebius which has not undergone a multiple interpretation. For one interpreter "the elder" was the apostle John; for another expositor, the spokesman in Papias remained an unknown leader.

The designation of Mark as the interpreter of Peter has been associated with assistance in Peter's mission as well as with his help in writing the gospel in

---

[9]Eusebius, *Historia ecclesiastica* 3.39.15:

The elder said the following: Mark having become the interpreter of Peter wrote down accurately whatever Peter recalled. He recorded, however, not in an orderly fashion, the things that both had been spoken and accomplished by Christ. He neither had heard the Lord nor had followed him until he finally spoke to Peter who shared with him the teachings as far as was needed. But he gave not a complete exposition of the Lord's words, so that Mark did not fail at any point. Having written as many things as he remembered he provided insight without either omitting anything of which he had heard nor falsifying anything in those words.

which he supposedly represents the message of Peter.

Papias's assessment of Mark's recording "in a not orderly fashion" has been explained as Mark's unfamiliarity with the gospel, or as reverence for the Gospel of Matthew, or as respect for John or the ecclesiastical tradition. The statement of disorderliness has been associated with the lack of organization of theological content as well as with a disorderly sequence of events. This qualification was applied to the whole document or to single elements in it.

The emphasis on Peter's teaching has been considered as a response to historical as well as to theological needs [in the churches of his day]. The question was namely whether the teaching of Peter was related to the words of Christ (λόγοι) or also to the deeds of Christ (πραχθέντα). Another discussion concerned the "many things" (ἔνια), whether these meant the total gospel or just parts in it. Did the two verb forms for Mark's recording point to two different writings or were both verbs referring to the same document? Was the purpose of this quotation from Papias polemic or apologetic in intention?

No wonder that with so much uncertainty [so many different interpretations emerged from this testimony]. Some scholars argued for a reference by Papias to the canonical Gospel of Mark, others saw in it a reference to a Proto-Mark, while again others found in this passage simply a reference to the preaching of Peter (κήρυγμα Πέτρου) without any connection with the second gospel. It would be impossible to select from these various interpretations one thesis that could claim a common endorsement or that could claim any degree of accuracy. Yet I would like to call attention to some points of clarification.

a. It is totally unknown in which context and with what purpose the statements about Mark and Matthew were written down by Papias. We will have to reconcile ourselves to assumptions and suppositions in this respect.

b. In both citations referring to Papias, Eusebius seemed to have found less concerning the *text* of the first two gospels than about their traditional authors. Yet it is probable, because of the lack of specific indications, that Eusebius detected indirect data concerning the history of the first gospels in the Papias reports. It is therefore not likely that Papias himself distinguished between the evangelists and the canonical writers. On the contrary, the additional words "having written the gospel" and later on the simple words "according to Matthew" would lead us to believe that Papias apparently referred to the canonical authors. Also the omission of information, or of a quotation, concerning the relation of these writings to the canonical gospels would indicate that Papias did not expect uncertainty concerning their identity.

c. The absence of specific references by Papias to Mark should not be explained as unfamiliarity with that gospel. On the basis of current text criticism it can hardly be assumed that a contemporary of Polycarp, who died in the second half of the second century, would be unfamiliar with the Marcan Gospel.

d. Concerning the purpose of Papias's information about Mark, one should keep in mind that it remains unknown who the "elder" was. It is equally unknown what this spokesman actually said. The testimony by Papias is formulated in a manner in which he renders the tradition according to his own conviction. In order to determine the possible objective of Papias this quotation has to be analyzed as an indirect reference to his own ideas.

e. The document under discussion enjoyed a high reputation, as is apparent from the prominent position of the adverb meaning "accurately" and by the deliberate explanation of the "disorderly fashion" in which the recording had been accomplished. Also the apologetic attitude of Papias seems to point in this direction. The document in question was in honor either among the readers of Papias or with himself as well. Consequently he hardly dared to mention any failures of that gospel to the readers, although Papias himself had no difficulty recognizing certain limitations in that gospel.

f. The pointing out of certain limitations seems to be the major concern in this quotation, since the writer immediately offers his apologies with the words "he neither [had heard the Lord nor had followed him]." The author summarizes his apology by saying that ["Mark did not fail at any point"].

g. In order to convey the meaning of the criticism expressed by the words "not in an orderly fashion," the following reasons are given by Papias. First of all, the evangelist had been neither an eyewitness nor a contemporary of Jesus; secondly his source was "not a complete exposition" of the words of the Lord. From the first point can be concluded that the desired order should be of such a nature that it could be considered a natural result of having been with the Lord on a day-to-day basis. Such a criterion would guarantee an orderly knowledge of Jesus' work and teaching. In order to clarify the second point [concerning the degree of completeness] it should be noted that the words "having written as many things as he remembered" are meant to interpret the preceding words, "not a complete composition." Furthermore, the term "the Lord's words" (κυριακοὶ λόγοι) have the same explanatory function when describing "the things that both had been spoken and accomplished by Christ."

These various points seem to indicate that the criticism of disorderliness comes down to the simple fact that the document in question did not include the complete Christian teaching concerning Jesus' words and ministry. As causes for this failure are given the facts that the author had not been a disciple of Jesus and that he had no written source that could fill that information gap concerning Jesus' life and words.

h. If this conception of Papias's criticism is correct then it is also clear that the norm for his assessment is nothing other than the commonly accepted tradition concerning the origin of the document in question. Papias's opinion may possibly have been based upon his observation of the relative sobriety of that document in comparison with the wealth of tradition.

i. One should furthermore take note that the original context of the words quoted from Papias is completely unknown. It was not an improbable conjecture when Baur related this statement concerning Mark and Matthew to some remarks by Papias quoted in Eusebius a few pages earlier. These remarks dealt with the value of books in comparison with "the living and abiding voice," which words refer to the tradition originating with the Lord being the truth itself. Through the apostles and their disciples this truth had been transmitted for the sake of the message of salvation.

Papias had a predilection for tradition as the best means for investigating "the truth and the commandments of the Lord" provided it was applied in a critical manner. This explains clearly why Mark was considered incomplete and why the Gospel of Matthew was not considered an original document. For his purpose the "exegesis" of the "words of the Lord," namely, the proclamation of Jesus in word and example,[10] would have little value if it were not for Papias's own labor.

---

[10]The acceptance of a free interpretation of the expression "the words of the Lord" (λόγοι κυριακοί) is justified in the first place by the synonymous use of the expression λόγοι κυριακοί parallel to the "things that both had been spoken and accomplished by Christ." Furthermore it should be noted that Papias shared information concerning Philip, Justus, the millennium, etc., which he in each instance derives from tradition. Papias draws only the commandments "given by the Lord for faith" from this tradition with the omission of the "other commandments." Also the term "commandments" (ἐντολαί) is used therefore in a very wide sense. In this we see again an evidence of how in earlier times history and a range of facts were included in the rule of faith. These facts were considered in a special light because of their arcane character. The Christian rule of faith included not only those doctrines that were considered to have originated with Jesus, but also those the Church had derived from his example and deeds. The rule even included such truths as had emerged merely from the history of the Christian church. For the fathers of the church an exposition of the Christian doctrine could therefore not be encapsulated within a few abstract concepts. Facts and historical accounts had to play a prominent role in this doctrine.

It should further be noted in the general approach of Papias that he does not consider tradition as the primary source of doctrine, but rather as a source in addition to others (cf. the conjunction καί). He draws from tradition in a critical manner: cf. συντάξαι ταῖς ἑρμηνείαις. If these words are translated "adding to the interpretations" the following train of thought results: Papias used the tradition in addition to such written sources as the gospels in order to supplement the available data. The insight obtained from both tradition and the gospels was used for exegesis and for the interpretations of the Lord's words. His own book would in this case differ from the incomplete gospels in that it dealt with the rule of faith and explained it in such a way that it would better meet the needs of his day. Papias could make use of more materials and of another method than the simple portrayal of Christ. His writings may well have been a transition from gospel literature to the later dogmatic expositions.

Summary

Summarizing the nine points observed in connection with Eusebius's quote from Papias we arrive at the following conclusion: it is unlikely that Papias would not have known the second gospel; one is not allowed to deduce from the emphatic interpretation by Eusebius that Papias would not have spoken about the author of that gospel; one cannot assume that in the original context no reference was made to the association of the document in question with the evangelist Mark. Therefore we necessarily arrive at the conclusion that Papias indeed referred to the author of the second gospel and to his work of gathering information.

This must be understood also in the light of the accusation against this document that it did not contain a historically complete account of the teachings of Christ. Such a statement could very well be applied to our Gospel of Mark if Papias's assessment is interpreted from his own presupposition. He esteemed the written documents less than oral tradition and furthermore was strengthened in this opinion by what he had heard concerning the origin of Mark.

From the context in Papias it may be concluded also that a relative respect for that particular document did not seem out of place. He seems to speak about a well-known ecclesiastical document that had received high esteem in Papias's day. [The references to its incompleteness and to its position of high esteem] seem to point to the canonical Gospel of Mark. It seems unlikely that these references would refer to a collection of loose notes or to a gospel that was only good enough to serve as a source for other gospels.

If this interpretation of the Papias's quote by Eusebius is correct, the proponents of the Marcan Hypothesis lose a powerful weapon in refuting the objections against their hypothesis arising from the canonical Gospel of Mark itself. Additional suspicious circumstances emerge when one remembers the origin of the thesis of an Ur-Mark. Schleiermacher was an advocate of the Fragment Hypothesis. He rejoiced in the supposition that he had found a confirmation of his theory in the words of Papias. He presumed to have found a reference to small collections of speeches and facts that had preceded our gospel literature.[11]

It is somewhat strange to see how later scholars have used Schleiermacher's conception. Papias's testimony was used merely as a pretext covering personal opinions concerning the origin of the Synoptic Gospels. By virtue of the criticism

---

[11]Friedrich Schleiermacher, "Über die Zeugnisse des Papias von unsern beiden ersten Evangelien," *Theologische Studien und Kritiken* (1832): 762. [This journal article was reprinted in *Friedrich Schleiermachers Sämtliche Werke* (Berlin: G. Reimer, 1835) 1:361ff.]

of disorderliness, one assumed to have discovered a reference to a document other than the canonical Gospel of Mark. But no scholar has ever taken seriously that concept of disorderliness, since a disorderly document would be of no avail in explaining the largely parallel gospels of Matthew and Luke.

Again it was Michel Nicolas among the proponents of the Marcan Hypothesis whose conscience was alerted. This fact explains why for him the limits of the Ur-Mark and of the Proto-Mark run together. Those scholars who start from the canonical text of Mark sometimes digress further from the canonical gospel than others who begin their argument from the disorderly document mentioned by Papias. The former theologians feel urged to stay further from the canonical text because of objections raised against the recognition of an Ur-Mark, while the latter theologians assume that a supposedly pristine document is the source for three Synoptic Gospels. The latter scholars ultimately came closer to the canonical text of Mark, because of the parallelism in Matthew and Luke.

Réville, for instance, proceeded from the "disorderly" Mark of Papias and soon described it in such a manner that there was "little difference between the original and the canonical Mark."[12] The Ur-gospel of Holtzmann, on the other hand, is quite different from its later canonical form. Yet, Holtzmann found it difficult to determine whether Papias referred to source A or to its canonical Marcan edition.[13]

The fact remains that scholars thought they had discovered the existence of an Ur-gospel in Eusebius. They emphatically stressed Papias's description and applied it to a totally different document than canonical Mark. Gradually, however, these scholars created a Marcan Ur-gospel by way of synoptic analysis. They did not care whether Papias's testimony would justify such a document or not. His reference was merely used as a nomenclature for their own fabrications.

Such manipulations of data added to the lack of critical interpretation of Papias's words has not been conducive to a strengthening of the position of the Marcan Hypothesis. The theory of a Proto-Mark is as questionable as the theory of an Ur-Mark based on interpolations. That the advocates of the Marcan Hypothesis are not quite aware of these two options but rather shift unconsciously from one form into another, is an additional reason for its dubious achievement.

With this discussion we have completed the third point of this chapter. The two major theses [based on the length and the style of this gospel] had no con-

---

[12]Albert Réville, *Études critiques sur l'Évangile selon Saint Matthieu* (Leiden: D. Noothoven van Goor, 1862) 151; please note Réville's definition of Papias's concept of order.

[13]Holtzmann, *Die synoptischen Evangelien,* 254, 370.

clusive force. [The third thesis claiming an original Marcan document distinct from the canonical Gospel of Mark has no historical or literary support either.] We have found the means illegitimate by which they attempted to undermine objections emerging from the text of the second gospel itself. Thus we designate the use of their argument arbitrary.

The reason I chose the title "Critique of the Marcan Hypothesis" as the heading for this part of my research lies in the fact that the three theses discussed constitute the core of this hypothesis. The thesis of brevity has been considered a powerful argument by its adherents. The literary imagery in its peculiar Marcan form could point to an eyewitness account, which in that case would be a proof for the priority of Mark. The Marcan Hypothesis has placed itself in a position, however, from which it cannot contribute to the further development of gospel history or of historical conception in general.

Secondly, the division between an Ur-Mark and a canonical Mark has a character of arbitrariness. This gospel is liable to any division under the pressure of a critic. Gaining the claim of priority for a document in this crude manner is not conducive to critical scholarship.

Now, let us proceed to gather the theological objections against the Marcan Hypothesis coming to us from the Marcan text itself. These have been considered of minor importance by the advocates of the Marcan Hypothesis but they cannot be ignored by merely referring them to an Ur-Mark.

Chapter 5

Theological Assessment
of the Gospel of Mark

Mark's Mature Christology

Introduction

The correlation of the Gospels of Matthew and Mark opens the possibility that either of these gospels can lay claim to greater originality. Since the proponents of the Marcan Hypothesis were conscious of this interrelation they assumed that one of these two gospels had an earlier stage of development. Following this assumption, these scholars assigned priority to the second gospel and ascribed its later portions to a redactor. The proponents of the Marcan Hypothesis were not aware they acted against all probability or, at least, they did not show evidence of any hesitancy in their choice of priority. They rather felt obliged to persist in their position because of the apparently strong proofs for Mark's very early date due to its brevity and its literary imagery.

So much weight was placed upon the observation of these two characteristics of the Gospel of Mark that the numerous objections against this position could not balance the scales. In the preceding chapter we have demonstrated under "Thesis One" (above, 97-104) that the argument based on brevity is ambivalent in determining the chronological place of Mark. The second thesis (above, 104-15) based on literary imagery might even prove the opposite of what the proponents of the Marcan Hypothesis attempted to derive from it. If these supposedly strong arguments are removed from the balance, the scales will tip [in the direction of Matthean priority]. Moreover, the improbable separation of the Marcan text into "earlier" and "later" elements creates a major objection against the Marcan Hypothesis. Therefore, the reader can already anticipate the direction in which the final decision will go.

We should mention at this time a series of facts that heretofore have received little attention. They would, indeed, be of little significance if the two first-mentioned theses were valid. At this juncture in our discussion, however, these additional data may become decisive in the argument regarding priority. Such data concern first of all the theology of the Gospel of Mark, to be discussed in the present chapter. [In the third major part of this dissertation, chapters 6-8, a variety of exegetical issues will be discussed, which provide additional arguments for Matthean priority.] Chapter 6 will compare the sequence of textual materials in Mark with the accounts in the other two Synoptic Gospels. Chapter 7 will be devoted to the peculiarities of the Marcan text emerging from a comparison with their parallels in the other two gospels. Finally, in chapter 8 the portions that are unique for the Gospel of Mark will be incorporated into our argument.

A Christocentric Approach

Before we begin a theological analysis of the Gospel of Mark one point should be broached immediately. Bernhard Weiss[1] considers the presumed theological neutrality of the Gospel of Mark to be the reason scholars thus far have searched in vain for a theological intention of this gospel.

Reuss[2] rejects out of hand the notion that Mark would have developed a theology in reaction to the historical materials furnished by Matthew and Luke. This rejection by Reuss is, however, based merely upon his unyielding conviction of Marcan priority. As long as this presupposition prevails we must give priority to address the synoptic problem. This must be resolved before we can deal with Mark's theological position within the context of the first century of our Christian era.

We will therefore at this time not discuss Schwegler's assertion that "the Gospel of Mark has such a pronounced dogmatic character that it left a strong theological impact in its train."[3] We rather want to concentrate on something more specific. Let us focus on the image of Christ that the author of the Marcan gospel has developed by the content as well as through the form of his account. Mark's conception of Christ sheds light upon various other characteristic concepts of his gospel as well.

---

[1]Bernhard Weiss, "Zur Entstehungsgeschichte der drei synoptischen Evangelien," *Theologische Studien und Kritiken* 34 (1861): 689.

[2]Eduard W. E. Reuss, *Histoire de la théologie chrétienne au siècle apostolique* [*A history of Christian theology in the apostolic age*] 2 vols., 2nd ed. (Strasbourg and Paris: Treuttel & Wurtz, [2]1854; [1]1852) 2:362.

[3]Albert Schwegler, *Das nachapostolische Zeitalter in den Hauptmomenten seiner Entwicklung* (Tübingen: L. F. Fues, 1846) 478; further developed by Schwegler, 474ff.; De Wette, *Einleitung,* 194ff.; Baur, *Kritische Untersuchungen,* 561ff; Baur, *Das Marcusevangelium,* 136ff.; Hilgenfeld, *Das Marcusevangelium,* 123ff.; Hilgenfeld, *Die Evangelien, nach ihrer Entstehung und geistlichen Bedeutung,* 145ff.; Köstlin, *Die Ursprung und die Komposition der synoptischen Evangelien,* 310ff.; Strauss, *Das Leben Jesu für das deutsche Volk bearbeitet* (1864) 1:132ff.

The starting point for Mark's Christology is furnished by Irenaeus. According to this church father the authority of the gospels was established by the fact that even heretics made use of them.[4] In this connection Irenaeus stated,

They assert that Jesus and Christ are to be distinguished, the former has suffered while the latter has not. These heretics can be refuted by a careful study of the same Gospel of Mark that is so beloved by them.[5]

Leaving aside the accuracy of the author's opinion we may conclude from this information that the Gospel of Mark did meet certain criteria that appealed to the Gnostics. This gospel certainly gives occasion for a Gnostic distinction between a terrestrial Jesus and a heavenly Christ.

Jesus as the "Son of God"

In the opening verse the evangelist announces his writing as a "gospel of Jesus Christ, the Son of God." It is not too audacious to assume that this solemn intonation is the perspective from which Mark visualizes in his gospel the total image of Christ. Like the concept "Son of David" in the Gospel of Matthew we encounter in Mark's "Son of God" the design for a complete Christology. The question needs to be raised, however, what meaning is expressed by these words. It is not likely that they would be nothing more than a product of traditional ideas. It is equally unlikely that these words would refer to Jesus' supernatural birth, since the account of the Virgin Birth is lacking in the Gospel of Mark.

We already took note above of the fact that in the second gospel Jesus was called the "Son of God" only by the Father, by the demons, and by himself. At the moment of death he was also recognized as such by the centurion.[6] This last incident is especially noteworthy. The cause of the officer's acknowledgement was that Jesus "thus cried out and breathed his last" (15:39). Tischendorf suggested removing the words "cried out" from the original text; Zeller considered this word a later insertion in order to explain the cause of the centurion's reverence.[7] This later redactional correction supposedly had been necessitated by the fact that the evangelist Mark had omitted the other information by Matthew [of the earthquake and the resurrection of the saints as

---

[4]Irenaeus, *Adversus omnes haereses* 3.11.7.

[5]*Qui autem Jesum separant a Christo et impassibilem perseverasse Christum, passum vero Jesum dicunt, id quod secundum Marcum est praeferentes evangelium, cum amore veritates legentes illud, corrigi possunt.*

[6]See above, 120.

[7]Eduard Zeller, "Zum Marcus-Evangelium," *Zeitschrift für Wissenschaftliche Theologie* 8 (1865): 388.

reasons for the officer's recognition of Jesus as the "Son of God"]. Such an emendation, however, does not show this verse (15:39) to its full advantage.

According to Mark the recognition of the centurion was caused by Jesus himself rather than by events [such as the earthquake and the resurrection] as they are summarized in Matthew and Luke by "the things that were happening" (Matt 27:54 and Luke 23:47). The relative clause in Mark 15:39 referring to the centurion, "who was standing right in front of Him," seems to point clearly to Jesus himself as the occasion for his exclamation. The use of the words "cried out" for Jesus' final moment is not unintentional either. It is not too farfetched to explain this term in reference to the loud screams by which the demons, upon Jesus' command, left their victims (1:26; 9:26). In accordance with such phenomena it is only natural that Jesus' sonship was evidenced in a similar manner. In his dying hour the Spirit of God manifested its presence [clearly and audibly].

The manifestation of the Spirit by the loud cry mentioned in 15:37, 39 explains also the meaning of the title "Son of God" used in the opening verse of this gospel. Jesus was the Son of God because of the indwelling of God's Spirit. From this perspective Mark's Christology becomes translucent. [According to the Gospel of Mark], only when we keep in mind that Jesus was attested by this Spirit can we understand his nature and his actions.

This Spirit "immediately drove him out into the wilderness" (1:12) after it had descended upon him at baptism. It was the same Spirit that enabled Jesus to know facts beyond common human knowledge. Jesus perceived "in his spirit" (2:8) the inner motivations of the scribes who witnessed the forgiveness of sins in the paralytic man. In a similar way Jesus was aware that he was under suspicion of a potential breaking of the Sabbath (3:3). In 9:35 Jesus showed himself cognizant of the ambitious interests of his disciples.

A comparison of these references with their synoptic parallels shows, indeed, that Mark stressed the spiritual insight of Jesus. For this reason he did not fail to include the stories of Luke about the entry into Jerusalem (11:4-6) and the selection of the guest room [where Jesus was to eat the Passover with his disciples] (14:13-16). Both stories confirm Jesus' power of prediction. This Christological approach explains also why Jesus' kinsmen wanted to seize him, because they said, "He is beside himself" (3:21). Similarly the accusation of a covenant with Satan becomes in Mark a definite charge of lunacy, a being "possessed by Beelzebul" (3:22), or having "an unclean spirit" (3:30).

This Christological approach explains also why Mark does not mention a blasphemy against the Son after having stated the blasphemy against the Spirit. Both Spirit and Son are one for Mark. [The implications of this blasphemy against the Spirit reflect Mark's unique position as well]. In Matthew it is unforgivable that one does not recognize the first workings of God's Spirit, the initial manifestations of the Kingdom (Matt 12:31); in Mark one commits an unforgivable sin against the Holy Spirit because one has cursed the indwelling Spirit of Jesus as a Beelzebul (3:29). This articulation is only possible for an author who has a conscious and definite conception of the Spirit [and the Spirit's relation to the Son].

Jesus as the Authoritative Teacher

A natural consequence of Mark's high Christology is that his description calls attention to Jesus' unusual conduct, a certain Johannine divine autonomy, as the following examples may illustrate. Simon and his friends had almost been left behind by Jesus the day after they had been called to be his followers. That is, Jesus had gone out alone to preach in the surrounding towns (1:37).

Later Jesus went up into the hills and "called to him those whom he desired" (3:13). At that time a company of twelve disciples, who permanently would accompany him, was established. After having supplied them with the power to cast out demons, Jesus assumed the authority to send them out to preach. To some of them Jesus gave new names without any apparent reason. Simon was called "Peter" (3:16), while the sons of Zebedee were named "Boanerges" (3:17).

[There are evidences that Jesus pursued his mission all on his own, for example,] when the disciples had wrestled with wind and waves since the preceding evening, Jesus wanted "to pass by them" about the fourth watch of the night without saying a word to them (6:45-48). In a later context, Jesus [simply ignored the Pharisees] by returning immediately in the same boat in which he had just landed, because he was disturbed about the request for a sign (8:12)

[Evidences of Jesus' teaching authority abound.] "Sitting down" Jesus called the twelve in order to address them (9:35). The verb "to charge" or to "warn sternly" (διαστέλλεσθαι) is Mark's favorite term expressing this authority.[8] When the fig tree in the season that it cannot bear fruit had only leaves to still Jesus' hunger, it was reason enough for it to be destroyed (11:14). Fortunately the evangelist added a command that would protect against such [potentially devastating] power of faith, [namely, the command to forgive (11:25). Some manuscripts add the warning "But if you do not forgive, neither will your Father who is in heaven forgive your trespasses" (11:26).] The tone in which Jesus rebuked his disciples when they thought of "bread" rather than of the "leaven" of the Pharisees (8:16), fits completely within Mark's theological frame of reference.

[According to Mark Jesus was a self-confident teacher.] He behaved in a composed manner when unruly crowds thronged around him. Jesus moved freely

---

[8]See Mark 5:43; 7:36; 8:15; and 9:9.

into and out of Capernaum in spite of a murderous plan by the Pharisees and the Herodians (3:6). Yielding to opposition was out of the question for Jesus. The verb form "withdrew" in 3:7 is not related to the preceding events as in the parallel passage in Matthew (12:15). Furthermore this verb does not occur again in the Gospel of Mark. When Jesus was seeking a lonely place in 6:31 he did this to provide rest for his disciples, not because he was haunted by the fate of John the Baptist as is recorded in Matthew (14:13).

The notion that Peter could be a hindrance to Jesus was considerably weakened by Mark by eliminating the words "you are a hindrance to me" (Matt 16:23). It seems that Mark transferred all potential annoyance of Jesus to the disciples by stating, "turning and seeing his disciples" (8:33).

In general we find in Mark an endeavor to keep Jesus aloof from human conditions. When in Matthew (17:19ff.) the disciples asked why they had not been able to heal the epileptic child, Jesus pointed to their lack of powerful faith. It would be possible to interpret Jesus' response in Mark 9:29 in a similar manner. Yet the Marcan text [leaves out a reference to the power of faith and simply] states, "This kind cannot be driven out by anything but prayer and fasting." This controversial statement, which may be out of context, could be viewed as a reproach against the dead religious formalism of Jesus' day. With such an interpretation Mark could, like Matthew, point to the power of faith which would have enabled Jesus to heal the epileptic child. Yet this possible interpretation is out of the question since Mark does not refer to the power of faith.

According to Mark's presentation the demon which vexed the epileptic child belonged to a peculiar kind that "cannot be driven out by anything but prayer and fasting" (the Vaticanus text has only "by prayer"). Since the disciples did not have this special insight they could not meet the conditions for healing. It should not be concluded, however, that Jesus would have to fulfill the requirements [of prayer and fasting] himself. He [lived on a higher plane] and was able to achieve miracles from the resources of his superhuman nature. No reference to this power was necessary; for Jesus there were no special requirements to facilitate an act of healing.

That the evangelist had, indeed, a high view of Jesus becomes evident also from the preceding request by the father of the epileptic child. Jesus showed himself surprised upon hearing the man's words, "If you can!" His answer was, "All things are possible to him who believes" (9:23). The intent of these words becomes evident from the hasty reply by the father: "I believe; help my unbelief!" This response implied a reproach for the man who apparently was not certain of Jesus' miraculous power, because [by his original remark] he betrayed a trace of unbelief. If he had fully believed he would have considered all things possible. No wonder that Jesus provided help not because of this partial unbeliever, but only because "a crowd came running together" (9:25). Jesus apparently wanted to avoid an annoying throng, without wasting more time.

Jesus as the Miracle Worker

Doubting the absolute miraculous power of Jesus was considered sinful by Mark; conversely faith included a belief in miracles. In his 1862 publication,[9] Réville points to a peculiarity of Mark, namely, that the result of Jesus' miraculous power was demonstrated mostly in a gradual manner. Mark presumably presented the healings almost as a natural process, which would be in conflict with his propensity for miracles. This alleged aspect of Mark's presentation is used by Réville as an argument for the greater originality of Mark's Gospel in contrast to Matthew's where the results of Jesus' miraculous actions follow instantaneously. This reasoning, however, seems correct only because Réville considers this peculiarity in Mark a result of Mark's tendency to present miracles as natural events.

Nothing seems to me more incorrect than this interpretation. Réville would certainly not maintain that Mark's description of the miracles suggests an eyewitness report. Also Réville views the gradual healing of the blind man in Bethsaida (8:22) and the slowly withering fig tree (11:20) as elaborations by Mark of the miracle stories of Jesus. [Indeed, the question should be raised why Mark gave additional details on these miracles.] For an evangelist who considers all things possible for Jesus as well as for God, it is not likely he would attempt to describe supernatural events in a natural way. Mark would rather provide these details in order to extol the miraculous power of Jesus to a still greater degree. One should give preference to any other explanation over a purely naturalistic approach! Mark is prone to concentrate on the miraculous rather than on a natural explanation.

This tendency of Mark caused him to mention the thronging crowds around Jesus, his fruitless attempts to remain secret, and the detailed descriptions of the intensity of diseases. This [same propensity for the miraculous] led Mark to dwell more on events than on messages. Reuss deduced from this last characteristic that a predilection for miracles could be an indication of an early date.[10] Such an assertion may be true in isolation, but it cannot be sustained within the context of the Gospel of Mark. In this gospel we are not merely dealing with a predilection for miracles but rather with a more or less developed Christological

---

[9]Albert Réville, *Études critiques sur l'Évangile selon Saint Matthieu* (Leiden: D. Noothoven van Goor, 1862) 136.

[10]Eduard W. E. Reuss, *Histoire du canon des saintes écritures dans l'église chrétienne,* 2nd ed. (Strassbourg: Treuttel & Wurtz, 1863) 181.

conception [calling for evidences of his power rather than specimens of his wisdom].

The relatively small number of speeches in Mark merely serves to set the stage and to create the perspective from which the miracle stories are to be viewed. Let us compare this aspect with the Gospel of Matthew in which we discern a variety of traits [emerging from the miracle stories, a variety] by which a pluriform image of Christ comes into view. Jesus is depicted as the Son of David with his multiple qualities; he takes upon himself weaknesses and diseases; he is the Good Shepherd of the oppressed and dejected crowds; he is the gentle Messiah who pursues his way in all quietness; he expresses himself by way of parables; he is the Prince of Peace to whom praise is offered by the mouth of children; he opens the eyes of the blind and the ears of the dead; because of him the cripple jumps as a hart and the tongue of the mute rejoices.

Thus the material used by Matthew for this multiple image of Christ consists of several strands. There are conceptions about forgiveness of sins, about the power of faith, about the observation of the Sabbath, about death, about the relation of the Messiah towards the Gentiles and Israel. All these elements give color to the miracle stories in manifold alteration. The reader discovers how historical recollections are merged with messianic meditations. All through the Gospel of Matthew one notices the seminal beginnings from which later conceptions have developed. The Gospel of Matthew is a fruit still rooted in its soil of origin.

In Mark the situation is quite different. The fruit has been picked and it has been detached from its historical context. One major theme is heard throughout this whole gospel; it is the elevation of Christ who has been wrested away from the world of humans. According to Mark, Jesus belongs no more to the circle of prophets nor can he be compared with prophetic figures. Through the possession of God's Spirit he has become a totally unique being who reveals his superhuman nature by his unlimited miraculous power. From this one perspective all miracles receive equal validity in Mark; they share the same significance, namely, that they are works performed by the divine Christ.

A few examples will underscore this last assertion. The story of the healing of a lame man in Matthew (9:1-8) makes sense only when one focuses on the Christian conception of forgiveness of sins. It displays the anger of the scribes who take offense at the act of forgiving sins while they do not mind the performance of miracles. This objective comes out clearly when the crowds praise God "who had given such authority to men" (Matt 9:8). Mark has abandoned Matthew's leading idea in order to focus on his favorite theme [of the exalted Christ]. Therefore, in his text the miracle itself receives the major attention. Upon Jesus' command the lame man rose, took up his pallet, and "went out before them all" (2:12a). The reason for amazement and glorification of God among the crowd was "We never saw anything like this!" (2:12b).

A second example [of different objectives among these evangelists] is Matthew's account of the Canaanite woman (15:21-28). The origin of this story was the question concerning the mission of the Messiah. Jesus was addressed by the title "Son of David" [and responded he "was sent only to the lost sheep of the house of Israel" (15:24)]; the faith of the Gentile woman was the compelling force to which he yielded. Mark shifts, [in this instance of the divine Messiah, from Jewish particularism to his major theme of the divine Messiah]. Mark wants to show that even outside Palestine Jesus cannot remain hidden. Also abroad Jesus cannot refrain from performing miracles. The emphatic confirmation that the demon had left the girl and that she was lying in bed (Mark 7:30) again shifts the attention from Matthew's messianic quest to the miraculous act accomplished by the universal Christ in Mark.

This focussing on one main theme can be found throughout the Gospel of Mark. At every occasion it is made clear that it was the divine Jesus who performed the miracles. The second gospel consistently points to the fact that Jesus is miraculously powerful, so that the complete content of this gospel is therefore to be interpreted from this perspective. It is therefore very difficult to presuppose that such use of the miracle stories as we find in Mark would represent the most original level of the gospels. It is equally difficult to assume that the variety of ideas in Matthew would have developed at a later date from this uniform theme in Mark. It is equally difficult to assert that the predilection for miracles in Mark could be more original than Matthew's interest in clusters of speeches, as Reuss averred.[11] [We conclude that] the Christ of the Gospel of Mark is God's gift prepared for all nations [rather than merely for Israel].

The Christology of Mark consists of components that have come into being through a variety of reflections and circumstances. Those components are incorporated into one purpose, namely, to depict the Son of God, equipped with the Holy Spirit in an ontological sense. This Son of God assumed a place in the creation that is exalted far beyond the world of humans; he was lifted up beyond any nationality in order to be beheld by all peoples on earth.

Mark's Doctrinal Approach

The New Didache

The answer to the question why the Gospel of Mark has so few speeches must be found in his Christological concern. One can hardly contend that doctrine would have no relevance for Mark. More than any other evangelist he

---

[11]Reuss, *Histoire du canon,* 181.

emphasized Jesus' teaching ministry. Repeatedly Jesus' teaching is mentioned, however, without unfolding the content of that teaching (1:21, 22; 2:2, 13; 6:4, 6, 34; 10:1). When the "sheep without a shepherd" aroused compassion in Jesus he expressed his feelings by teaching them "many things" (6:34). It is indeed strange that the actual words received so little attention from an evangelist who attached so much importance to Jesus' doctrine and teaching ministry.

One explanation of this fact seems to be offered in Mark 1:27. As soon as Jesus appeared as a teacher in Capernaum he evoked amazement because of the authority of his teaching (1:22). But when he performed his first miracle, the casting out of a demon, his teaching was called "new." Jesus' authority had been shown to extend itself to "unclean spirits." These spirits may be seen by Mark as symbols for the Gentiles, in which case this story would point to the universal character of Jesus' teaching.

This teaching of Jesus would be considered "new" because of this message to the Gentiles, or also because of the integration of message and miracle. The "didache" mentioned in the opening chapter of this gospel thus seems to have a wider range of reference than just to Jesus' personal instruction. This teaching rather refers to the total manifestation of Christianity and to the Christian message in a universal sense.

The Christocentric Didache

Christianity was seen by the evangelist Mark as a totally new phenomenon conceived as a new doctrine. Its movement owed its origin to the powerful Jesus as depicted in his gospel. Jesus was the teacher who proclaimed the gospel in the fullness of time (1:15). The truth of the Christian teaching stands or falls with the validity of his personality. The certainty of the imminent future was equally dependent upon him. To this very viewpoint the evangelist of the second gospel had arrived [after contemplation and through the missionary movement]. Furthermore, Christianity had been established as a new doctrine. It was now of utmost importance to provide a guarantee for the divine character of this doctrine in the transcendent origin of its founder. [For his Gentile readers] Jesus evoked infinitely more interest by his being than by his words and teachings, which would keep him more associated with his Jewish surroundings.

Only certain speeches were adopted by Mark and then in a form characteristic for him. Whatever factors may have been involved in his selection of materials one will certainly have to attribute a major role to Mark's Christological viewpoint. [Other factors for inclusion of certain speeches may have been] his love for a balanced presentation, his neglect of secondary elements, theological considerations, and also his sources must have played a role. The more the person of Christ had been crystallized into dogma, the more a doctrinal relationship to him became a point of interest to the readers.

The more the relation between Christ and [ecumenical] Christianity became a focus of attention, the more the historical position Jesus occupied within his Palestinian surroundings was lost to sight and neglected. The more emphasis was placed upon belief and upon the theological relation to Jesus, the more his Jewish and moral requirements tended to be disregarded.

The Kingdom of Heaven was moved more distinctly into the future while the terrestrial form of Christianity was considered a time of preparation. The requirements for entrance into the Kingdom received different meaning as well. Of the many words and speeches known from Jesus only relatively few had direct relevance [for the generation for which Mark was writing]. The grand transposition of the Gospel of John, which gave new content to the didache by placing Christ himself into its center, had not yet taken place in Mark but we do discern traces of transition.

[The following examples may illustrate this change of focus.] In the other two Synoptics we notice that Jesus regularly reminded his disciples of his impending suffering; in Mark this prediction had been transformed to composed instruction. The message about his suffering is introduced in 8:31 with the words: "he began to teach" and in 9:31: "he was teaching." Such a transition has changed the historical prediction of Christ into a theological exposition.

Mark 12:35 [furnishes another illustration of theological questioning]. "As Jesus taught" he asked how people could call Christ the Son of David, while he is rather David's Lord. [Also by Mark's arrangement of materials Christ is moved to the center of his message.] Mark placed the parable of the lamp, which had to be placed upon a stand (4:21), between the one about the sower and the one about the sprouting seed. This arrangement indicates that for Mark Christ began to introduce himself as the subject of his universal message.

The Universal Didache

Sometimes Mark seems to detach the original words from their temporal and geographic context. The words by which the money changers were driven from the Temple, according to Matthew, have been used by Mark as a separate specimen of Jesus' teaching (11:17). The Temple is called a house of prayer "for all the nations," which must be more that a routine amplification. Those were the words that angered the chief priests and the scribes, while the multitude "was astonished at his teaching" (11:18). The whole issue of the Jerusalem Temple seems to have been transported to a higher plane.

The Christ of Mark has been disengaged considerably from his original historical context. He has become the unique teacher who called Christianity into being. Christ initiated the new teaching. For this reason Mark highly valued a contemplative approach, since the divinity of Christ's nature is a guarantee for his teaching. His supernatural character, his impressive and often incomprehensible appearance, his divine Spirit which manifested itself in every situation—all these were aspects deserving special attention. The total content of Mark's gospel should be viewed from the perspective of the exalted Christ.

Mark's Salvation History

Jesus' Relation to John the Baptist

Christology and its crystallization into doctrine had their implication for the manner in which Mark portrayed Jesus in relation to a variety of persons and powers. Whatever natural causes may have contributed to the omission of the birth narratives and the genealogical tables by Mark, there certainly was also the theological consideration. The gospel of the Son of God could only begin in the moment when Jesus was formally endowed with the Spirit. The enigma of the baptism of Jesus had finally satisfied the minds of his followers by defining it as the real hour of Christ's birth. This interpretation caused, however, a devaluation of all preceding history.

One point, however, could not be omitted from the gospel, namely, the reference to the "herald" of the Kingdom, although his role in relation to Christ is portrayed by Mark in a scarcely original manner. John's personality as well as his preaching appear rather insignificant in Mark when compared with Matthew's account. The first gospel introduces John with his message in the desert: "Repent, for the kingdom of heaven is at hand" (Matt 3:2). Matthew justifies the work of John (γάρ) by referring to Isaiah's prophecy concerning the voice which was to prepare the way of the Lord. The message of repentance in the desert is the content of "the voice" that had been expected.

The evangelist Mark conceived the work of preparation [by the ministry of John the Baptist] quite differently. He viewed the role of John as the "herald" of the coming Christ. This change of approach also caused a different sequence of thought in his gospel. According to Mark, the beginning of the gospel is not the message of repentance but the announcement of the prophetic Christ, not the voice crying for repentance but the messenger (φωνή) himself steps into the foreground. Thus the second verse in Mark concerning the messenger receives its meaning [in the context of the total gospel]. Commentators have no good explanation for this verse (1:2); they either attributed it unjustly to Isaiah or they tried to eliminate it from the original text. Mark intentionally derived this verse from Matthew 11:10 quoting Malachi 3:1 [about God's messenger] and inserted this before Matthew's quote from Isaiah 40:3 (see Mark 1:3 and Matt 3:3). By leaving out the sermon to the Pharisees and Sadducees, Mark introduces the main subject of John's preaching (Mark 1:7-8) with a description of John's life and work (Mark 1:4-6).

Mark's major interest focused on the words of John: "After me comes he who is mightier than I," followed by the promise of a baptism "with the Holy Spirit" (1:7-8). In order to grasp the intent of those words the reader has to consult the Gospel of Matthew. Matthew records that the Pharisees and Sadducees hoped to escape the wrath to come through a baptism of repentance (Matt 3:7). It will be of no avail, however, if they do not bear fruit that befits repentance. The message [as presented by Matthew] is urgent: the axe is laid to the root of the trees and the fire is ready for the dead wood.

The Pharisees and Sadducees may presume to mislead the powerless penance preacher who has merely water at his disposal, but they will not be able to deceive the mightier one coming after him. The announced Messiah will have the Holy Spirit and fire available for his baptism, which referred to Jesus' majesty as Messiah and to his final judgement.

The context in Matthew makes it clear that the baptism "with the Holy Spirit and with fire" should be interpreted metaphorically. John's ministry is used as a model for the work of the Messiah, who will come as a judge with the winnowing fork in his hand in order to burn all the hypocrites, as chaff at harvest time. This beautiful imagery is totally lost in the Gospel of Mark. The contrast in Mark is not the weakness [of the messenger] and the power [of the Messiah], but water baptism and spirit baptism. The terms "mightier" and "with the Holy Spirit" therefore receive a totally different meaning. The omission "with fire" underscores this point. [John the Baptist served merely to elevate and prefigure the divine Christ.] The baptism of John is expressed by an aorist form thereby indicating a completed event, while Jesus' baptism is expressed by the progressive tense (1:8), [thus leading into the distant future].

It is highly unlikely that Matthew would have created his beautiful imagery from the syncopated verses in Mark. It is equally improbable that Mark's conception of John as the herald for Christ would be more original than Matthew's more historical presentation. The latter has incorporated the baptizer and his message in his gospel because here the first trace of a preaching of repentance was found in connection with the imminent Kingdom of Heaven. It is inconceivable that the contrast of water and spirit baptism would be earlier than the contraposition of John's weak appeal for repentance over against the mighty appearance of a messianic judge. Mark's presentation of the relation of John the Baptist to Jesus shows the same development of thought as his Christological conception described above.[12] [Salvation history has replaced the record of sacred history.]

---

[12]See above, 132-37.

Jesus' Relation to His Disciples

The same development can be detected in the relation of Jesus to his disciples. Réville called attention to the lowly position the disciples occupy in Mark.[13] For him this psychological immaturity is an indication of greater historical originality in comparison with the other gospels.

Réville wants to preclude theological implications in this contrast between Jesus and his disciples. But upon closer investigation such an implication cannot be avoided. The so-called "Unwissenheitfragen" (questions or remarks from ignorance) are a characteristic phenomenon in gospel literature. Whatever their origin may be,[14] in the form they have in the gospels they generally cannot be considered genuine historical recollections that had been preserved in spite of the later reverence for the apostles. These "questions" are rather conscious peculiarities of the authors. Matthew used this literary device as well and in the Gospel of John these questions have strongly increased.

The frequency of these questions seems to parallel the higher level of Christology. In the Gospel of Mark the naiveté of the disciples as described above[15] serves simultaneously as a backdrop for the glorious personality of Christ. The hypothesis may even be ventured that the low profile of the disciples implies a slight antiapostolic tendency. This trend may also be detected in the transferal of the privileges of the twelve to a larger circle of believers. The "disciples" mentioned in Matthew 12:49 are called the true "mother and brothers" of Jesus. In Mark these disciples even had to share their honor with a crowd sitting about Jesus (3:32, 34). [In the same manner Mark states in chapter 4 that] the privileged persons to whom the secret of the parables was given, as distinct from "those outside," were "those who were about him with the twelve" (4:10).

Furthermore, we observe that in the Gospel of Mark the illustrious triumvirate had to adopt a fourth person. Mark refers namely to four witnesses of Jesus' glorification, and of his agony in Gethsemane as well as of the resuscitation of Jairus's daughter. The accentuated story of the calling of the two pairs of brothers in 1:29 seems to have been a reason for Mark to grant Andrew equal honor with Simon, John, and James. Andrew was, together with Simon, co-owner of a house; it was in this house that the two sons of Zebedee witnessed the healing of Simon's mother-in-law (1:31). When in 1:36 "Simon and those with him"

---

[13]Réville, *Études critiques,* 134.

[14]These questions may have developed spontaneously from the teaching situation: questions are raised in order to give Jesus an occasion to respond. Cf. in this respect Matt 18:21.

[15]See above, 118ff.

were searching for Jesus we have to assume that Andrew was included in this group. Andrew was also among those sitting on the Mount of Olives when they were asking questions privately concerning the parousia (13:3).

From these passages we may conclude that the triumvirate did not exist for Mark [as a sacrosanct cadre]; at a later date it would purposely be dissolved by the fourth gospel. Mark's deliberate mentioning of the twelve in support of the cause of missions (3:14) was a means of harmonization with Matthew.

The origin of the concept "the twelve," even though it is repeatedly mentioned in the Gospel of Matthew, is still unclear. It seems to have been part of the Matthean tradition. Even though Mark followed this tradition, he ascribed a wider area of activity to the larger circle of Jesus' disciples.

Neither the concept of the twelve nor that of the three were vivid concepts for Mark. They were not clearly circumscribed in his sources either. On the one hand Mark made an attempt to delineate more sharply the origin and purpose of those associations; on the other hand he allowed a diffusion of their distinctiveness because of circumstances and other ideas. For instance, in order to focus attention upon the exalted Jesus, Mark had to stress the low degree of understanding by the apostles and their immaturity. There is nothing unusual in this literary method but it does suggest that Mark's approach is far from an eyewitness report. Such a literary device is rather an indication of a much later time of composition.

Jesus' Relation to the Demons

Concerning the relation of Jesus to the demons, I could refer to [Eduard] Zeller's article in Hilgenfeld's journal.[16] This relation is more pronounced in Mark than in Luke. The casting out of evil spirits is reported by Mark as a continuous activity by Jesus and by the apostles, while for Matthew the redemption of the possessed is only part of the many healings of sickness and diseases among the people. In Matthew the demons only occasionally express their awareness of the purpose of Jesus' appearance (Matt 8:29). This occasional testimony even though it included a recognition of Jesus as the Son of God, is still not of major importance to Matthew.

In Mark, however, the professions by the demons have become theological formulas. The evangelist points emphatically to the fact that they know "the Holy One of God" (1:24, 34; 3:11; 5:7) and that they are subservient to Jesus. The demons preceded the humans in this insight. [According to Mark], Jesus took pains to prevent a broadcasting of this insight until after the exorcism at Gadara

---

[16]"Zum Marcus-Evangelien," *Zeitschrift für Wissenschaftliche Theologie* 8 (1865): 308-28, 385-408.

when the reason for such secrecy seemed to be removed. In Gadara the man is clearly told to proclaim what has happened to him. For Mark the awareness among the evil spirits of their adversary is not just accidental. The explicit theological affirmation by the demons has a totally different character in Mark from the one demonic testimony mentioned in Matthew. [Also in this respect,] Mark's descriptions clearly indicate a later time of composition.

[During the early Christian era] the range of action by Christ began to extend itself beyond the world of humanity. One reason for this extension was the emerging Gnostic movement. In Paul's letter to the Ephesians Christ has accomplished God's will by uniting "all things in Heaven and on earth" (Eph 1:10). In his letter to the Romans Christ "descended to the depth of the earth" and "ascended above all heavens" (Rom 10:6-7 and Heb 4:14). These quotations do not imply that similar profound thoughts are also found in the Gospel of Mark.

There is in Mark, indeed, the imagery of the battle between the Holy One of God and the evil powers in the air. This conflict is articulated on the one hand by the insight and submission of the demons, and on the other hand by the power of Jesus over such violently possessed persons. Mark stays aloof, however, from any historical traits in the healing of such psychotic diseases. Over against the plain description of demon possession by Matthew the evangelist Mark cannot claim any historical priority [with his mythological imagery].

The representation of Jesus as the dreaded adversary of all satanic powers betrays a developed demonology. Christ is the victorious Lord recognized by the servants of Satan from the moment of their first encounter. A developed demonology implies a high Christology as well. [The relation to John the Baptist, to the disciples, and, as well, to the demons] bear out the same high Christological view in the Gospel of Mark.[17]

Jesus' Relation to the Angels

If Jesus is the Son or the Holy One of God exalted high above the realm of evil spirits, he also has been assigned a position higher that the angels. The gospels generally agree that Christ will send angels as his messengers in the day of the parousia. No wonder that also during his earthly existence angels were serving Jesus in the desert (Matt 4:11) and in Gethsemane (Luke 22:43).

In comparison with the other gospels Mark more emphatically attributes to Jesus a higher place than the angels. Viewed from the total context of Mark the

---

[17]Please note how in the Greek text the term "unclean" occurs not only as an adjective with the noun "spirits," but also as an independent noun, as a kind of proper name (1:27; 3:11; 5:13; 6:7).

perceptive explanation that Zeller gave of Mark 13:32 is not correct.[18] Mark does indeed state in that verse, "But of that day or that hour no one knows, not even the angels in heaven, nor the Son, but only the Father." Much attention has been given by scholars to the words "nor the Son." But the absence of these words in some versions of Matthew cannot be interpreted as an evidence of reverence for the Son by the supposedly later evangelist Matthew.

Zeller's remark is correct that Matt 24:36 eliminates any knowledge of the day and hour of the parousia. The ignorance of the angels precludes anyone else except the Father from having any insight into those data. There was thus no viable answer regarding the question of the disciples: "When will this be?" (Matt 24:3). Mark, however, raised the possibility that the Son might be able to indicate the day and hour, which was unknown even to the angels. When Mark thus negated this possibility he gave evidence of a later Christological development than we see in Matthew. Mark does not need to be accused of a lack of reverence, which, according to Zeller, was to be rectified in Matthew by eliminating these sensitive words [from the earlier Ur-Mark text].

Summarizing the results of this chapter we see in the Gospel of Mark the following image of Christ: Jesus is the Son of God because of the indwelling Holy Spirit. He is exalted above the angels and is feared by the host of demons. He is a Christ who for his ministry needs nothing else than a messenger to announce his coming. Jesus is a miracle worker whose power is beyond doubt for any believer. He is the subject of continuing amazement and astonishment for thousands of admirers. Jesus is beyond understanding for everyone; he is beyond comprehension also for his disciples. Jesus is self-reliant and self-sufficient in his actions.

Such a Christological image certainly cannot boast an early date. The Gospel of Mark is not an initial statement of impressions like the Gospel of Matthew in which all these theological aspects have a totally different, a much simpler, and a more naive character. The proponents of the Marcan hypothesis overlook these evidences when they give priority to the "Son of God" of the second gospel over the "Son of David" of the first gospel. By implication they must accept Matthew's description of the fulfiller of the prophecies as a later development. They also must accept Matthew's concept of the Good Shepherd for the oppressed and defeated multitudes of Israel a later development than Mark's concept of the superhuman miracle worker.

The proponents of the Marcan hypothesis have not seriously analyzed the difficulties arising from a theological comparison of the first two gospels. Historically as well as theologically I can see only strong arguments *against* the Marcan hypothesis.

---

[18]Zeller, "Zum Marcus—Evangelien," 308-28.

[The advocates of this theory had expected to find their strength in the historical-literary arguments of brevity and literary imagery; they had to assume an Ur-Mark or a Proto-Mark in order to explain the passages of later date. Theologically, however, the Gospel of Mark has shown a strong unity in its Christology, its doctrinal approach, and its interpretation of salvation history, and there is no need to find unity in either an underlying or later document.]

Part Three

Exegetical Assessment of the Gospel of Mark

Chapter 6

The Sequence
of the Narrative Materials
in Mark

A Synopsis of the First Three Gospels

A Comparative Chart

The next point to be raised against the Marcan hypothesis involves an analysis of the Marcan text itself: [we will deal with the sequence of its materials, its pecularities, and finally with its unique passages.[1] By way of introduction to the discussion on the sequence of textual materials] I want to present first the issue of sequence in a most concrete manner by presenting the content of the Synoptic Gospels in graphic parallels. I intend to demonstrate in what sequence Mark's narratives have been arranged in comparison with those of the other two evangelists.

[To indicate parallel texts vertical lines have been drawn between the columns of pericopes.] A line that runs vertically on the right or left side of the pericopes in Mark will indicate when its text agrees with Luke and when with Matthew. In the same manner the vertical lines alongside the materials in Matthew and Luke will by their length indicate to what extent their materials agree in detail with the Marcan text. Finally, interruptions in those vertical lines will indicate interruptions in the succession of the accounts of each gospel. Such interruptions may have been caused either by insertions or by omissions.

From Mark 14 on it is difficult to continue the same analysis. The profound thought Luke used for his passion narratives caused him to deal more freely with the text, which largely runs parallel in Matthew and Mark. What I want to demonstrate visually in the chart is the way in which the Gospel of Mark winds its way as a thread through both parallel gospels. It happens in such a way that the reader can derive the second gospel, with some exceptions, from the two parallel gospels and come out with the same sequence of Mark's present text.

---

[1]See above, 132.

Matthew		Mark	Luke	
11:10	3:1-4:17	1:1-15	3:1-4:15	7:27
	4:18-22	1:16-20		5:1-11
	4:23; 7:28	1:21-22	4:31-32	
		1:23-28	4:33-37	
	8:14-15	1:29-31	4:38-39	
	8:16	1:32-34	4:40-41	
		1:35-39	4:42-44	
8:1-4		1:40-45	5:12-16	
	9:1-8	2:1-12	5:17-26	
	9:9-13	2:13-17	5:27-32	
	9:14-17	2:18-22	5:33-39	
	12:1-8	2:23-28	6:1-5	
	12:9-14	3:1-6	6:6-11	
	12:15-16	3:7-12		6:17-19
10:1-4		3:13-19	6:12-16	
	12:22-32	3:20-30		11:14-23; 12:10
	12:46-50	3:31-35		8:19-21
	13:1-9	4:1-9	8:4-8	
	13:10-17	4:10-12	8:9-10	
	13:18-23	4:13-20	8:11-15	
		4:21-25	8:16-18	
	13:24-30	4:26-29		
	13:31-32	4:30-32		13:18-19
	13:34-35	4:33-34		
8:18, 23-27		4:35-41	8:22-25	
8:28-34		5:1-17	8:26-37	
		5:18-20	8:37-39	
9:1, 18-26		5:21-43	8:40-56	
	13:54-58	6:1-6		4:16-30
10:1, 7-11, 14		6:7-11	9:1-5	
		6:12-13	9:6	
	14:1-2	6:14	9:7	
		6:15-16	9:8-9	
	14:3-12	6:17-29		
		6:30-31	9:10	
	14:13-14	6:32-34	9:11	
	14:15-21	6:35-44	9:12-17	
	14:22-23	6:45-52		
	14:34-36	6:53-56		
	15:1-20	7:1-23		
	15:21-28	7:24-30		
	(15:29-31)	7:31-37		
	15:32-38	8:1-9		
	16:1-4	8:10-13		
	16:5-12	8:14-21		12:1
		8:22-26		
	16:13-20	8:27-30	9:18-21	
	16:21	8:31	9:22	

Matthew	Mark	Luke
	16:22-23	8:32-33	
	16:24-25	8:34-35	9:23-24
	16:26	8:36-37	9:25
		8:38	9:26
	16:28	9:1	9:27
	17:1-8	9:2-8	9:28-36
	17:9	9:9-10	
	17:10-13	9:11-13	
	17:14-21	9:14-29	9:37-43
	17:22-23	9:30-32	9:43-45
	18:1-5	9:33-37	9:46-48
		9:37-40	9:48-50
10:42		9:41	
	18:6-9	9:42-48	
		9:49-50	
	19:1-9	10:1-12	
	19:13-14	10:13-14	18:15-16
		10:15	18:17
	19:15	10:16	
	19:16-26	10:17-27	18:18-27
	19:27, 29	10:28-30	18:28-30
	19:30	10:31	
	20:17-19	10:32-34	18:31-34
	20:20-28	10:35-45	
	20:29-34	10:46-52	18:35-43
	21:1-9	11:1-10	19:29-38
21:17-19		11:11-14	
	21:12	11:15-16	19:45
	21:13	11:17	19:46
		11:18	19:47-48
	21:20-22	11:19-26	
	21:23-27	11:27-33	20:1-8
	21:33-46	12:1-12	20:9-19
	22:15-22	12:13-17	20:20-26
	22:23-33	12:18-27	20:27-40
	22:34-40	12:28-34	
	22:41-46	12:35-37	19:41-44
	23:6,7,14	12:38-40	19:45-47
		12:41-44	21:1-4
	24:1-8	13:1-9	21:5-11
10:17-22	24:9, 14	13:9-12	21:12-16
	24:9-19	13:13-17	21:17-23
	24:20-25	13:18-23	21:24
	24:29-30	13:24-26	21:25-28
	24:31	13:27	
	24:32-35	13:28-31	21:29-33
	24:36	13:32	
		13:33-37	

The remarkable point is that the sequence of the used materials is not disrupted even though half of Mark's gospel has parallels either with Matthew or with Luke. By combining and compressing both parallel gospels the reader will obtain nearly the complete Gospel of Mark. Let us work through both Matthew and Luke pursuing the continuing thread of Mark's gospel.

A Telescopic Combination of Two Gospels

Mark 1–3:6. [The first two chapters in Mark are basically an example of single parallelism.] The first fifteen verses of Mark's Gospel contain in outline everything which has been recorded by Matthew and Luke about John the Baptist, about Jesus' baptism, and about his temptation. The beginning of Jesus' ministry is portrayed as in Matthew and includes the calling of the first disciples (1:16-20). Even though verses 21 and 22 remind the reader of the opening and closing statements of the Sermon on the Mount, they are the beginning of a consistent parallel with Luke and in deviation from Matthew up to Mark 3:6 and Luke 6:11. The evangelist Mark does eliminate from his Lukan materials the selection of the four apostles (Luke 5:1-11). The section Mark 2–3:6 has double parallels, at least in the sequence of materials.

Mark 3:7–6:6. [The next section demonstrates the "winding thread" of Mark's gospel by its frequent changes in parallelism.] Mark first follows Matthew (3:7-12) then Luke for the institution of the circle of the apostles (3:13-19). The series of parables (3:20–4:20) are again parallel to Matthew; then Mark shifts to Luke in order to include the parable of the "Lamp under a Bowl" (4:21-25). The closing section of this portion dealing with the journey to Gadara, the exorcism, the request of the healed man to follow Jesus, and the return to Galilee again follows Luke's text (Mark 4:35–5:43). When in 5:43 Mark leaves Luke, he immediately returns to Matthew in joining him in the account of the rejection at Nazareth (Mark 6:1-6).

Mark 6:7-34. [Mark 6 at first follows the pattern of alternate parallels.] The instruction of the twelve and their commission (6:7-13) is a pericope following Luke. The opinion of Herod about Jesus (6:14) is taken from Matthew, but the opinions of others about Christ (6:15, 16) are again from Luke. The decapitation of John the Baptist (6:17-29) follows the Matthean text, while the return of the disciples (6:30-31) is basically following Luke. Finally, the departure to a lonely place (6:32-34) borrows from Matthew. This pattern of alternate parallelism shows a combination of materials from both parallel gospels in swift succession. If these parallel sections from Matthew and Luke were telescoped together they would equal the material in Mark 6.

Mark 6:45–10:40. [The next major section of the gospel demonstrates Mark's method of deviation.] A long series of pericopes concluding with the healing of the blind man in Bethsaida (6:45–8:21) runs parallel to Matthew but is missing completely in Luke. This series is followed by a considerable portion of double parallels (8:27–10:40). In this last portion there are several deviations from Matthew in which he sides with Luke (see 8:38; 9:32-33); and conversely he shares his deviations from Luke with Matthew (see 8:32-33; 9:9-10; and 9:11-13).

Mark 10:1-52. Chapter 10 is significant as an illustration of insertions and omissions. Mark has inserted his admonition to receive the kingdom as a child (10:15) in the material he used from Matthew, namely, between Matthew 19:14 and 19:15. This insertion follows the example of Luke (see Luke 18:17). On the other hand Mark omits Matthew 19:30–20:17, again upon Luke's example. Mark then turns around and makes insertions in Luke's text, namely, between verses 17 and 18, 30 and 31, 34 and 35 of Luke 18; at this time Mark follows the example of Matthew. Also in his omissions from Luke's text Mark agrees with Matthew (see Luke 18:43 and 19:29).

Mark 12:1-44. The same pattern of insertions and omissions can be discerned in Mark 12. The question about the greatest commandment is inserted after the material from Luke 20:40 similar to Matthew. The warnings against the teachers of the Law (Mark 12:38-40) and the story of the widow's offering (Mark 12:41-44) agree in context and content with Luke. When Mark in these sections omits Matthew 21:28-33 and 22:1-15 we again find the same situation in the parallel places in Luke.

Mark 13:1-37. [The eschatological sermon in Mark provides a combination of various patterns. Only the insertions and omissions in view of the parallel texts will be considered here.] Following Luke, Mark inserts after Matthew 24:9 a statement about the persecution of the disciples. Mark then omits the words about the sudden appearance of Christ and about the general revelation of the parousia (Matt 24:26-28), again like Luke. However, Mark inserts some verses in Luke 21 between verses 24 and 25 dealing with the shortening of days and the appearance of false Messiahs (Mark 13:20-23). The same insertions can be found in Matthew!

These examples should illustrate first of all how Mark used his parallel materials. [He, indeed uses a variety of editorial methods. The single, the alternate, and the double parallels indicate he used both Matthew and Luke.] His insertions and omissions are significant illustrations of his editorial approach as well. Secondly it is important to observe that the sequence of Mark can be recovered from the parallels almost without interruption, as was demonstrated in chapter 3 above. The Marcan text winds its way as a thread through the Synoptic Gospels Matthew and Luke. This fact can be pursued throughout the Gospel of Mark, as was demonstrated by the followers of Griesbach, who unanimously concluded that Mark was composed by using both Matthew and Luke as his sources.

The Problem of Omissions

The Omissions by Matthew

The conclusion that Mark used Matthew and Luke has been combated vehemently by the advocates of the Marcan hypothesis.[2] The reason for this resistance basically was the conception these scholars had of the work of the evangelists and their idea of the respect they owed to these evangelists. [This presupposed conception caused a major grievance against the theory of Griesbach.] If Mark indeed had known the two other Synoptics and had used these as his sources, he supposedly would have been guilty of an inexcusable frivolity. On the other hand, the omission of so many passages from his sources, which generally were highly honored as authoritative gospels, would have been tantamount to an intentional rejection of authentic apostolic tradition. According to the proponents of the Marcan hypothesis such a course of action would have been inexplicable for the earliest era of Christianity because of the need to record the wealth of available tradition, while such procedure would have been unnecessary during a later period because of the existence of recognized well-informed gospels.

It is not my intention to refute this reasoning after what I have expounded about the implications of the brevity and the theology of the Gospel of Mark.[3] Furthermore, a study of the omissions of so many verses by Mark would require a special research project on the second gospel. At this juncture I intend rather to use the argument concerning the supposedly unlikely method of omissions against the advocates of the Marcan hypothesis themselves.

When a scholar rejects the possibility of omissions by the evangelist Mark and when this scholar refuses to give Mark the role of an epitomizer, he must proceed from a definite conviction concerning the evangelist and his predecessors. All advocates of the Marcan hypothesis share the persuasion that the evangelists intended to expand the materials of their predecessors rather than abridge them. The case presents itself, however, that Matthew as well as Luke also omitted pericopes from their presumed source. These omissions of course created major problems for the champions of the Marcan hypothesis. They were well aware that if their quantitative argument against Griesbach[4] and his

---

[2]See Eduard W. E. Reuss, "Études comparatives sur les trois premiers évangiles au point de vue de leurs rapports d'origine et de dépendance mutuelle," *Revue de théologie et de philosophie chrétienne* 11 (1856): 163ff. [this is the second part of Reuss's four-part study]; Bernhard Weiss, "Zur Entstehungsgeschichte der drei synoptischen Evangelien," *Theologische Studien und Kritiken* 34 (1861): 678ff.; Heinrich Julius Holtzmann, *Die synoptischen Evangelien: Ihr Ursprung und geschichtlicher Charakter* (Leipzig: W. Engelmann, 1863) 113ff.

[3]See above, 97-104, 139-42.

[4]See above, 23ff.

followers was to be sustained, they should not be guilty of the same supposedly inexcusable procedure by Matthew and Luke.

Reasons had to be devised, therefore, which would explain omissions of verses and whole paragraphs from Mark by Matthew and Luke. First of all the difference in the number of omissions in Matthew and Luke had to be a matter of consideration. It is clear which author had the strongest tendency to omit passages, because there is quite a disparity between Matthew and Luke in this respect. This observation, however, does not solve the problem itself. Whether one leaves out much or little material, the practice of omission is present in either case. The proponents of the Marcan hypothesis had to set themselves the task to explain away at least some of these omissions in both Matthew and Luke.

Reuss has given special attention to four pericopes, namely, the healing of the deaf and dumb man (Mark 7:32-37), the healing of the blind man at Bethsaida (Mark 8:22-26), the healing of the man with an evil spirit in Capernaum (Mark 1:23-28), and the story of the widow's mite (Mark 12:41-44). None of these stories is included in Matthew. The first two stories are similar in that Jesus used a medium, producing the effect of His authoritative word. Moreover, the blind man at Bethsaida only gradually received his ability to see. Reuss is of the opinion that both these aspects—mediation and gradual healing—could by Matthew be considered detrimental to belief in the miraculous power of Jesus.[5] [This could have been a valid reason for omission, according to Reuss. He feels supported by further similar omissions in Matthew,] namely, the case of the exorcism of the man at Gadara (Mark 5:7ff.) [where the evil spirits were sent into the swine], and the healing, as practiced by the disciples, by way of applying oil to the sick (Mark 6:13).

This rationalization of Matthew's omissions, however, still provides no answer for the two other pericopes mentioned by Reuss, [namely, the healing of the man with an evil spirit and the story of the widow's mite]. For these omissions he simply assumed the possibility that they had been left out in the editorial process of rearrangement and transformation.[6] I prefer not to formulate a value judgement on such conclusions; I merely want to remark that these explanations do not suffice in safeguarding Matthew from the suspicion of frivolous disregard for apostolic records.

[Moreover, if one assigns priority to Mark, there are several other omissions from the Marcan text by Matthew.] After the events at Capernaum [Mark has the following account which is not in Matthew]: Jesus left the town early in the

---

[5]Eduard W. E. Reuss, "Études comparatives sur les trois premiers évangiles au point de vue de leurs rapports d'origine et de dépendance mutuelle," *Nouvelle revue de théologie* (Deuxième série) 2 (1858): 28.

[6]Ibid., 38.

morning; when Simon and his companions overtook him and urged him to return, Jesus indicated his intention to preach also in other towns (Mark 1:35-38). Other examples are Matthew's three omissions in connection with the apostles: their mission (Mark 3:13-14), the report about their taking off for their own mission (Mark 6:12,13), and their return (Mark 6:30,31). Finally, according to Mark the man at Gadara requested to become a disciple of Jesus, which was followed by Jesus' reaction of sending him to his friends in order to proclaim what had happened to him (Mark 5:18-20). [This example of mission is also omitted by Matthew.]

[Several other incidental omissions could be mentioned.] The opinion of Herod about Jesus leads Mark to add the opinions of others and to restate emphatically the tetrarch's opinion (Mark 6:15, 16), which Matthew left out. Also left out are other passages such as the following: Jesus' reprimand of his disciple John when he was troubled over the fact that men who did not follow Jesus yet used his name in order to cast out demons (Mark 9:38-40); the scribe being near to the kingdom of God (Mark 12:32-34); the conclusion of the eschatological speech with the admonition to be alert (Mark 13:33-37). Finally, Mark 14:51-52 speaks about a young man running away and leaving behind his linen cloth.

Some of these passages do have parallels elsewhere in Matthew's gospel. For instance, Matthew does have an admonition to be alert and it also has the commission of the twelve in a certain form. Some verses occur at other locations in Matthew in more or less exact parallels. The proponents of the Marcan hypothesis have not failed to advance such facts and to present anything that can be used to demonstrate the presumed insignificance of the omitted passages and verses by Matthew.

There are, however, additional features missing in the stories that Matthew and Mark do have in common. Mark added circumstances to the miracle stories which enhanced their significance considerably. He depicted how the lame man was let down through the roof (Mark 2:4); he quoted the words of Jesus to the man with the withered hand after the latter had stepped into the center of the congregation (Mark 3:3-5a); he described the behavior of the demoniac, his name Legion, and his healing (Mark 5:3-10, 15-16); he recorded the dialogue about the touching of Jesus' garment after Jesus had perceived power had gone forth from him (Mark 5:29-33); he mentioned the messenger who announced to Jairus that his daughter had died (Mark 5:35-37); he related the conversation with the doubting father of the lunatic child (Mark 9:20-26); he recorded the circumstances of the disciples when they were untying the colt for the entry into Jerusalem (Mark 11:4-6); he reported the prediction by Jesus plus its fulfillment when the disciples had to find a place for the Last Supper (Mark 14:13-16). All of these contributing features were left out in the composition of the Gospel of Matthew.

But even more is left out! There is a whole series of verses dealing with crucial concepts like those of the lamp (Mark 4:21-25), of salt (Mark 9:49-50), of receiving the kingdom as a child (Mark 10:15) and of similar parabolic terms.[7] The total of these omitted passages and verses comprises one hundred verses which would be equal to the material for three chapters. All these verses have been more or less ignored by the adherents of the Marcan hypothesis. Their lack of effort to discover the motivations for these omissions clearly indicates their embarrassment about the issue of omissions by Matthew.

My question at this point is whether the recognition of omissions in the Gospel of Matthew does not completely undermine the Marcan hypothesis itself. When Matthew is allowed to summarize stories of Mark by omitting characteristic features, [he is clearly not contributing more detail]. When Matthew leaves out supposedly controversial passages for theological reasons, [how can he be safeguarded from the accusation of disrespect of apostolic tradition?] When Matthew overlooks materials in the process of arrangement and transformation, why could not Mark be given this liberty?

[In other words, the quantitative thesis holds to Marcan priority because it is the shortest gospel. Matthew and Luke supposedly have added to their sources. If the advocates of the Marcan hypothesis grant Matthew the liberty of omitting 100 verses from his source, why not allow Mark to leave out Matthean material and thereby allow Matthean priority as an option]? Indeed, a case could be made for the priority of that gospel which left out the least materials. But if the argument against the Griesbach theory hinges on the question of omission, the proponents of the Marcan hypothesis cannot pride themselves on being free from flaws in their construction of canon history.

The Omissions by Luke

Thus far I have mentioned only the omissions by Matthew from his presumed source of Mark. With respect to Luke's use of Mark "the number of omissions are minimal," according to Reuss.[8] The situation changes, however, when the omissions by Luke become a crucial argument for the opponents of the Griesbach theory. Indeed, the number of omitted passages by Luke is rather extensive.

The following pericopes of Mark are lacking in the Gospel of Luke: the growing seed (4:26-29); the execution of John the Baptist (6:19-29); Jesus' walking on the water (6:45-53); the healings in Gennesaret (6:54-56); the

---

[7]See Mark 1:45; 2:27; 8:38.
[8]Reuss, "Études comparatives," *Nouvelle revue* 2:27.

washing of hands and other purity laws (7:1-23); the Canaanite woman (7:24-30); the healing of the deaf and dumb man (7:31-47); the feeding of the four thousand (8:1-9); the request for a sign (8:10-13); the warning against the leaven of the Pharisees (8:14-21); the healing of the blind man at Bethsaida (8:22-26); the rebuke of Peter (8:32-33); the messianic secret (9:9-10); the expectation of the coming of Elijah (9:11-13); the causes for sin and the salt of faith (9:43-50); the teaching about divorce (10:1-12); the question by the sons of Zebedee (10:35-45); the withering of the fig tree (11:11-14, 19-26); the question about the greatest commandment (12:28-31); and the scribe near to the kingdom (12:32-34). Furthermore, a series of often-significant verses have been omitted by Luke.[9] These verses plus the passages listed in the footnote comprise one-fourth of the Gospel of Mark!

In this list of omitted materials I have not included the stories of Jesus' ministry in Nazareth (Mark 6:1-6), the miraculous catch of fishes (Mark 1:16-20), and the anointing in Bethany (Mark 14:3-9). These pericopes were not included because the proponents of the Marcan hypothesis consider the random parallels in Luke[10] as substitutes for similar pericopes in Mark and Matthew. I also did not mention the last three chapters of Mark which embody the passion narratives. The passion story is so radically different in Luke that Reuss had difficulty in discovering any points of agreement with the Gospel of Mark.

The fact that the remarkable parallelism between Mark and Luke comes totally to a halt with chapter fourteen of Mark led Reuss to a new presupposition. He presumed that Luke had a copy of Mark in which the passion narrative was missing; Reuss then developed the conjecture that the complete series of stories in Mark 6:45-8:26, which should occur between Luke 9:17 and 9:18, was also absent from his Marcan source. Reuss was somewhat surprised himself by this discovery.[11] He did not find many supporters among his associates. But their rejection of his conjectures required them to find other solutions to the problems identified by Reuss. The proponents of the Marcan hypothesis were confronted with the challenge to discover the motivations for the omission of so many parts of Mark by Luke.

It is most remarkable how scholars have explained the omission of the large section of Mark 6:45–8:26. After Holtzmann had attempted to find substituting parallels for some pericopes, he continued in the following manner:[12]

---

[9]Mark 1:5-6; 4:33-34; 8:37; 9:21-26, 28-29, 41; 10:16; 13:10, 18-20, 21-23, 32, 33-37.
[10]Luke 4:16-30; 5:1-11; 7:36-50.
[11]Reuss, "Études comparatives," *Nouvelle revue* 2:60.
[12]Holtzmann, *Die synoptischen Evangelien,* 105.

The omission of some sections between the feeding of the five thousand (Luke 9:10-17) and the profession by Peter (Luke 9:18-27) must have had a definite reason. From source A the following stories have not been adopted: Jesus' walking on the water, which seemed unnecessary after the other account of a storm (Luke 8:22-25); the miracles in the area of Gennesaret, which were skipped because Luke did not like condensed reports; furthermore, he assumed he had covered similar miracles in other places of his gospel; the washing of hands was left out in order to make space for a speech against legalism (Luke 11:37-52); the Canaanite woman was for Luke a dubious story which also had become superfluous after the account of the healing of the centurion's slave in Luke 7:2-10 justifying the acceptance of the gentiles, and after the account of Elijah's mission to Zarephath in Sidon (Luke 4:24-26); the healing of the deaf and dumb man was replaced by the story of the casting out of a demon that was dumb (Luke 11:14); the feeding of the 4,000 seemed of no importance after the story of the feeding of the 5,000 (Luke 9:10-17); the section on the signs of the times was substituted by the interpretation of the sign of Jonah in Luke 11:29-32 and by the section on the interpretation of signs (Luke 12:54-56); the warning against the leaven of the Pharisees was expressed later in Luke 12:1; the healing of the blind man in Bethsaida seemed an unnecessary introduction to the later story about the blind man in Jericho (Luke 18:35-43). The motivation for all these omissions was therefore obvious. It was the drive for efficiency which caused the leaving out of this series of pericopes.[13]

Many readers will still find this exposition an unusual solution for the complete omission of a section in Mark which is not only extensive but also forms a consecutive series. The reader will deem it a strange contrast, noticing the "drive for efficiency" in this section, against a backdrop [elsewhere in Luke] of an abundance of exorcisms, or resuscitations, of offenses against the Sabbath, of healings of lepers, and so forth. Perhaps the reader will side with Reuss, but then only as the lesser of two evils. [Ultimately one either accepts the arguments of Holtzmann or Reuss, or otherwise questions the whole proposition of Marcan priority].

My query again is—if the proponents of the Marcan hypothesis miss a considerable portion in Matthew and almost half of their Marcan source in Luke—whether they are not actually denying the whole concept of quantitative canon criticism. When these scholars have to conjecture all kinds of meaningless reasons to explain the disturbing reality of omissions, their Marcan hypothesis

---

[13]See also Lambrechts's dissertation, "An exegetical-theological study in which the diversity of messages and narrations indicates Luke's use of Mark's text," *Specimen exegetico-theologicum,* 229ff.

does not seem to be able to explain the actual relationship of the gospels. When they take refuge in presuppositions about the history of the Gospel of Mark, these are then rejected and refuted even by their own partisans.

If the quantitative hypothesis has become untenable, its argument against the Griesbach hypothesis [is weakened and] it might be advisable to discontinue it. But in this case the Marcan hypothesis has lost a strong argument. Nicolas indeed was correct when he denied the advocates of the Marcan hypothesis the satisfaction of a final solution to the issue of canon history.[14] If there remains a certain uneasiness within the circle of the advocates of the Marcan hypothesis, how much less can they satisfy the queries of their opponents!

The Alternating Omissions by Matthew and Luke

At one point especially, the Marcan hypothesis cannot give a satisfactory solution. Let us imagine two evangelists drawing upon the same source. For personal reasons or because of a peculiar procedure of composition, both exercise a certain liberty. Repeatedly they seemingly intentionally leave out important paragraphs. According to the proponents of the Marcan hypothesis, they are unfamiliar with one another's work. Yet it is established that these evangelists never found occasion to leave out, with few exceptions, the *same* pericopes. Furthermore, we see that their gospels have alternately adopted materials from their presumed common source in such a way that they supplement each other. After all these observations, the reader must feel urged to come to the conclusion that he is encountering here an unusual kind of coincidence. One would sooner believe the story of the seventy rabbis individually translating the Torah into the same Septuagint text [than this coincidence of alternating source references by authors who were not familiar with each other's work].

The relation of Matthew and Luke is, indeed, one of alternating parallels, as was demonstrated in the synoptic chart above.[15] A good example of such parallels is Mark 6 [of which Matthew allegedly adopted or rejected the following numbered pericopes:] (1) He considered the first six verses of this chapter useful because they dealt with Jesus' ministry in Nazareth; (2) the following seven verses about the mission and instruction of the twelve were supposedly less suitable because of his own extensive missionary speech in chapter 10; (3) Matthew then used verse 14 which reported how Herod had heard about Jesus and what his opinion about Jesus was; the following statements of opinion by others seemed superfluous because of the various opinions mentioned as an introduction to the profession of faith by Peter in Matthew 16:14-20; (4) the

---

[14]See above, 61-63.
[15]See above, 151-53.

verses dealing with the execution of John the Baptist were again appropriate after the reference to Herod's assumption about Jesus as John the Baptist having returned to life (Mark 6:17-29); (5) Matthew then had to leave out the return of the exhausted disciples (Mark 6:30-31) because he had not adopted their commission from an earlier location in Mark 3:13-14; (6) the departure to a lonely place (Mark 6:32-34) could not be omitted, however, in connection with the feeding of the multitude. In such manner one could rationalize Matthew's procedure of alternately omitting and including some verses from the Marcan account in the arrangement of his own gospel.

Let us now consider the Gospel of Luke in its use of the sixth chapter of Mark: (1) the ministry in Nazareth (Mark 6:1-6) could be left out since it had been mentioned before in Luke 4:16-30; (2) the mission of the twelve could be included as a balance to the mission of the seventy later on (Luke 10:1-12); (3) the various opinions about Jesus could nicely be inserted in association with Herod's opinion (Mark 6:14-15); (4) the execution of John the Baptist seems unnecessary after the account of his imprisonment in Luke 3:19-20; at this location Luke had not mentioned Herod's murderous plot specifically but he had stated in general terms "all the evil things that Herod had done" (Luke 3:19); (5) the return of the disciples was very appropriate after the statement concerning their mission in Luke 9:10; (6) the departure to a lonely place, however, Luke did not want to depict in the same fashion as Matthew did in making use of Mark's words. Thus we find that Luke adopted from Mark 6 the pericopes 2, 3b, and 5, while Matthew incorporated the pericopes 1, 4, and 6. This certainly should be called a case of coincidence!

As a second example I would like to use Mark 9:33-50 for which the parallels in Matthew and Luke are quite complicated (Matt 18:1-9; Luke 9:46-50). (1) Mark introduced this section by the question of Jesus after they had entered a house in Capernaum. Jesus asked them what they were discussing on the way (9:33). The disciples realized he knew about the substance of their conversation and therefore kept silent. Jesus then taught them that if anyone wanted to be first in the Kingdom of heaven he had to be willing to be a servant (Mark 9:34-35). (2) Thereupon Jesus placed a child in their midst in order to exhort them to a childlike love (Mark 9:36). This exhortation was underscored by the affirmation that the acceptance of a child was equal to the acceptance of Christ or of his sender (Mark 9:37). (3) Thirdly, Jesus reprimanded his disciple John who only wanted to allow the followers of Jesus to cast out demons in Christ's name (Mark 9:38-41). (4) In the next pericope Jesus condemned as an abomination to cause little children to sin; and (5) he continued with the words that it would be better to miss a hand or a foot causing sin than to be thrown into hell (Mark 9:42-48). (6) Finally, Mark added two verses about the true salt of faith (9:49-50). There is no inner connection between the first and second pericopes; the association between the second and third pericopes could be the words "in the name"; between pericopes three and four there again is no connection; and the connecting link between four and five is in the verb "causing to stumble" (σκανδαλίζειν).

The parallel passage in Matthew 18 has a long series of words, all connected by word association. (1) In Matthew Jesus begins with an admonition to humility (Matt 18:1ff.). (2) Also in this chapter a child is placed in the center of the group of disciples who are admonished by Jesus to become like children (Matt 18:4-5). (4) [After skipping Mark's third pericope about Jesus' reprimand of John] Matthew records Jesus' warning against causing "one of these little ones" to sin (Matt 18:6-7). The term "causing to stumble" becomes a connecting link with the one who causes to sin, and (5) with the hand, foot, and eye that have the potential to cause sin (Matt 18:7-9). Matthew adds a new statement about despising "one of these little ones" (Matt 18:10), which evokes the thought about the value of these little ones, namely, that none of these should perish (Matt 18:14). So the parallel section from Matthew moves from one word association to the next. From the pericopes in Matthew 18 the ones numbered 1, 2, 4, and 5 correspond to those in Mark 9, while the third pericope is omitted by Matthew.

Luke has only two pericopes corresponding with the materials of Mark 9:33-50. They are Luke 9:46-48 dealing with the acceptance of a child parallel to Mark's second pericope (Mark 9:36), while the other passage is Luke 9:49-50 refuting John's notion about the casting out of demons (Mark 9:38-41). This second parallel corresponds to Mark's third pericope which Matthew omitted. Conversely Luke rejected pericopes four and five which Matthew adopted for his text (Mark 9:42-50). [Again we can establish a certain alternation of parallels: Luke used pericopes 2 and 3, while Matthew used 1, 2, 4, and 5.]

[The second pericope is common to both Matthew and Luke but is interpreted differently.] Matthew stressed the words about humility from Mark's first pericope (Mark 9:33-35) and used the second pericope about the child as a model of humility. Luke, on the other hand, made the acceptance of the kingdom his key idea and integrated the second pericope into the exhortation of receiving Jesus and the one sending him (Luke 9:48). The reference to the ambition among the disciples has been replaced in Luke by a contrast of great and small in terms of accepting Christ or not.

Hermann Weisse asked ironically, "After all this, what do those theologians say who [with Griesbach] consider Mark the successor of the other gospels?"[16] We would concede that such dividing of the Marcan text by Matthew and Luke is strange, indeed, especially if they did not know one another's work. It would

---

[16]Christian Hermann Weisse, *Die evangelische Geschichte: Kritisch und philosophisch bearbeitet,* 2 vols. (Leipzig: Breitkopf und Härtel, 1838) 1:73-79.

be even more peculiar if they did know one another's gospel. But we would maintain that on the basis of the examples above the advocates of the Marcan hypothesis have no right to reject offhand the Griesbach hypothesis. The Marcan hypothesis apparently has not been capable of explaining the omission by Matthew and Luke of numerous components from their so-called common source Mark. The champions of the Marcan hypothesis cannot account for the unusual coincidence of the alternate omissions by both Matthew and Luke. [The problem of omission combined with the phenomenon of alternation is the Achilles heal of the Marcan hypothesis, whereas, though there remains the problem of omission on the view that Mark is third, the phenomenon of alternation is readily explained if Mark is third.]

The Issue of Mark's Use of Sources

Mark's Independent Approach

The critics of the Griesbach theory have used a second major argument in addition to their quantitative theory. The peculiar use by Mark of his two synoptic sources was for them an occasion of hilarity. There is a sense of exaggeration in the notion these scholars formed of Mark's use of his sources. They speak of a "romping around"[17] from one source to the other. With amusement they quote Lachmann's assertion that Mark was skipping around in the most unusual manner and that he wandered through the Gospels of Matthew and Luke without any design.[18]

These critics aver that Mark never used his sources simultaneously and that his skipping from one source to the other was occasioned by mere accidental circumstances. Such a notion of Mark's literary work excludes him from being considered a creative author. His "laborious turning over of pages"[19] is a typical expression by the critics of the Griesbach interpretation of Mark's work. These critics point to unexpected insertions from Matthew where the context has been provided by Luke and the other way around. These opponents cynically ask whether it would not have been burdensome for Mark to abruptly consult another source at the moment when he was deeply absorbed in one document.

The critics continue querying why the result of Mark's work turned out in this form rather than into some other structure. Why did Mark not simply leave out the complete Sermon on the Mount [instead of just quoting the opening and

---

[17]The German is "herumtümmeln."
[18]Karl Lachmann, "De ordine narrationum in Evangeliis synopticis," *Theologische Studien und Kritiken* 8 (1835): 577.
[19]The German is "mühevoll blättern."

closing verse,] they ask. Why did he not continue with Matthew's text rather than switching over to Luke? Why did he begin with Luke 4:31 [Jesus at Capernaum] rather than with 4:16 [dealing with Jesus' rejection at Nazareth]? And many similar questions are being raised. These opponents of the Griesbach hypothesis point to the number of stories that are unique for Mark in order to derive from this the conclusion that Mark was not a dependent author and that his work does not show a major dependence on sources. After all these queries about the procedure of Mark's work as Griesbach viewed it, the critics rhetorically ask, "When has anyone ever written this way?" They conclude with the outcry, "That goes against the grain for me!"

This exaggerated and inaccurate presentation by the opponents challenges us to respond to the issue of authorship. Indeed, the notions of "laborious turning over of pages," of "being absorbed," and of being just a copyist should be kept far from any evangelist. The reader should try to imagine the situation of these evangelists! They were men with intense interest in their church, they had a deep concern for theological and practical considerations. Men who were involved in these concerns should be respected highly as leaders among the early Christians.

The evangelists must have been brilliant minds who knew how to wield their pen for the sake of the church and its members. In the public worship services they were frequently engaged in the reading and the exposition of the Scriptures. The sacred scrolls must have been the focus of their concern. If there were scrolls available they will not have missed an opportunity to acquaint themselves with these. The evangelists must have been eminently familiar with the religious literature of their day. Whenever there were authoritative gospels available they certainly would have read and reread these.

The memory of the early Christian scholars had not yet been weakened by an overload of literary studies. It was for them, therefore, easier to absorb and retain the content of a gospel. They were saturated by its message and their lives were influenced by each detail of these gospels. The evangelists were the theologians of their day. Though the study and the work habits of the authors in those days had their peculiar character, the evangelists were excellent exponents of their craft. Even though it may be difficult for posterity to form an idea of their motivations [we may presume that] these authors were truly dedicated men.

Even if a writer remains close to his sources, he should not be regarded as a slavish copyist. If the reader wants samples of the way sources were used, he merely should compare parallel quotations by the evangelists from the Old Testament. Their deviations in form betray a thorough knowledge of the original text, irrespective of which evangelist should be held to have priority. It might be possible to demonstrate the same freedom in the use of other sources, for instance the document of the Wisdom of God.[20]

An example that strikingly characterizes the independence as well as the dependence of Matthew and Mark are the accounts of the feeding of the multitude, again irrespective of the priority of either author. After the feeding of the 5,000 (Matt 14:13-21 and Mark 6:30-44) the pieces that were left over were gathered in baskets (κόφινοι) in both accounts; after the feeding of the 4,000 (Matt 15:32-39 and Mark 8:1-10) another Greek word was used for the baskets (σπυρίδες). Both accounts agree in their description that the 5,000 sat down "upon the green grass," while the 4,000 sat down "on the ground." In the first story about the 5,000 Jesus "looked up to heaven" in blessing the loaves, while in the second story neither Matthew nor Mark make reference to a blessing but rather to a giving of thanks (εὐχαριστήσας).

Thus Matthew and Mark followed one another faithfully even in minute details, yet each of them kept his own characteristic approach. Matthew, for instance, remained faithful to himself by consistently using the perfect tense of the verb "to give" (ἔδωκεν), while Mark preferred to use the imperfect tense (ἐδίδου). In Matthew and Mark the crowd was identified as "those who ate" but they use different verbs for the word "to eat."[21] In Matthew's stories the disciples gave the morsels to the crowd, while Mark had Jesus give them to the disciples "in order that they set them before the people." Mark consistently mentions the loaves and the fish while Matthew only mentions the loaves in the remainder of his stories.

There are more distinctions between the two accounts in Matthew and Mark. When Jesus, because of a misunderstanding later on referred to both events, the same distinction between the two Greek words for basket is used in Matthew 16:9-10 as well as in Mark 8:19-20. Mark, furthermore, added detail by referring to "baskets full of broken pieces" and "the broken pieces, seven baskets full," but stays with the distinctions κόφινοι and σπυρίδες used in 6:43 and 8:8.

If one does not want to assume that authors compared their text word for word with their sources as well as with their own earlier statements one must arrive at the following procedure. On the basis of our example about the feeding of the multitude in Matthew and Mark we must assume a certain time lapse between what the author read in his source and what he wrote down in his gospel; this intermediate period gave occasion for recollections and meditations, [which

---

[20]Cf. Matt 23:34-39 with Luke 11:49-51; 13:34-35.

[21]Matthew used ἐσθίοντες while Mark used φαγόντες. [In previous verses where they are eating, both Matthew and Mark use the same verb. When they refer to the crowd as those who ate, Matthew changes verb forms; Mark does not. However, in current critical texts only Matthew refers to the crowd as those who ate; in Mark the phrase is relegated to the apparatus. Meijboom used some form of the Stephanus/Elzevir Greek text. —ed.]

then were inserted in the final text]. In this way the subject matter of the sources was rendered with a certain freedom in spite of adherence to the original text.

This relative freedom of the evangelists in the assimilation of the materials from their sources can be noticed everywhere in their work. One only needs to look at any random page of the Synoptic gospels and carefully compare its parallels. The reader will immediately observe how on the one hand peculiar constructions and turns of phrases have unnoticeably persisted in the new text and how even sudden breaks of thought in the middle of a sentence have been taken over. On the other hand the agreement between source and new text is seldom exactly the same without any discrepancy. The new text always is a new version; it may be a peculiar text but it is never a thoughtless copy of the original.

If these observations are applied to our discussion of canon history we would insist that the evangelists must be assigned a certain independence in any case. They were so familiar with their sources and so at home in their literature that they could enrich them with their own insight. They certainly proceeded with ample consideration and mature deliberation. This profile of the authors is to be given preference above the caricature given by scholars who represent the evangelists as "being absorbed" in the writings on their desk, laboriously trying to find their way among their massive notes and documents, or meandering through their sources led by occasional circumstances.

Mark's Coordinating Approach

The work of the evangelists was, indeed, a result of mature thought. What would be more normal than an author wanting to develop a third document making use of two gospels of which each had its own characteristic approach in form and content. This author most likely would intend to avoid the sharp theological edges of both the other gospels by bringing together the essential elements or the parts which were of more universal importance. He would try to present the various stories from a new perspective and with new vitality. He would attempt to give his gospel an integrated unity by presenting it in a new, though literary structure. Finally, he would feel impelled to meet specific needs which could not be met by the earlier writings. [All of this could very well have been Mark's intention.]

It is incorrect to assert that Mark followed only one source at a time. Each pericope with double parallels shows clearly the influence of both sources, which demonstrates how the author has assimilated his materials. It is furthermore inaccurate to contend that Mark shows a careless attitude in dealing with factual statements while being meticulous in his structure. The author should not be blamed that he intentionally merged the style and idiom of both sources. His detailed description of circumstances should not be attributed to a predilection for particulars. The merging of source materials was characteristic for authors of those days. The emphasis on detail is part of the new structure by which Mark planned to revitalize the traditional materials.

Why should the Gospel of Mark have to show obscure passages, traces of previous transitions, and signs of interrupted context in order to be acceptable as a later author? In the next chapter we will demonstrate that Mark does indeed have its obscure passages. The argument based upon signs of an interrupted context assumes that the sources had a harmonious text composition. What texts are available in Matthew and Luke that are not susceptible to being interrupted without damage? Finally, we should not overlook the fact that abrupt transitions were not frequent in Mark since the evangelist expended so much care on harmonious unity.

But [even if we assume a continuous text in Mark,] we can meet the challenge of proving some abrupt transitions. [Let us follow the sequence of a few events in Matthew and then compare these with parallels in Luke and Mark.] The author of the first gospel tells us in outline form how Jesus after his first appearance and the election of his apostles (1) traveled through Galilee (Matt 4:23). To a large crowd, which had followed him from all around, Jesus then proclaimed the Sermon on the Mount. As soon as Jesus had come down the mountain the crowds followed him again. (2) At this point in time a leper asked him for cleansing. Jesus satisfied his desire by healing him. (3) "As he entered Capernaum" (Matt 8:5), a Centurion besought his help for his paralyzed son (Matt 8:6). After some other healings Jesus went over to the other side of the lake to the country of the Gadarenes. (4) In Matt 9:1 Jesus returned "to his own city" where he granted forgiveness to a paralytic man.

Luke has three events in common with Matthew. The author of the third gospel has (1) Jesus traveling around the towns of Galilee (Luke 4:42ff.); (2) "while he was in one of the cities" a man full of leprosy requested his help (Luke 5:12); (3) then "on one of those days" a paralyzed man was brought to him (Luke 5:17). Both Matthew and Luke give a few examples of Jesus' ministry and connect them with appropriate transitions. There is nothing strange in the fact that only a few select events are touched upon.

In Mark the events are closely knit together—as I have demonstrated earlier[22] leaving much room for interruptions. After the verses that, like Matthew and Luke, speak of (1) his traveling around (Mark 1:35-39), there follows a statement of transition, (2) "And a leper came to him." This transition agrees with Matthew who also lets this incident follow the initial period of traveling ministry (see Matt 8:2). Luke simply indicates "while he was in one of the cities" (Luke 5:12). After this event Mark immediately continues with the words

---

[22]See above, 111ff.

"And when he returned to Capernaum" (Mark 2:1). This transition introducing (4) the story of the paralyzed man demonstrates how Mark has tightened the context. In Matthew the return to Capernaum introduces (3) the story of the centurion (Matt 8:5), while (4) the healing of the lame man is introduced by the words of Matthew 9:1: "he came to his own city." This demonstrates that Mark has used Matthew's introduction to the third pericope for the story of Matthew's pericope. Leaving out Matthew's third pericope means that Mark follows Luke at this point.

[Evidence of an interrupted context is found also in Mark 6.] The author of the second gospel does not explain the need for the feeding of the 5,000 because of a long journey along the lake northwards. According to Luke this journey was used for teaching the multitude and ended with the feeding in Bethsaida (Luke 9:10). In following Matthew, however, Mark locates the feeding of the 5,000 across the lake, although he retains Bethsaida as the final destination after the storm and Jesus' walking on the sea (Mark 6:45). Because of his combination of materials, Mark has Jesus cross the lake to Bethsaida on the western shore, while the boat lands, as in Matthew's account, on the eastern shore at Gennesaret (Mark 6:53; Matt 14:34).

[Other obscure passages occur because of a misunderstanding of the source materials.] After the feeding of the 4,000, according to Matthew 15:39, Jesus went to the regions of Magadan. According to Mark, however, Jesus went to Dalmanutha (Mark 8:10). Since no one knows where Dalmanutha is[23] we are free to bring it in relation with some other location. Mark expressly states that the return from the area of Tyre and Sidon took place "through the region of the Decapolis" (Mark 7:31). We also notice that Mark has associated Matthew's report about the disciples reaching "the other side" (Matt 16:5) with the preceding words "he left them and departed" (Matt 16:4) rather than with the journey by boat mentioned in Matthew 15:39. Because of this misunderstanding Mark developed two journeys across the lake (Mark 8:10 and 8:13,14). In consequence he needed two places of destination: Dalmanutha on the eastern shore and Magadan on the western shore.

[Disparities occur when Mark uses a unique story and attempts to fit this into the general synoptic context.] He narrates the healing of a blind man (Mark 8:22-26), a story that has no parallels in either Matthew or Luke. Mark chose Bethsaida as location for this miracle, most likely through the influence of Luke who in 9:10 mentions healings and a message about the Kingdom of God in this town. Luke continues to use Bethsaida as the place for the first profession of faith by Peter (Luke 9:18-22). Mark, however, follows Matthew at this point and

---

[23]Some suggestions can be found in Heinrich Ewald, *Die drei ersten Evangelien übersetzt und erklärt,* 2 vols. (Göttingen: Vandenhoeck & Ruprecht, 1850) 268.

identifies the area of Caesarea Philippi as the location of the first profession of faith. Thus Mark has used Bethsaida twice, once in 6:45 and then in 8:22.

[Somewhat peculiar introductory phrases result when Mark leaves out a story that is not considered relevant to his readers.] He tells how Jesus asked his disciples what they were discussing "on the way" (9:33). To use a long road through Galilee up to Capernaum as the setting for a single ambitious argument is carrying it a little too far. That the question itself was asked in a house is typical for Mark and is consistent with the arrival in Capernaum, mentioned deliberately by Mark. In Matthew, by contrast, the complete narrative is recorded including the question concerning the temple tax as well as the question concerning the Kingdom (Matt 17:24-18:5).

Matthew's introductory words, "when they came to Capernaum," are used also by Mark. Matthew's sequence of events is in keeping with his introduction while the same opening words in Mark are a somewhat peculiar setting for just the one question concerning the Kingdom. It is rather obvious that Mark wanted to leave out the question about the temple tax as being of too much temporal and local interest [for Gentile readers].

[At other times a peculiar introductory phrase is caused by Mark's drive for concreteness while rejecting the general description of his sources.] He introduces, for instance, the feeding of the 4,000 with the words "In those days, when again a great crowd had gathered, and they had nothing to eat" (Mark 8:1). This is an elaboration in order to restore the context that had been disrupted by the specific story about the healing of a deaf and dumb man instead of Matthew's general report of healings (Matt 15:29-31). Matthew depicts the hills of Galilee as the backdrop for the blessings coming through Israel's Messiah, and he portrays the crowds bringing all kinds of sick people and praising God for their healing. All of this has been eliminated by Mark because of his report of a specific case. This procedure necessitated, however, an explanation for the "hungry crowd."

I could go on like this in order to prove that not only transitions and introductions have been changed by Mark, but that there are even traces of disruption of the context in spite of the fact that Mark took great care to avoid these. [The gospels are free arrangements of events and speeches and Mark followed that pattern. All of these comparative studies have demonstrated Mark's coordinating approach indicating Marcan posteriority rather than Marcan priority.]

The Motivations of Mark

What do the critics want with questions like Why did Mark formulate his gospel this way and not differently? Why was Mark not always equally elaborate, or why did Mark, the epitomizer, apply so much effort on detail? Why this particular sequence of his stories, or why his use of parallels in this specific way and not differently? To give an exposition of the motivations of Mark at each instance is not part of the objective of this dissertation [but the following case studies can provide a general idea].

First of all, we cannot expect to track down the motivations behind each particular story. We cannot presume to penetrate the inner mind of the author either. The demand that such analysis should be possible, and that potentially an answer could be found for each question, is very presumptuous indeed. Such an attitude among our opponents can only be explained by their overbearing posture. Posterity is not to judge what an author from early times could and should have written differently. If this is true in general how much more so for gospel literature in particular. What would the proponents of the Marcan hypothesis say when we would direct our criticisms and questions so bluntly to them? When we would cry out in exaggeration how difficult it must have been for Matthew shifting abruptly to Mark while he was engrossed in his Logia source?

[A glance at Matthew 8 raises many questions about the motivations behind his selection of materials.] Having just finished the Sermon on the Mount, Matthew had to insert a few words from another source (Matt 8:1). [Up to 4:22 Matthew had followed his Marcan source to Mark 1:20.] In chapter 8 Matthew picks up his source but skips several stories of Mark in order to join him again with the healing of the leper (Matt 8:2-4; Mark 1:40-45). A few verses later (Matt 8:14-15) Matthew backs up in his source material to Mark 1:29 and not to Mark 1:20 where he had left off. Then, in chapter nine, Matthew jumps forward after having incorporated some pericopes from another source to Mark's story of the healing of the paralytic man in Capernaum (Matt 9:1-8; Mark 2:1-12).

That must have been quite a tumbling through his sources for Matthew going back and forth from one document to the other! The many studies by our opponents, which are intended to explain this rearrangement by Matthew, prove only that apparently also within the circle of the champions of the Marcan hypothesis no unanimity has been reached [regarding Matthew's use of his sources]. The fact is that the proponents of the Marcan hypothesis cannot find the answers to the questions raised by friend and foe alike.

[Because of this state of affairs in Matthew] we could expect answers from our opponents on questions like these: why Matthew attempted to embellish the stories of Mark in spite of the fact that he adopted these in abbreviated form; why an evangelist like Matthew who so frivolously treated information and important facts from his apostolic sources, attempted scrupulously to weave together the terminology of both his sources.

Indeed, it is again a matter of degree. The great resistance our adversaries have against the notion that Mark could have used both of the other Synoptics as sources can be explained from the fact that they observe the same issue in Mark more clearly than in Matthew. The issue centers on the nature and origin of gospel literature as was mentioned above.[24] The proponents of the Marcan hypothesis do not want to adopt our position because it conflicts with their basic assumption of the quantitative theory. Yet their own hypothesis is more than half dependent upon an explanation of the quantitative phenomena [of abbreviation and omission].

There is a creative independence combined with a high degree of dependence in the way the evangelists used their sources. These authors conflate passages of smaller size and leave relatively few portions unused. They edit larger sections with great freedom while smaller units are adopted almost verbally. Such literary methods are marks of relative independence, which we must assume for Mark too. Mark's use of the parallel gospels in this manner may be a beam in the eyes of our opponents; the friends of the Marcan hypothesis are not free from the splinter in their own eye either.

The truth is that no hypothesis can be devised that would not have to deal with the problem of editing documents, since it is essential to the character of gospel literature. This conviction, however, is not appreciated by the champions of the Marcan hypothesis, because it would acknowledge an attitude in the evangelists different from their persuasion. They would have to recognize a totally different motivation from the notion they have of the early witnesses of salvation history. No wonder that our view appears to them foggy and negative. Our opponents cannot reconcile themselves with the results of clear arguments based upon the phenomena of the text.

[The problem of omissions as well as the free use of sources are two characteristics common to each of the synoptic authors.] Also the advocates of the Marcan hypothesis have to incorporate in their theory these characteristics which they consider objectionable. The arrangement of materials and the transitional formulas necessitate a recognition of Mark's late origin, while an argument for an early date is unsatisfactory. Even if they assume that Matthew and Luke have used Mark as their source they still have to deal with the freedom with which [these two synoptic gospels used their Marcan] source. There is an abundance of expressions and insertions, and a more limited number of rearrangements and inconsistencies which manifest the literary license of these authors.

It remains remarkable, even peculiar, that both compilers, Matthew and Luke, hardly ever inserted or omitted the same passage. They rather give the appearance of careful collaboration in their process of compilation. The same can be said about the arrangement of material. Matthew accepted the sequence of Mark 1:1-20 while Luke retained the last four verses for another context. When

---

[24]See above, 156ff.

Luke agreed completely with the long series of events recorded in Mark 1:21 until 3:6, Matthew disagreed with this sequence. The latter could use only a few clusters of events without rearrangements; for the rest this long series of events was chopped up in Matthew by transpositions and insertions.

After Mark 3:6 Matthew again was satisfied with the sequence of his presumed source. Mark's third and fourth chapter could be used by Matthew almost completely and in the same sequence, while Luke inverted the general report of Mark 3:7-12 and the following pericope. Luke transferred the covenant with Satan (Mark 3:20-27) to his eleventh chapter, the visit of Jesus' relatives (Mark 3:31-35) to his eighth chapter, and the parable of the mustard seed (Mark 4:30-33) was moved to the thirteenth chapter. [Then follows a shift in parallelism] when Matthew moved the material of Mark 4:35–5:43 to an earlier context, while at this time Luke left the sequence untouched. So each of the compilers rearranged the materials that the other had adopted without change. Depending on their motives, the evangelists freely reversed and replaced the passages from their sources. They never rearranged the same pericopes simultaneously, however, even though their rearrangements followed one another immediately.

We can ascertain a similar state of affairs at less important points. When Luke inverted the sequence of the conversations at the Last Supper, Matthew found no reason for change (Luke 22:32-39; Matt 26:30-35). Luke gave a deviating version for Jesus' ministry in Nazareth (Luke 4:16-30), the selection of the apostles (Luke 5:1-11), and the anointing (Luke 7:36-50), while Matthew again retained the Marcan text. On the other hand Luke adopted the list of names of the apostles at the same place (Luke 6:13-16), the commission (Luke 9:1-6), and the prediction of persecution as part of the eschatological sermon (Luke 12:1-12), which, for a variety of reasons, were moved by Matthew to other places.

Such a shifting interdependence of two evangelists in relation to their source is highly peculiar. These authors were independently taking the liberty of free arrangement and yet seemed to collaborate in their work. The rearrangements, insertions and omissions are evidence of different objectives, which clearly indicate that the authors have no knowledge of each other's work. [It is peculiar that either Matthew or Luke will begin quoting Mark when the other stops. It seems more likely that Mark is the coordinating author using his two sources Matthew and Luke alternately. In fact,] when the Marcan parallels in these two gospels are telescoped into one document an almost complete gospel of Mark emerges in form as well as in content. These facts of compilation remain an unexplainable enigma for the proponents of the Marcan hypothesis. The data of text compilation definitely point to a later origin of the second gospel and are therefore a strong argument against the Marcan hypothesis.

Chapter 7

Text Studies in Mark

Text Conflations

The Galilean Period

The following chapter will deal with details of Mark's text. In the same manner as we investigated the issue from a theological[1] and literary[2] viewpoint, we will now explore to what extent arguments arise against the Marcan hypothesis from a linguistic perspective. This will bring us automatically to an analysis of the peculiar relation of Mark's text to the readings in both other Synoptic Gospels. Mark's text shows so many points of agreement with both parallel gospels that its style has been claimed to have a "combined nature."[3] Here again the most characteristic feature is the double agreement of Mark's text with the other two Synoptics, which has caused the followers of Griesbach to recognize its *posteriority* rather than its *priority* among the Synoptic Gospels.

The reader will repeatedly be struck by Mark's text merging the riches of both other synoptic versions. When comparing three parallel pericopes verbally one will observe locations where, in a few phrases, the words and turns of phrases of both parallels are united into one text. [It is, of course, easier to understand how two versions were conflated into one than how the components of one text were distributed over two later documents.] A strange coincidence must have prevailed in order to explain how the expressions of Mark would independently have been so neatly divided by Matthew and Luke [so that Luke would have used from Mark what Matthew accidently had left untouched and vice versa]. In the present chapter I want to present the main examples of Mark's conflations [from the Galilean as well as from the Judean period]. After this I will discuss the significance that proponents of the Marcan hypothesis attribute to this phenomenon.

The prophecy of the mightier Messiah who was to come after John the Baptist is an example of such a conflation. The first words of the proclamation in

---

[1]See chap. 5, above.
[2]See chap. 6, above.
[3]In German "combinierte Beschaffenheit."

Mark 1:7, "After me," are taken from Matthew. The following words, "comes he who is mightier than I," are adopted from Luke. Also the loftiness of the coming one agrees with Luke's description: "the thong of whose sandals I am not worthy to untie." [Thus elements of both Matthew and Luke are merged into one Marcan text.]

[An example involving theological content is found in the baptismal account.] Matthew reports that Jesus "saw the Spirit of God descending like a dove." Jesus is the subject of the vision. The following statement, "This is my beloved Son" (Matt 3:17), does not explicitly state whether Jesus or the general public was the subject of the hearing of these words. Luke, however, states as an objective fact that the Spirit was descending and the words were being spoken (Luke 3:22). Mark combines both the subjective and the objective emphases. In agreement with Matthew he states in 1:10 that Jesus was the subject of the vision, while in 1:11 Mark records the words from heaven as an objective affirmation: "Thou art my beloved Son; with thee I am well pleased."[4]

[Another conflation is found in Mark 1:21-22 dealing with Jesus' teaching.] Mark 1:21 states, "And they went into Capernaum; and immediately on the Sabbath he entered the synagogue and taught." This verse uses the same verbs for "going into" or "entering" as Luke 4:30-31; the teaching in the synagogue may be a reminder of Matt 4:23, which is the introduction to the Sermon on the Mount; the response of the astonishment to Jesus' teaching in Mark 1:22 agrees with Luke 4:32; and the teaching with authority, "and not as the scribes" is taken from Matt 7:29, the conclusion of the Sermon on the Mount.

Conflations can cause inconsistencies, as this last example may illustrate.[5] The context in Mark has been adjusted to Luke to indicate a wider time span than Matthew, as is obvious from the plural "on the Sabbaths." Even though Mark adopts this plural he changes the meaning of these verses to a description of a singular teaching event by adding the words "immediately" and "he entered the synagogue." The response of astonishment about his authority changes, therefore, from a public response to a particular reaction in one synagogue. The tension between a general and particular description is not relieved by Mark's next verse (1:23) where he reiterates the location as "in their synagogue" which Mark may have adopted from Luke's next story (Luke 4:33).

[The following conflation may reflect cultural differences among the readers of the respective gospels.] In the parallel passage to Mark 1:32-34 we read in Matthew 8:16 that the people "towards the evening" brought to Jesus many who were possessed with demons. Matthew continues by stating that Jesus cast them

---

[4]Cf. Friedrich Bleek, *Einleitung in das Neue Testament,* ed. Johannes F. Bleek (Berlin: Reimer, 1862; [2]1866; [3]1875; [4]1886) 246.
[5]See above, 168-71.

out and that "he healed all who were sick." The sequence of diseases has been reversed in Luke 4:40-41. He reports that "when the sun was setting" all those "who had any that were sick with various diseases" brought them to him. In the following verse Luke then refers to the casting out of demons. Mark merges both types of disabilities in what is for him a characteristic manner. His text reads:

> That evening (Matt), at sundown (Luke), they brought to him (Luke) all (cf. Luke) who were sick (Luke, cf. Matt) or possessed with demons (Matt) [33]And the whole city was gathered together about the door (Matt). [34]And he healed many who were sick (Matt) with various diseases (Luke) and cast out (Matt) many (cf. Luke) demons (Luke).

The conflation of the passages from Matthew 8 and Luke 4 is evident first of all from the double indications of time. Secondly, where Matthew mentions first the demon possessed and Luke gives priority to the sick, Mark gives both disabilities equal emphasis. Thirdly, it may seem inconsistent that according to Mark Jesus only healed "many" people and cast out "many demons" (v. 34), although the people brought "all" who were sick or possessed (v. 33). This can be explained, though, from the texts in Matthew and Luke where the former refers to "many" and the latter refers to "all" being brought to Jesus.

[Another example of cultural difference in understanding a disease may be found in Mark 1:42.] In this verse we read the words of Matthew 8:3, "And immediately the leprosy was cleansed," but also the words of Luke 5:13, "And immediately the leprosy left him." These words are combined by Mark in such a way that his version reads, "And immediately the leprosy left him, and he was made clean."

Conflations also can mean a harmonization of sentence structure in addition to the merging of materials. An illustration of this is Mark 3:7-12 which contains a detailed portrayal of Jesus' followers and his healing ministry. The sources for this pericope must have been Matthew 12:15-16 and Luke 6:17-19. In Matthew the occasion for these verses was Jesus' withdrawal after the evil scheming of the Pharisees. Many people followed him and he healed all the sick, but Jesus ordered them also not to make him known. In Luke the situation is different. Jesus had just selected the twelve from the circle of his disciples and he was about to proclaim a message on a level place.

The great crowd is portrayed by Luke by way of an elliptical sentence:

> . . . and a great crowd of his disciples and a great multitude of people (was present . . . people), who came to hear him and to be healed of their diseases; [18]and those who were troubled with unclean spirits were cured. [19]And all the crowd sought to touch him, for power came forth from him and he healed them all.

Mark connects the transition of Matthew concerning the withdrawal from the Pharisees with Luke's portrayal of the crowds including the disciples. He does this in such a manner that the "disciples" are singled out from the crowd in order to be more closely associated with Jesus, while only the "great multitude" (Luke) becomes the subject of the verb "followed," the verb used in Matthew. When Mark in the following verse (Mark 3:8) enumerates the different places from where the crowds gathered, he concludes rather demurely, "a great multitude, hearing all that he did, came to him." Here the reader discovers traces of Luke's elliptical sentence, especially the dependent clause: (people) "who came to hear him." Mark 3:8 became consciously or unconsciously a means of eliminating the ellipse in Luke.

The thronging of the crowd was caused by the desire to touch Jesus, according to Luke (6:19). For Mark, however, the thronging becomes the occasion for the unusual command to have a boat ready to protect Jesus against the potential danger to life, [which may hark back to Matthew's context concerning the threats by the Pharisees]. Mark's story can be fully explained from both parallels, but it is hardly possible to explain how Matthew and Luke could have deduced their accounts from Mark as their source.

[Also grammatical mistakes in the Marcan text can sometimes be explained from a conflation.] For instance, there is an inaccurate construction in the list of names of the apostles in Mark 3:13-19, which only can be understood from the simultaneous use of Matthew and Luke. Matthew lists the names of the apostles in the nominative before he records the commission (Matt 10:5-42) which was addressed to these twelve. Luke, however, has the names of the apostles in the accusative because they were the object of Jesus' election (Luke 6:13-16). Mark's description is then as follows:

> [13]And he went up on the mountain, and called to him (cf. Matt 10:1) those he desired. And they came to him (cf. Matt 5:1). [14]And he appointed twelve, to be with him, and to be sent out to preach [15]and have authority to cast out demons (Matt 10:1): [16]Simon whom he surnamed Peter; [17]James the son of Zebedee . . . etc.

The names of the apostles then follow in the accusative which can hardly be interpreted as being dependent from the verb "appointed." The explanation of this incorrect grammatical construction can only be that Mark used the construction of Luke for the listing of names he found in Matthew.[6]

[Conflations may weaken the original content of the source materials rather

---

[6]Cf. Eduard Zeller, "Zum Marcus-Evangelium," *Zeitschrift für Wissenschaftliche Theologie* 8 (1865): 396-408.

than contribute to their vigor.] The pericope of Herod's opinion about Jesus is a case in point (Mark 6:14-16). In the parallel passage of Matthew, Herod is the one who expresses the suspicion that Jesus is the resuscitated John the Baptist (Matt 14:1-2). In Luke's parallel passage the tetrarch is concerned about the rumors among the people that Jesus was John the Baptist raised from the dead (Luke 9:7-9). Mark first reports Herod's reaction to the rumors among the people, as in Luke, and then allows Herod to express his own suspicion, as in Matthew. Herod's statements in Mark are rather dull in comparison with Luke. Mark quotes, "John, whom I beheaded, has been raised" (Mark 6:16), while Luke has, "John I beheaded, but who is this . . . ?" (Luke 9:9).

A similar loss of vigor can be noticed in Mark 6:31 where Jesus says to the just-returned apostles, "Come away by yourselves to a lonely place, and rest a while" (parallel to Luke 9:10) followed immediately by the statement "And they went away in the boat to a lonely place by themselves" (parallel to Matt 14:13).

[In conclusion, one more instance of cultural differences in understanding demonic possession.] Matthew 17:14-18 contains the story of the lunatic boy who, because of his illness, endangers his life by throwing himself into fire or water. The healing process is described by Matthew as the emerging of a demon, which is basically a Jewish notion of disease. Luke, on the other hand, describes this illness as a case of epilepsy where the patient foams because of convulsions [and where the healing is a calming down] (Luke 9:37-43). Only a combination of the two accounts can explain Mark's narrative (Mark 9:14-27). Like Luke, he first portrays the manifestations of epilepsy in order then to proceed with Matthew, noting that the boy "often is cast into the fire and into the water" (Mark 9:22). The Markan record demonstrates also by other features its later character in comparison with its two synoptic parallels.

The Judean Period

[The Judean period and the Passion narratives also reflect the coordinating role of Mark.] The incident of the blind Bartimaeus outside Jericho is introduced by Matthew with the words, "And as they went out of Jericho" (Matt 20:29). Luke, however, places the incident before the entry of the city, "As he drew near to Jericho" (Luke 18:35). Mark is again the coordinator of these passages by stating in 10:46, "And they came to Jericho; and as he was leaving Jericho. . . . "

The following example of conflation deals with the question concerning the resurrection of the dead (Mark 12:18-27). In the parallel passage from Matthew (22:23-33) Jesus substantiates the resurrection of the dead with the observation that God is not a God of the dead, but of the living. In this connnection the question is raised, "have you not read what was said to you by God . . . ?" (Matt 22:31). Luke, in his parallel passage 20:27-40, calls to the attention of the reader that "even Moses showed, in the passage about the bush," that the dead are being raised. Both elements are brought together in Mark 12:26: "have you not read in the book of Moses, in the passage about the bush, how God said to him . . . ?" Since the words "about the bush" fit more harmoniously in the text of Luke, the Marcan text must be the conflation of both other synoptic texts.

[An example of loss of vigor can be found in Mark 13:1-4 voicing the prediction of the temple.] According to Matthew, the occasion for the eschatological message was the admiration of the disciples for "the buildings of the temple" (Matt 24:1-3). For Luke the prediction was occasioned rather by the "noble stones" (Luke 21:5-7). Mark combines both features by his rather dull exclamation, "Look, Teacher, what wonderful stones and what wonderful buildings!" In the question concerning the sign, Mark contributes neither to Matthew's personal expectation formulated as "the sign of your coming" (Matt 24:3) nor to Luke's historical hope expressed by his words "the sign when this is about to take place" (Luke 21:7). Mark's conflation therefore loses in distinctiveness when he states, "what will be the sign when these things are all to be accomplished" (Mark 13:4).

Some theologians find a syntactic irregularity in Mark 13:9 which is part of the section on the beginning of the tribulations (Mark 13:9-13). Verse nine reads:

> they will deliver you up to councils; and you will be beaten in synagogues; and you will stand before governors and kings for my sake, to bear testimony before them.

The irregularity is "you will be beaten" which presumably should be connnected with "in the synagogues" in order to maintain a balanced sentence structure.[7] In comparison with Luke 21:12-17 and Matthew 10:17-22 the reader will discover a striking agreement with both parallel texts. Whenever Mark deviates from his closest parallel, Luke, he agrees in this deviation with Matthew.[8] This parallelism will explain the syntactic irregularity just mentioned. In Matthew we read "they will deliver you up to councils, and flog you in their synagogues" (Matt 10:17). Luke's version is "delivering you up to the synagogues and prisons, and you will be brought before kings and governors" (Luke 21:12). It seems that Luke's version ("to the synagogues," accusative) has replaced Matthew's reading ("in their synagogues," dative). Mark follows Luke in the delivering of the Christians to councils, but adds Matthew's statement about the martyrdom of being beaten in synagogues. Grammatically a shift from εἰς to ἐν happened easily.

[Several conflations, though, improve the content by constructively combining the data of both parallel gospels. Mark 14:1 is a sample of such a construc-

---

[7][The Revised Standard Version (1946, ²1971) adopted this construction. —ed.]
[8]See above, 152-53.

tive conflation.] The imminent feast of Passover in Matthew 26:2 is called by Luke "the feast of Unleavened Bread" (Luke 22:1). Mark integrates this information into the statement "It was now two days before the Passover and the feast of the Unleavened Bread." The chief priests and the scribes took counsel together in Matthew 26:4, "in order to arrest Jesus by stealth and kill him." As a variant Luke has "how to put him to death" (Luke 22:2), while Mark describes their scheming as a deliberation "how to kill him after arresting him by stealth."[9]

[Another example of a constructive combination is Mark 14:12-16, dealing with the preparation for the Passover.] According to Matthew, on the day before the Passover the disciples approached Jesus with the question, "Where will you have us prepare for you to eat the Passover?" Jesus responded to this question with specific instructions (Matt 26:17-19). In Luke, on the other hand, Jesus takes the initiative by charging Peter and John to find a room for the Passover meal. In response they ask for further instructions (Luke 22:7-13). In Mark both approaches are intertwined in such a way that the disciples first approach Jesus with their question, as in Matthew, after which two of them are deliberately being sent by Jesus with specific instructions, as in Luke. [This conflation again disproves Marcan priority.] The formal assertion "So Jesus sent Peter and John," without any word of introduction, fits better in Luke's context than in Mark who first allows the disciples to raise a question about the location for the Passover meal and then makes a reference to two disciples being sent. It is hard to deny that Luke's version is more original than the reading of Mark.

Conflations may create a pleonasm like the literal statement in Mark 14:30, "today this night" (σήμερον ταύτῃ τῇ νυκτί).[10] This literary form has come into being by combining Luke 22:34 referring to "this day" with Matt 26:31 stating "this night." Another pleonism is found in Mark 15:32 where Jesus mockingly is called "Christ, the King of Israel." This statement brings together the words of Matt 27:42 where Jesus is mocked as "the King of Israel" and Luke 23:35 where Jesus is called "the Christ of God."

Other conflations may create a complete incomprehensibility as in one of Mark's episodes describing the death of Jesus on the cross (15:33-37). The evangelist assumes an association between "a sponge full of vinegar" offered to Jesus by one of the bystanders and the words "Wait, let us see whether Elijah will come to take him down." In order to understand this line of thought one has to consult the parallels (Matt 27:45-56; Luke 23:36-38). The vinegar is mentioned by Matthew as a means of anesthesia which Jesus had refused in verse 34 and which is offered him again by one of the bystanders after his bitter lament (vs. 48). In Luke the soldiers are the ones offering the vinegar to Jesus,

---

[9][According to the RSV translation. —ed.]
[10][The RSV translates as "this very night." —ed.]

"saying, 'if you are the King of the Jews, save yourself'!" In the latter case the vinegar may have been meant either as a pain reliever or as a form of torment. Mark, at least, has understood it to be an act of torture. His strangely conflated verse (Mark 15:36) has used Matthew's information concerning one of the bystanders presenting the sponge with vinegar and addressing Jesus with the disrespectful words by the soldiers mentioned in Luke's Gospel.

[There may be theological overtones in the next conflation.] Matthew closes Jesus' life with the profession by the centurion who because of the events surrounding Jesus' death felt compelled to exclaim, "Truly this was the Son of God" (Matt 27:54). Luke underscores the humanity of Christ by having the centurion cry out, "Certainly this man was innocent!" (Luke 23:47). Combining the humanity and the divinity of Christ, Mark wrote in 15:39, "Truly this man was the Son of God."

[Finally there is a conflation resulting in a different factual outcome.] According to Matthew the women went out to meditate near the sepulchre "after the sabbath, toward the dawn of the first day of the week." (Matt 28:1). Luke reports a different purpose for their visit, namely, an act of homage for which the women had prepared spices on the day of Jesus' death (Luke 24:1). Though agreeing with Luke on the purpose of their visit, Mark takes the names of the women from Matthew, as well as the indication of time. However, he separated the night into two periods. The first part, "when the sabbath was past," is considered the time of the preparation of the spices (Mark 16:1), while the second part, "very early on the first day of the week," is indicated as the time of implementing the plan of the women (Mark 16:2). The result of this double time indication is that the spices have been prepared before the Sabbath (Luke 23:56).

The Enigma of Text Conflations

[Conflations have a variety of purposes and results. They may provide more comprehensive information or they may reduce the narratives to the bare essentials. In the process they may contribute to the theological or historical content of the text, or they may mean a loss of clarity and literary expression.] This chapter merely listed some examples, which could be increased with several others. These samples are meant merely to illustrate as clearly as possible the peculiar reaction of Mark's text to both of its parallel sources. It is a consistent characteristic of the second gospel that it shows a great degree of similarity in vocabulary and syntactic construction with both synoptic parallels.

This similarity is of such nature that the reader is faced with the alternative of accepting either a peculiar division of Mark's text by two compilers or of affirming the ingenious compilation by Mark from his two sources. The same alternative was encountered in chapter 6 by discussing the sequence of narrative materials and by analyzing the quantitative theory.[11] With an impartial assessment of this state of affairs the final conclusion should be beyond any doubt, especially since frequently incorrect or unclear turns of phrases can only be explained by referring to their sources.

The champions of the Marcan hypothesis have no solution for these text conflations. On the one hand some of their representatives declare there is some justification for the conclusion we have drawn from these conflations. On the other hand our critics use the strongest words possible to vent their aversion to this inference. "These arbitrary and hair-splitting blendings which are to explain the most inexplicable enigma of canon history are not capable of making Griesbach's hypothesis acceptable," according to Bernhard Weiss.[12]

Our opponents raise questions concerning places where no conflation was used by Mark. They cite Mark 14:17 which indicates the time of the Last Supper. Matthew reports its taking place "when it was evening" (Matt 26:2); Luke simply states, "And when the hour came" (Luke 22:14); while Mark only writes, "And when it was evening." Our critics cannot reconcile in Mark a conscientious effort concerned with minute details with occasional oversights. Such an exaggerated notion of Mark's literary labor, as we already discussed above,[13] is not endorsed by the followers of Griesbach either. The allegations by our opponents can only be ascribed to a definite bias.

The same Weiss who calls this "word splitting" and "enigma," does not hesitate to refer to text conflations in Luke. In this gospel he discovers traces of an Ur-Matthew and Mark influencing the text simultaneously. Weiss lists Luke 8:25, 9:5, 11, and 13, which are samples that could not stand up against the examples given in this chapter about Mark.[14] Thus the proponents of the Marcan hypothesis are themselves not averse to the notion of conflations, when two sources influence an author simultaneously so that the words and turns of phrases blend together. When they accept this for Luke we may invite them to consider without excessive meticulousness the justification of Marcan posteriority on the basis of comparable text conflations.

Such a conclusion is the most acceptable solution for the so-called enigma of conflations in Mark. One can hardly deny that it is a simpler solution than the

---

[11]See above, 97-104.

[12]Bernhard Weiss, "Zur Entstehungsgeschichte der drei synoptischen Evangelien," *Theologische Studien und Kritiken* 34 (1861): 685.

[13]See above, 165-74.

[14]Weiss, "Zur Enstehungsgeschichte," 86; together with others Weiss especially emphasizes Luke 8:25 as an argument against conflations by Mark. The question is, however, whether the words "the men marveled" (Matt 8:27), "and they were afraid, and they marveled" (Luke 8:25), and Mark 4:41 "and they were filled with awe," are not a development of ideas of Christology and apostolic authority in Mark.

accidental distribution of Mark's expressions over two evangelists [independent-ly] using his gospel as their source. Some advocates of the Marcan hypothesis have not failed to draw this conclusion for some cases in Mark. The way in which these theologians presented their case, however, was merely to acknowl-edge exceptions to a hypothesis which already had been considered proven on other counts.[15] Since we have not found a valid proof for the Marcan hypothesis we are fully justified in giving a natural explanation for the blending of texts by Mark. We are therefore entitled to place the argument of conflation together with all our other arguments on the scales of the balance, which [on balance] will turn completely in favor of the Griesbach hypothesis and against the Marcan hypothesis.

Crucial Texts in Mark

Implicit Statements

As has been mentioned above[16] Réville assigned a number of these conflations to a later editor, the canonical or the Proto-Mark. It hardly needs mentioning that the priority of Mark is seriously undermined when one is convinced of Mark's internal unity, or of its being formulated all at one time, as some of our opponents aver. With any conception of Mark's unity, one has precluded a potential analysis of Mark into an original text supplemented by later canonical texts.

The list of such texts by an assumed canonical editor is long. I do not want to dwell on these texts since there is a general agreement on their late date. At this time it is only of importance to demonstrate the late date also of the so-called Proto-Mark. In addition to the conflations mentioned above,[17] there are a few other phenomena to be taken into consideration. There are, namely, peculiar verses in Mark that can only find their explanation in the text of one of the synoptic gospels rather than being traces of a Proto-Mark.

Among these phenomena I would like to include [those statements in Mark that imply the information given by the other synoptic gospels]. One of these is the way in which Mark consistently describes Jesus' teaching by way of some samples that are to be characteristic of the spirit of the total content of Jesus' teaching. We read, for instance, in Mark 4:2, where Jesus presents his teaching

---

[15]Weiss, "Zur Enstehungsgeschichte," 683ff.; Heinrich Julius Holtzmann, *Die synop-tischen Evangelien: Ihr Ursprung und geschichtlicher Charakter* (Leipzig: W. Engelmann, 1863) 113ff.

[16]See above, 56-57.

[17]See above, 175-84.

on the lakeshore by way of parables: "And he taught them many things in parables, and in his teaching he said to them. . . . " With these words of introduction Mark informs the reader that the following pericopes are merely samples of Jesus' teaching.

Indeed, only a few parables are given from the complete series in Matthew. At the end of his selection of parables Mark concludes in 4:33, "With many such parables he spoke the word to them." Also the message against the Pharisees (Mark 12:38-40) seems to have been condensed into a few verses, which are meant as a summary or a larger unit introduced by the words "And in his teaching he said. . . . " [Another example of a statement implying information from the other two Synoptics] can be found in Mark 8:32. After Jesus' first announcement of his suffering, Peter "began to rebuke him." Such a reprimand by Jesus does not completely explain the charge that Peter was merely "thinking about the things of men." the reason for Jesus' words of rebuke can be found, however, in Matthew 16:22 where Peter exclaims, "God forbid, Lord! This shall never happen to you."

[The following paragraph of Mark implies additional information from Luke.] Mark reports in 14:54 that Peter was sitting in the courtyard of the high priest "warming himself at the fire." The word for "fire" used by Mark is the Greek term for light (φῶς), which generally designated a fire used by an army for the purpose of providing light. For heating purposes another Greek word was mostly used for fire, namely, πῦρ. Luke's text provides the explanation for Mark's use of "light." The third gospel tells us that the guards had kindled a fire around which they assembled themselves. Peter had joined the circle of soldiers in such a way that the fire illuminated his face. According to Luke, this circumstance was the reason a servant girl recognized him as a follower of Jesus (Luke 22:54-57). Mark conceived of the fire kindled by the guards as a source of light. On the basis of Luke's text Mark imagined the place of Peter "near the fire" in such a way, that he sat down with the guards and warmed himself in the light of the fire.

[Another statement implicitly referring to Luke] is Mark 14:65. When the people in the courtroom mocked and abused Jesus they urged him to "prophesy." Such a demand could be seen as a form of mockery of Jesus' prophetic ministry. But why did they "cover his face," as is reported in the same verse? We touch here upon the notion of a prophet as someone who knows what is hidden to others. Most likely the request to prophesy was related to a specific question requiring an answer. Again we need Luke for more information on this passage. In Luke 22:64 the blindfolded Jesus is being asked, "Prophesy! Who is it that struck you?"

These examples of statements [implying additional information from the other Synoptics] may be sufficient. They are a strong argument against the priority of Mark. The collection of implicit statements published by De Wette[18] would require a complete study of Mark's dependence on the other two Synoptics, which would lead us too far afield at this time.

Anacoluthons in Matthew

Besides analyzing conflations and implicit statements the question of priority in canon history can by studied on the basis of anacoluthons, a word meaning abrupt changes of thought within a sentence or paragraph. [The thesis is that anacoluthons are an indication of a secondary text needing the source materials for further explication. Volkmar claimed that Matthew, because of his anacoluthons, shows his dependence on Mark as his source.]

The first pericope to be discussed may be the account of the execution of John the Baptist.[19] It has been called the "deceptive pericope,"[20] which has been claimed by Volkmar as the strongest conclusive argument for the priority of Mark. The account in Matthew (14:1-14) is unclear, according to this scholar, because this gospel does not mention what happened to explain why Jesus was called to the attention of Herod. The immediate context refers to the unbelief of the people in Nazareth which prevented Jesus from doing many signs "at that time" (Matt 14:1). [There would be no reason, therefore, that such an ineffective ministry should come to the attention of Herod!]

Furthermore, this exegete does not understand how Jesus could take a boat in Nazareth [which is far from the Lake] (Matt 13:54; 14:13). He wonders how Jesus' departure could be presented as a result of the message concerning John's death. Since this message is mentioned in an insertion, Volkmar argues that it should not have any influence on the course of events. He avers it is difficult to imagine how the crowds could follow Jesus "from the towns" (Matt 14:13), and how in the next verse Jesus seems to notice them for the first time. Finally, Volkmar considers the withdrawal to a lonely place rather futile since the crowds were there as well.

To explain these anacoluthons our opponents point to Mark as the source which is to explain all these inconsistencies. First of all, I would like to raise the question whether the story in Matthew is actually so incoherent that it needs further explication. The introductory phrase "At that time" (14:1), is used

---

[18]Wilhelm Martin DeWette, *Lehrbuch der historisch-kritischen Einleitung in die kanonischen Bücher des Neuen Testaments,* 6th ed. (Berlin: G. Reimer, [1]1826; [2]1830; [3]1834; [4]1842; [5]1848; ed. Hermann Messner and Gottlieb Lünemann, [6]1860) 185ff.

[19]Matt 14:1-14; Mark 6:14-33; Luke 9:7-9; cf Luke 3:19-20.

[20]Gustav Volkmar, *Die Religion Jesu und ihre erste Entwicklung nach dem gegenwärtigen Stand der Wissenschaft* (Leipzig: Brockhaus, 1857) 377.

frequently by Matthew (see 11:25; 12:1) and is an indication of a loose context. A connection between the two pericopes (Matt 13:53-58 and 14:1-12) certainly can be detected. The first pericope deals with the relationship of a prophet to his own country: the people of Nazareth did not understand from where that wisdom and power came [to the carpenter's son]. The second pericope expresses the opinion of Galilee's tetrarch about Jesus: Herod is convinced that Jesus has these powers because he is the risen John the Baptist.

The point of connection between both pericopes may have been the question for the source of "the powers," or the fact that both stories associate Jesus with Galilee, his "own country." Such associations are very common for a gospel like that of Matthew. That the execution of John the Baptist is reported after the reference to his having been "raised from the dead" (14:2) is not uncommon for gospel literature either. It is also very common for an author to lose the thread of his narrative because of some intermittent elaboration, for example, on John the Baptist.

When we pay closer attention to the verses 13 and 14 of Matthew 14 we notice that what Jesus heard must have been the news about John's death. Jesus' withdrawal seems to have been related to the same event since it is described as the consequence of Jesus hearing the news about John the Baptist. The Greek verb translated "withdrawing" (ἀνεχώρησεν) does not always have this connotation (cf. Matt 9:24; 15:21; 27:5). It is significant in this connection, though, that also Jesus' departure to Galilee and his ministry in that region are called a "withdrawal" using the same Greek verb (Matt 4:12).

There seems to have lingered in the memory of the early Christians a close tie between the ministry of Jesus and the apprehension of John the Baptist. But even though Matthew seems to know of this tradition, he does not make it a strong point: the fate of John the Baptist is only presented as the occasion for the public ministry of Jesus (Matt 4:17). The crowds followed Jesus immediately after this withdrawal and a miracle was performed in the presence of thousands of spectators (Matt 12:14).

This ambiguous manner of narration and that unconscious association of materials by the evangelist is also the reason for his unexpected reference to a boat in this context. It would be naive to expect from the evangelist an accurate account of geographical details. When Matthew mentions the withdrawal "from there" he does not necessarily think of Nazareth: the immediately following words, "in a boat," may have created a new association for the evangelist. In this connection, as anywhere else in this gospel, the reader should not ask for geographical or chronological details. The words "from there" have been used in a general sense also in Matthew 9:9-27; 11:1; 12:9, 15; 13:53; and 19:15. One could also ask the question from where the boat so suddenly originated in Matt 14:13; 3:23; 13:3. [Each of these features tells something about the literary approach of Matthew. These traits are not necessarily anacoluthons, but rather a literary sequencing based upon association.]

The presence of crowds is a natural feature for Matthew who could not imagine Jesus deserted at any time. Repeatedly it is stated that large crowds followed him (Matt 4:25; 8:1; 12:15; 15:30; 19:2; 20:29). The crowds are even mentioned routinely without letting the reader know whence they came (see Matt 8:18; 9:8). The crowds sometimes are inadvertently presented in different formations: for instance, the crowd following Jesus after the Sermon on the Mount (Matt 8:1) seems different from the crowd listening to that sermon (4:25). The larger the crowds the more impressive Jesus' teachings.

The "great throng" mentioned in Matt 14:14 seems also to be a different crowd from the multitude mentioned in the preceding verse, where it is not identified as a "great throng." The ambiguous and indefinite presentation is quite in agreement with the character of Matthew's Gospel. Our few examples should sufficiently answer the question concerning potential anacoluthons in Matthew [resulting from his method of association of ideas and his routine usage of indications of time and place]. Therefore, we do not need the Gospel of Mark as a tool for interpreting the "deceptive pericope" in Matthew!

But let us assume that Mark 6:14-33 could provide us with a unique opportunity for clarifying the loose connections in Matthew 14:1-14. We will discover to what degree this will be helpful. The preceding pericope in Mark tells about the twelve having been sent out on a teaching and healing mission, which would have been an opportune time for Herod to hear about the fame of Jesus. The apostles returned wearied and hungry after Mark's report about the execution of John the Baptist. At that time they shared their experiences (Mark 6:30, ἀπήγγειλαν), which caused Jesus to seek solitude in order to provide a moment of rest to the apostles.

If these verses from Mark 6 are to be the clue to the interpretation of Matthew 14:1-14 we get the following picture. The return of the disciples is, indeed, mentioned in Matthew 14:12—"they went and told Jesus"—but these disciples actually belonged to John the Baptist. The time indication in Matthew 14:1, "at that time," could refer to the omitted charge to the apostles mentioned in Mark 6:7-11. The words "from there" in Matthew 14:13 supposedly has reference to the place where the twelve returned to Jesus, mentioned in Mark 6:30. The presence of a boat in Matthew as well as in Mark could presumably be explained from Mark 6:6 where Jesus is reported as traveling around the villages of Galilee. The "going ashore" and the "great throng" awaiting them are mentioned in both Matthew and Mark. The latter even tells us how the great throng flocked together from all the towns surrounding the Lake of Galilee (Mark 6:33).

If the anacoluthons in Matthew are to be explained from the Gospel of Mark we find only limited help, [since some of these inconsistencies are also in Mark].

Whether we are at liberty to compare merely Mark and Matthew will have to be determined on the basis of a careful comparison of all three synoptic gospels. [Since Mark 6 is an example of alternate parallelism,[21] we should take the text of Luke into consideration as well.]

When Mark deviates considerably from Matthew he agrees with Luke; the diverging paragraphs between Mark and Matthew are the charge to the apostles, the return of the twelve, and the enumeration of various opinions about Jesus; in each of these cases Mark resembles Luke more closely. I do not want to raise the issue whether Luke or Matthew had the strongest impact on Mark; I just want to follow Mark's text as regards his presumed originality or to ascertain whether or not sources have been used.

The "Deceptive Paragraph"

The introduction to John's beheading is presented by Mark in the form of a dialogue exchanging opinions about Jesus (Mark 6:14-16). Herod expresses his opinion that Jesus is John the Baptist raised from the dead. He feels so strongly convinced that he reiterates emphatically his opinion after he has listened to the opinion of others. Such a dialogue could be a vivid presentation, but in content it is somewhat repetitious.

Now, it is noteworthy that this dialogue is composed of elements occurring separately in Matthew and Luke. The first affirmation by Herod is also in Matthew, while Luke leaves the tetrarch in uncertainty by having others voice various opinions. He does this in such a manner that Herod's final question concerning Jesus precludes the possibility that he would be John the Baptist: "John I beheaded, but who is this . . . ?" (Luke 9:9). A somewhat similar approach is used in the next pericope when the disciples report to Jesus regarding the public opinions about him (Luke 9:19).

Comparing the three synoptic texts, we may ascertain that Mark first adopted Matthew's text almost completely and then continued his account using Luke's materials. We notice that the words "John I beheaded" (Luke 9:9) fit perfectly in the context of Luke as Herod's response to the opinions of others. Also the public opinions are a necessary component of Luke's story, even though he uses these again in the next pericope (Luke 9:19ff.). In Mark, however, the opinion of others seems out of place: [verse 15 begins rather abruptly—"But others said"—and the response of Herod in verse 16 does not react to these public opinions either]. According to Mark, his flat remark was simply, "John, whom I beheaded, has been raised" (Mark 6:16). All this contributes to the likelihood

---

[21]See above, 152-53.

that Mark is a combination of both the other more vivid presentations rather than their source.[22]

There is an additional point of comparison. In the story of Peter's profession of faith as well as in the public opinions mentioned to Herod, Luke assigns Elijah a distinctive place among "the old prophets" (Luke 9:8, 19). Matthew allows Jeremiah a share in this distinction as well (Matt 16:14). Jeremiah was the prophet of God who so fervently prayed for the people and their holy city (2 Macc 15:14).

Mark first shares Luke's suggestion that Jesus was Elijah according to public opinion; as a second possibility Mark intimates, "He is a prophet, like one of the prophets of old" (Mark 6:15). It seems that the difference between Elijah and the other prophets is not very clear to Mark. It may also be that for him the return of Elijah was not any more alive as an eschatological expectation. For Mark, Elijah was just one of the prophets; Jesus was either one of the prophets of old or he was a new prophet of essentially the same authority as the old prophet, according to Mark's interpretation of the public opinion of Jesus' day. The messianic notion of Mark seems inferior to the conceptions of the parallels in Matthew and Luke.

The story of John's beheading is justifiably referred to as a sample of Mark's graphic literary style. This literary quality, however, does not give him a role of historical priority. Matthew could have used Mark since the motivations for the act of execution are so clearly articulated. His vagueness at other points cannot be excused, however, if he used Mark as his source.

According to Matthew, fear for the people prevented Herod from having John the Baptist killed, although he had no fear of having him apprehended. This seems somewhat paradoxical, especially since "the king was sorry" (Matt 14:9) about the necessity to have John beheaded. In contrast to Matthew, the reader will find detailed information in Mark about the reason for Herod's sorrow and about the occasion for his daughter's wish. Behind these elaborations we clearly see Mark's intention of wanting to clarify the gospel material of his day.

After having compared Mark with Matthew let us now turn briefly to Luke (9:7-9). In his gospel the absence of the twelve on their mission created space for a description of Herod's uncertainty concerning Jesus. When the apostles returned, Jesus withdrew with them to a lonely place. The influence of Luke is evident by the use of the term "apostles" which Luke uses frequently, but which Mark has only at this location (Mark 6:30). Jesus' invitation to the returned apostles to take some rest seems strange within the context of Mark, especially since the lonely place still had to be found. To this end they had to take a boat and by the end of the day the apostles even had to supervise a meal for 5,000 people!

---

[22]See above, 165ff.

[The invitation "Come away by yourselves to a lonely place, and rest a while"] has an overly graphic and concrete style. It conveys to us the impression of a later edition of Luke's words "he took them" (Luke 9:10) or of Matthew's words "he withdrew" (Matt 14:13). Also the reason for withdrawal in Mark has been widened and transferred to the twelve by the words "Come away by yourselves." The "coming and going" of people added honor and respect for Jesus as well as for his disciples. This comparison shows us that Mark's story ought to be read in the light of the account in Luke and Matthew. Mark combined their texts in an excellent way when he wrote, "Come away by yourselves to a lonely place (elaboration of Luke 9:10) . . . and they went away in the boat to a lonely place by themselves (parallel to Matt 14:13).[23]

[From 6:34 on,] Mark uses Matthew again as his major source. The flocking together of the crowd is described in a vivid style. Mark's statement "As he landed he saw a great throng" (Mark 6:34) can only be interpreted from the parallel section in Matthew where we find similar words (Matt 14:14). The phrase "because they were like sheep without a shepherd" (Mark 6:34) has been evoked in association with the word "compassion," which also in Matthew is followed by the beautiful image of the shepherd (Matt 9:36).

Mark gives expression to this compassion by having Jesus "teach them many things" (Mark 6:34), which is in complete agreement with his approach. Matthew, on the other hand, always points out how the Messiah heals all diseases among the people and how he alleviates their suffering. Mark has replaced the thought of benevolent messianic ministry by the concept of the power of the Son of God. Mark mentions, therefore, only those healings that are manifestations of God's miraculous work. The major aspect of Christ's ministry remains for Mark, however, his teaching.[24]

When Matthew describes Jesus' ministry in general terms he always combines teaching and healing (Matt 4:23; 9:35); Mark, on the other hand, only speaks of Jesus' teaching ministry (Mark 6:6; 10:1). He repeatedly mentions that Jesus was teaching (Mark 2:13; 4:1-2; 12:35). While Matthew uses words like "Jesus said" or similar expressions as introductions to Jesus' sayings, Mark always introduces Jesus by the words "he taught" (Mark 8:31; 9:31; 11:17). In Matthew the apostles received power to cast out demons and to heal all diseases (Matt 10:1); in Mark these same men return from their mission reporting about "all that they had done and taught" (Mark 6:30). It is therefore totally in line with Mark's approach when he portrays Jesus "teaching many things" out of compassion for "sheep without a shepherd."

---

[23]See above, 179.
[24]Cf. above, 139-42.

Taking all this into consideration and considering that the content of this pericope (Mark 6:30-34) is divided over both parallels [we are again confronted with the question of the interrelatedness of the gospels]. It seems most likely that the Gospel of Mark is the result of its use and assimilation of both synoptic parallels. This is more likely than that Luke would have used from Mark what Matthew accidentally had left untouched and vice versa. The anacoluthons in the first gospel can very well be interpreted from its own approach; the Gospel of Mark provides only limited help to this effect. The most reasonable solution for the issues in canon history is [the Griesbach theory] where Matthew and Luke serve as sources for the Gospel of Mark.

One objection remains, however. Herod is called a tetrarch in Matthew 14:1 but a king in 14:9. Verse 9 looks like a routinely copied text from Mark, [which could mean Marcan priority!] Matthew could, of course, have confused the terminology of tetrarch and king himself, and Mark could have copied the mistake. One has to be careful, however, not to draw major conclusions from such incidental mistakes. It is a well-known fact that later copyists have attempted to emend parallel texts and in the process have expanded certain mistakes.

The process of textual emendation was practiced several centuries before the time of our oldest manuscripts. This is evidenced in verses we can clearly identify as glosses, although they are not listed as such by the copyists. Reminding the reader of this fact is not an effort to avoid an inescapable issue. It should only serve to caution us. Irregularities and remaining questions should have the same weight as the solid facts established in our study of canon history. [The "deceptive pericope" should deceive no objective researcher of gospel history.]

Distinctive Pericopes in Canon History

The Parable of the Sower

[Our text studies in the gospels have dealt with the phenomena of conflation, of implicit statements and of anacoluthons. Our present section will deal with two pericopes that clearly illustrate the development of canon history.] The parable of the Sower (Matt 13:10-23; Mark 4:10-25; Luke 8:9-18) provides us with such an informative comparison. This parable is one of the clearest examples of the interrelatedness between the Synoptic gospels. After Matthew has told the parable of the Sower and before he gives its explanation, he inserted an exposition about the use of parables as a method of teaching. The occasion for this discussion was a question to this effect by the disciples.

The structure of their question—"Why do you speak to them in parables?"—suggests immediately that the objective of the discussion is the relevance of parables for the crowds. According to Matthew's account, the prophecy of Isaiah is to be fulfilled, which proclaims that the blind will see and the deaf will hear (Isa 6:10), but which also forewarns that the people will hear and not understand (Isa 6:9).

By way of introduction to this prophecy two sayings are included indicating the privilege of the disciples in comparison with the crowds, and also their opportunity to receive further insight into the meaning of the parables. The first saying asserts that it is given to the disciples to know the secrets of the Kingdom of Heaven and that the crowds will not share in these secrets (Matt 13:11). The second saying expresses both aspects again: "For to him who has will more be given . . . but from him who has not, even what he has will be taken away" (Matt 13:12). Both sayings affirm that the secrets must be presented in such a way that those who do not belong to Christ will not have the opportunity to understand. Those who do understand will also receive further insight by way of an explanation of the parables. All this is clearly focussed upon the fulfillment of the prophecy from Isaiah 6.

In Mark and Luke the text has been considerably expanded in such a way that a later development can clearly be recognized. The decisive issue is, therefore, to establish which gospel has the most original content. In Luke the question of the disciples does not anymore create an occasion to speak about Jesus' method of teaching. The question leads directly to a statement about the secrets of the Kingdom given to the disciples. Luke emphasizes the revealing aspect of the parables while Matthew struggles with the revelation hidden from the masses. Consequently, the words of prophecy regarding the dullness of the people's heart are left out by Luke and the intervening sayings are shortened. In 8:10 Luke does mention the revelation hidden for "others," but this is much less direct than Matthew's statement concerning the crowds: "to them it has not been given" (Matt 13:11). Luke also leaves out Matthew's second saying about those who have and those who do not have. For Luke the point of the sayings is that the disciples have a right to the explanation of the parables!

The intention of Luke is clearly to minimize the negative aspect of teaching in parables, even though it was mentioned by the prophet Isaiah. Luke rather wanted to focus on the positive instructive function of the parables. This is underscored by a brief parable about the lamp on the stand, which he inserted immediately after the explanation of the parable of the Sower. "No one after lighting a lamp covers it with a vessel. . . . For nothing is hid that shall not be made manifest . . . " (Luke 8:16, 17). These words are quite different from Matthew's emphasis: "that . . . hearing . . . they do not understand" (Matt 13:13). This last thought is the core of Matthew's quest and an application of Isaiah 6.

Luke continues by inserting at this point the previously omitted second saying in Matthew 13:12: "Take heed then how you hear; for to him who has will more be given, and from him who has not, even what he thinks he has will be taken away" (Luke 8:18). Because of the relocation, this saying has gained a totally different meaning from that in the Matthean context, although the same words are being used. Matthew quoted this saying in order to indicate the reason why esoteric language was used in view of the crowds and why the disciples should have an explanation. Luke did not see any sense in covering a lamp with a vessel and has, therefore, no place for anyone not understanding the gospel unless that person does not "take heed." [Matthew's saying about "him who has not" has been reinterpreted in the eschatological context of the secrets of the Kingdom which will be revealed. Luke does not refer anymore to the crowds in Palestine] but to the Christians [in the diaspora] and their insights into the Gospel and its eschaton.

We would suggest that Matthew's presentation, associating the Gospel explicitly with the fulfillment of the prophecy over Israel is more original than Luke's. The latter's intentions are motivated by more pragmatic reasons [and include the secrets of the eschatological future]. As soon as we have decided upon the secondary nature of Luke we have by implication made the same conclusion about Mark [who followed Luke in the arrangement of the pericopes in this context]. Mark, however, surpasses both Matthew and Luke in theological development, as I will show below.

In Matthew the emphasis was on the hidden revelation; Luke by contrast underscored the revealed revelation; in Mark both ideas receive equal attention. When Jesus answers the question concerning the meaning of parables he says, according to Mark, "To you has been given the secret of the Kingdom of God, but for those outside everything is in parables" (Mark 4:11). Jesus then proceeded to ask about the understanding of the disciples themselves: "Do you not understand this parable? How then will you understand all the parables?" The disciples as well as the crowds are dealing with the hidden revelation, but only the disciples have access to revealed revelation.

Emphatically Mark assures [that] "for those outside, everything is in parables, so that they may indeed see but not perceive" (Mark 4:11b). The lack of insight by the disciples is not because of the parables but is determined by their willingness to listen to the explanation. For them the word of Mark 4:11 is valid: "To you has been given the secret of the Kingdom of God." Therefore Jesus admonishes them to gain insight by listening to the explanation (vs. 13), [which for Mark may well have referred to early Christian preaching]. The presupposition that the disciples would be able to understand a parable without further interpretation is foreign to Mark. In Matthew explanations of parables are the natural privileges for the disciples; Luke stresses that they have a right to this explanation. Mark, with his low view of the disciples, questions their ability to understand and stresses the need for further interpretation.

This progression of emphasis makes it difficult for me to assign priority to

Mark's text in comparison with its parallels. Also the wider context of the parable of the Sower confirms this. After Mark has completed his theme with the explanation of the parable of the Sower, he continues like Luke with the two small parables about the Lamp under a bushel or on the stand, and about giving the right measure. But Mark gives these additional parables a meaning of their own by introducing each of them with the words "And he said to them." Such a loose arrangement of parables, each having their own meaning, is typical for Mark (cf. Mark 3:23 and 4:34), but it equally reveals his dependence on other sources.

The parable of the Lamp (Mark 4:21-23; Luke 8:16-18) is changed by Mark in such a manner that it points directly to Christ or to Christianity as the light of the world. Mark concludes this parable with a solemn exhortation: "If any man has ears to hear, let him hear," which suggests a spiritual concern. The author intended that the light was to be placed upon the stand in order to become manifest worldwide.

In these two parables Mark combined Luke 8:18 and Matt 7:2. From the former passage he used the exhortation "Take heed what you hear," and from the latter, "the measure you give will be the measure you get." The Matthean saying was connected with the passing of judgement on others. In Mark this saying receives a totally different meaning in connection with the admonition "Take heed what you hear." This saying now conveys the verity that in accordance with the measure of knowledge which one has gained will one receive greater insight. Mark adds to this thought, "For to him who has will more be given; and from him who has not, even what he has will be taken away." This means that if one is able to measure his insight with large measures he will greatly benefit by this spiritually.

We are inclined to see in these two unique parables about the Lamp and about the Measure an affinity with Gnosticism. In any case it is difficult to find in this line of thought the original version of the Gospel, from which both other characteristic presentations of Matthew and Luke would have been developed.

The Expectation of Elijah

Let us briefly concentrate on Jesus' words about the expectation of Elijah's return (Matt 17:9-12; Mark 9:10-13). Hitzig used the comparison of these pericopes to prove the originality of Mark.[25] The difference between Matthew and Mark in this section consists mainly in the conception of Elijah's relation to Christ. The preceding account about the transfiguration is so identical in both gospels that either Matthew or Mark must have known the gospel of the other.

---

[25]See above, 27-32.

The connection [between the transfiguration and the discussion about Elijah] is extremely loose; all attempts to discover a connection have failed thus far. Matthew first depicts the transfiguration on the mountain and concludes with the command to tell no one about the vision (Matt 17:9). Then follows the question by the disciples: "Then why do the Scribes say that first Elijah must come?" (Matt 17:10). Jesus answers that their assertion was correct and that the words of Malachi 4:5, indeed, contained a truth: ["Behold, I will send you Elijah the prophet before the great and terrible day of the Lord comes"]. This prophecy was fulfilled, however, in John the Baptist. Jesus proceeded by saying that since the Scribes did not recognize John the Baptist as a fulfillment of prophecy, neither would they accept Jesus as the fulfillment of messianic prophecy. Both John and he himself would suffer and be rejected by the leaders of Israel.

The intention of the author is to share Jesus' interpretation of the prophecy concerning Elijah. This interpretation is connected with the account of the Transfiguration by the conjunction, "Then why" (τί οὖν). In the preceding account on the Transfiguration Jesus is proclaimed as the Messiah, the final fulfillment of the Law and the prophets. The conjunction οὖν introduces the deduction, If Jesus is the Messiah who then was the promised Elijah?

Such a merely psychological connection could not occur with two authors simultaneously. If we find the same arrangement of pericopes in Matthew and Mark, it must point to an interrelatedness between the two authors in some way or other. In Mark the connection between the two accounts on the transfiguration and Elijah is more tenuous than in Matthew, since no conjunction is used. On the other hand, Mark has inserted after the command to secrecy the information, that the disciples pondered over the meaning of "rising from the dead" (Mark 9:10). This insertion separates the accounts in a natural manner. With the introductory words of verse 11, "And they asked him," the question concerning Elijah follows as a completely new pericope. This arrangement seems to indicate that no internal connection has been intended by Mark.

There is another difference between Matthew and Mark. The issue for Matthew is especially the question whether or not Elijah must "come first" [in order to suffer and to be rejected]. Mark has pushed this aspect of the question into the background in order to focus on the question of the resurrection [or of the second coming,] a question which Matthew leaves untouched. From the perspective of the resurrection Mark demonstrates the inconsistency between a first and a second coming. The Scriptures predicted suffering for the Son of Man and could, therefore, not simultaneously promise a resurrection because it would then make that suffering meaningless. Elijah has come [in the person of John the Baptist] and has been mistreated according to the Scriptures. [There is no reason anymore to discuss an eschatological resurrection.]

Comparing the discussions of both evangelists it soon becomes evident that there is more reason to consider Matthew's presentation as the original text than to ascribe priority to the Marcan text. It is highly conceivable that Mark has inserted the question about the resurrection by the disciples. It would be consistent with Mark's custom to show a contrast between the profound sayings of Jesus and the low level of understanding among his disciples. Because of this change in content Mark eliminated any connection between the account of the Transfiguration and the dialogue on Elijah. It is quite conceivable that he felt the tension between the cross of Christ and the resurrection, and that he wanted to balance Matthew's account which emphasized the suffering of Christ. Mark's statement that Elijah has come (Mark 9:13) must have been adopted more or less routinely from Matthew, because we do not notice any attempt to prevent a potential conflict with his own eschatology.

If all these observations are correct, then Mark does not take a stand against Isaiah's prophecy but against Matthew's interpretation. Matthew grants the Pharisees the validity of their Elijah expectation. But Mark, on the contrary, presents the whole Elijah expectation as an erroneous idea that Jesus had already rejected.[26] Mark's revision, however, left some traces of the original Matthean thrust; Mark still retained the fact that Elijah had come (Mark 9:13), and that Elijah must come first (Mark 9:11-12). Both of these reminders of Matthew cannot be harmonized with a "second coming" because of their isolated position within the pericope.

These observations allow a reasonable explanation of the Elijah pericope in Mark as a revision of Matthew. It would be much more difficult to assert that Matthew in using Mark's text would have omitted Mark 9:10 [regarding the disciples pondering about the resurrection] and that he would have replaced it by the simple conjunction "then." It would also be difficult to assume that Matthew would have overlooked the whole elaboration on the resurrection and, on the basis of the suffering of John the Baptist, would have added the suffering of the Son of Man as a supplement, introduced by the words "So also the Son of Man will suffer" (Matt 17:12). Such considerations of both accounts preclude the possibility of granting Mark the epithet of being the original gospel.

A Comparative Evaluation of Mark and Matthew

Continuing our comparison of distinctive pericopes in Matthew and Mark is highly tempting, especially since there is such an abundance of such pericopes. All these bear the stamp of a later development in Mark, so that it is not difficult to make up one's mind on this issue. Above we already noted how the story of

---

[26]See above, 190.

the lame man and of the Canaanite woman were less articulate in Mark.[27] [Instead of discussing additional pericopes I would like to raise the following questions.]

(a) Is there any notion left in Mark of the profound idea originally expressed in the withering of the fruitless fig tree (Mark 11:12-14, 20-26)?

(b) Does Mark sufficiently explain the fear of the disciples during the transfiguration (Mark 9:2-12), which in Matthew comes forth from the genuine Jewish experience of the presence of God manifested by the bright cloud and the voice (Matt 17:1-13)?

(c) Can priority be attributed to the dialogue about divorce in the form it obtained in Mark, in which neither the question nor the answer applied to the Palestinian situation (Mark 10:1-12)? And, does the concluding conversation about remarriage in Mark (10:10-12) not give the appearance that it took the place of Matthew's ideas about the fact that it was "not expedient to marry" (Matt 19:10)?

(d) Should one regard Jesus' answer equally probable when speaking to the disciples concerning their inability to cast out demons in Mark 9:28-29 as his response in Matthew where it agrees with the situation of Israel expressed in the words "O, faithless generation" (Matt 17:17)?

(e) Can one see in Jairus's request and in the agony about his dying daughter anything else than the result of simultaneous use of Matthew and Luke (Mark 5:22-43)?

(f) Will the reader understand the appeal to the starving David in the account where the disciples made their way through the fields breaking the law of the Sabbath (Mark 2:23-28)?

All these pericopes and many more I would like to develop in order to demonstrate how the character and content of Mark speak against the Marcan hypothesis, even if their champions freely cut away from their beloved gospel every trace which might create doubts of its early date. For the reader's sake, I will not give in to this inclination. I only would like to discuss the sections that are unique for Mark. When also these uniquely Marcan texts appear to be of later date than the two other Synoptic gospels, they also will speak out against the Marcan hypothesis. Even its proponents are not anymore inclined to regard these "Singularia Marci" as later supplements to the second gospel.

---

[27]See above, 138, 139.

Chapter 8

The Uniquely Marcan Materials

Personal Identifications

Identifications in Mark

The advocates of the Marcan hypothesis regard it as evidence of an early date when Mark lists with great accuracy the names and circumstances of the principal figures in his account. It is, indeed, correct that the disciples or followers of Jesus are consistently identified by name; the blind man outside of Jericho is called Bartimaeus (10:46); the cognomen of the sons of Zebedee is only known because of the Marcan Gospel (3:17); the Canaanite woman is called a Syrophoenician by birth (7:26); the Cyrenean who was compelled to carry the cross is identified as the father of Alexander and Rufus (15:21); the event of the starving David is dated—although incorrectly—by Mark "when Abiathar was high priest" (2:26).

The conclusion that these personal identifications are evidence of the priority of the Gospel of Mark implies that at a later date the interest in such data was waning. The fact that Matthew and Luke do not provide such information would then be characteristic of later gospel literature, when such accuracies gradually faded. Thus the implication of the Marcan hypothesis is that the interest in names and places decreased and finally disappeared completely from the record.

Identifications in Early Christianity

This conclusion can be disputed, however, on the basis of early Christian literature. The question to what degree we may accept the historical reliability of these identifications is not of first importance. In this connection it is only necessary to become aware of the fact that the early church certainly did not become indifferent to proper names. On the contrary, we encounter during the first centuries of Christendom the tendency to associate later circumstances with persons and events in the gospel stories. Similar tendencies can be detected in the various Christian nations of Europe that derived their origins from the first apostles: as a rule the boldest claims were made!

The saints of the Syrian church performed the same miracles and spoke the same words as Jesus and his apostles. About Ignatius we are told that he was the child who was embraced and blessed by Jesus.[1] Philip was the man desiring to bury his father before following Jesus.[2] Justa was identified with the Syrophoenician woman known for her great faith.[3] Her sick daughter was thought to be the same person as Bernice.[4]

It is in this frame of mind that Mark reminded his fellow Christians, that Simon of Cyrene, who carried the cross for Jesus, was the father of Alexander and Rufus (Mark 15:21). The same mind set did not shrink from the boldest contentions. A clear evidence of this tendency is found in Celsus when he emphatically claims Panthera as the father of Jesus.[5] These examples could certainly be increased by examining more pages from early Christian literature.

The examples prove that the further one is removed from the historical facts the greater the interest grows in precise circumstances and concrete persons. Nor was there any hesitation to create new names when appropriate. The reader should be cautioned, therefore, against rash judgments about [the date of] Mark and [attributing too much historical reliability] to dubious proper names.

Unique Marcan Pericopes

The Parable of the Growing Seed

The parable of the Growing Seed (Mark 4:26-29) has been called by Strauss "a being without hands and feet,"[6] which emerged from the parable of the Weeds in Matthew (13:24-30). The "enemy" could conceivably have been the apostle Paul in analogy to the Clementine homilies. Because of his association with Paul, Mark allegedly left out the enemy mentioned in the Matthean parable. Strauss may have been partly correct in tracing the origin of the Marcan parable in this manner. There certainly are many points of agreement in both parables.

In the first place, both parables occupy the same position in the series of parables by the two evangelists. Secondly, they agree in imagery and terminolo-

---

[1]Nicephorus Callistus Xantopoulos, *Ecclesiasticae historiae* (Antverpiae: Joannis Steelsius, 1560) 2:35.

[2]Clement of Alexandria, *Stromata* 3.4; see *Patrologia Graeca*, 4th ed., ed. J. P. Migne (1857–1887) 9:1129.

[3]*Pseudoclementine Homilies*, ed. P. A. de Lagarde (1865) 2.19.

[4]Ibid., 3:73; 4:1.

[5]Origen, *Contra Celsum* 1.32.

[6]David Friedrich Strauss, "Das Gleichnis vom fruchtbringenden Acker (Mark 4:26-29). Ein Beitrag zur Charakteristik des Markus Evangelium," *Zeitschrift für Wissenschaftliche Theologie* 6 (1863): 209-14.

gy: they are both parables dealing with the Kingdom; in both cases it is "a man" who scattered the seed upon the ground; both parables speak about the sleep of the man; and the sprouting of the seed and the succeeding harvest also occur in both parables. We have to assume, therefore, a certain affinity between these parables.

It is difficult, however, to assume that the beautiful parable of Matthew and its interpretation (Matt 13:36-43) originated from the simple Marcan parable. There is, on the other hand, evidence that Mark was familiar with the Matthean text. It can be deduced from the way in which Mark incorporated the sower's sleeping in his presentation. In Matthew the night is the most opportune time for an enemy to sow the weeds among the wheat. Mark also mentions the sleep of the man but it plays no role in the process of the growing seed. When he attempts to make it functional by adding "and rise night and day," we are not terribly impressed by his clarification. [The omission of the thief and the additional comment in Mark's parable] can only find its explanation in the Matthean prototype.

The Healing of the Deaf and Dumb Man

It may seem strange that the stories of the healing of the deaf and dumb man (Mark 7:31-37) and of the blind man in Bethsaida (Mark 8:22-26) have been omitted by both Matthew and Luke. These typical healing accounts were supposedly left out by the other two Synoptics merely because these healing miracles used a medium and consequently could be interpreted in a naturalistic manner. This, at least, is the reasoning of the proponents of the Marcan hypothesis concerning the elimination of both accounts.

In response to this assertion we can trace for at least one of these accounts a source in Matthew. We find a portrayal of Jesus' messianic healing ministry in Matthew 15:29-31. While he is sitting on a hill, the crowds bring to him their "lame, the maimed, the blind, the dumb, and many others," all of whom had disabilities of which healing could be expected on the basis of Isaiah 35:5 and 61:1. It is, therefore, quite natural that the crowds glorified "the God of Israel" when they in astonishment heard the dumb speak and saw the lame walk and experienced the healing of the maimed and the blind.

Mark's parallel to this general portrayal of healing is the particular case of the healing of the deaf and dumb man. The Greek word used for this case of disability is κωφός. In classical Greek this term was used only for the state of "dumbness," but in later Jewish and early Christian literature it gained also the meaning of being "deaf." In this story Mark used this concept in both meanings simultaneously. The man is deaf as well as dumb and is healed from both disabilities. When the astonished bystanders witnessed this healing they exclaimed, "He has done all things well; he even makes the deaf hear and the dumb speak" (Mark 7:37). The division into the two aspects of one disability and the generalization of one case to all deaf and dumb people, can only be explained from Matthew's portrayal just mentioned. It is not quite accidental that Mark selected from the many diseases in Matthew one disability that by its double nature could represent the multiple aspects of Jesus' healing ministry.

The Synoptic Apocalypse (Matt 24-25, Mark 13, Luke 21)

Characteristic of Mark's apocalyptic message are the following verses from Mark 13:33-37.

> [33]Take heed, watch; for you do not know when the time will come. [34]It is like a man going on a journey, when he leaves home and puts his servants in charge, each with his work, and commands the doorkeeper to be on watch. [35]Watch therefore—for you do not know when the master of the house will come, in the evening, or at midnight, or at cockcrow, or in the morning—[36]lest he come suddenly and find you asleep. [37]And what I say to you I say to all: Watch. [RSV]

These verses occur at the point where Mark abandons his parallels in order to join his sources again in 14:1 where the passion narratives begin with the scheming of the enemies of Christ.

In the interim, Matthew has collected a long series of components dealing with the second coming and with the obligations for all those looking forward to the eschaton. Matthew reminds his readers of the days of Noah (24:37-41) and challenges to alertness against the coming "as a thief in the night" (24:42-44); he proceeds to portray the faithful and the unfaithful servants (24:45-51), the foolish and the wise maidens (25:1-13), the faithful and the lazy managers (25:14-30), and concludes with the picture of the final judgment (25:31-46) by the Son of Man.

Luke has these stories at other places but he does have three verses (Luke 21:34-36) reflecting the content of Mark 13:33-37. The agreement between both gospels is so great that one immediately asks the question which of the two authors has influenced the other. The Lukan passage undeniably has the same warning against dissipation, comparing the parousia with a "snare" coming suddenly upon the inhabitants of the earth. Luke also has a plea for the prayer that one may have strength to bear the "labor pains" of the second coming. Furthermore, the reader will notice that the words "all these things that will take place" refer back to similar references in the preceding verses, 31 and 32. Luke's eschatological passage, therefore, fits its context and cannot be regarded as an insertion.

By contrast, it is difficult to discover a cohesive context in Mark. What intention does "the man going on a journey" have (a) placing his servants in charge and (b) commanding the doorkeeper to be alert? Such imagery can hardly be an occasion for the admonition "Take heed, watch; for you do not know when the time will come." There is a certain paradox between the responsibility given to each of the servants and the work each of them has to do. There also is a certain superfluity in the repeated admonition to watchfulness. The strong reminders of the sudden coming of the Lord do not seem to square with the emphasis on work.

These phenomena in the Marcan text can be understood when compared with both parallel passages. Mark 13:33-37 reflects at each point and in its various components a rich acquaintance with gospel literature. The parallelism with the Lukan passage is evident. The admonition in Mark 13:33 ("Take heed") expresses the same challenge as Luke 21:34 ("take heed to yourselves"). By the words "watch and pray"[7] in Mark the reader is reminded of Luke's words "watch at all times, praying. . . . " Mark introduces the eschatological events in verse 34 with the words "it is like . . . " just as Luke does in verse 31. "Watch therefore" (Mark 13:35) is parallel to Luke's "watch at all times" (21:36). Both versions speak about "the hour" (καιρός), although with different meanings. The different Greek words, ἐξαίφνης in Mark and αἰφνίδιος in Luke, are both translated "suddenly." Luke's line of thought and his vocabulary can be recovered completely in Mark in a somewhat less articulated manner.

The question now is, from where do those extraneous components come by which Mark dissolves the unified Lukan admonition? In order to answer this question let us survey the parallel text in Matthew (24:42-46). Again it is remarkable at how many points we discover agreement with Mark. The coming of the Lord is first compared with the days of Noah (24:37-39) leading up to the admonition "Watch therefore, for you do not know on what day your Lord is coming" (Matt 24:42). These words are similar to the words we found as alien elements in Mark's context.

Throughout these Matthean chapters we encounter imagery similar to the Marcan pericope (13:33-37): the "unexpected return" is expressed in Matthew 24:44 and 25:13, 19; in Matthew 25:14 "a man going on a journey" is mentioned and also the distribution of talents among his servants; Matthew 24:13 refers to "his house" and 25:14 refers to the servants to whom the talents are given. A specific servant is in charge of the others in Matthew 24:45; in the middle of the night the bridegroom comes (25:6) expected by the maidens. "A door" is mentioned in Matthew 25:11, "sleeping" persons in Matthew 25:6, and the "finding" by the master in Matthew 24:46.

---

[7][The RSV has only "watch" in the text and relegates "and pray" to the margin. —ed.]

There is no need to discuss these eschatological images in detail. They only demonstrate that Mark's pericope has been formed by ideas originating from the eschatological parables in Matthew. In order to clarify this point I want to remind the reader what Luke (12:35-40) has in common with Matthew. Luke speaks of servants waiting for the return of their master from the marriage feast, so that they open to him when he comes and knocks. These servants play the role of doorkeepers. Luke continues with the words "Blessed are those servants whom the master finds awake when he comes"; his coming may take place in the second or in the third watch. Again we recognize imagery reminding us of the verses in Matthew and Mark.

I conclude from these data that Mark in the verses under discussion has condensed the eschatological expositions in Matthew. I also conclude that the structure of Mark's pericope was strongly influenced by Luke. The integration of the various materials has been carried out with so much creativity that it even left space for personal memories and impressions. Consequently, Mark's brief pericope shows on the one hand a certain terseness but on the other hand a certain richness of detail.

Mark's Message for the Early Church

The Meaning of Salt and Fire

Finally, I would like to present a conjecture concerning the two verses in Mark 9 that always have been considered a hermeneutical key (9:49-50). Thus far the exegetes have not come to a point of agreement on this passage. The many interpretations listed by Meyer as well as his own comment on this passage cannot satisfy the reader. They all end up in abstruse ideas which are difficult to grasp and even more difficult to imagine coming from the mind of an evangelist. The words I have in mind are

> [49]For every one will be salted with fire and every sacrifice will be salted with salt. [50]Salt is good; but if the salt has lost its saltiness, how will you season it? Have salt in yourselves, and be at peace with one another.[8]

It immediately strikes the eye of the reader that there is a contrast between salt which can lose its savor and salt which is not subject to loss of strength, between external and internal salt. Having "salt in yourselves" is recommended, while a warning is raised against merely external salt. The internal salt produces mutual peace while external salt is also described as fire.

---

[8][Quoted according to some Greek texts; RSV relegates to the margin the phrase "and every sacrifice will be salted with salt." —ed.]

The first question coming to mind concerns a definition of salt in this context. The fact that everyone and every sacrifice is salted with fire, does not necessarily indicate that salt would have the meaning of consecration. On the contrary, it is quite possible, even likely, that the meaning of "being salted" should be found in verse 50. The parallel verses in Matthew 5:13 and Luke 14:34 use the image of salt for the normative and preserving power of the followers of Christ in this world.

In Matthew and Luke the subject of the process of being salted is not quite clear. Mark, however, expresses in no uncertain terms who is accountable with his question "how will you season it?" Salt that can lose its taste is of no use since it cannot be seasoned again. We will have to think in this context of an incentive that becomes the source of power for the Christians. This incentive challenges them to be proud of their profession of faith and to preserve them from discord and backsliding. Dissension has the opposite effect of salt, according to verse 50. First of all peace is needed among the Christians themselves. Furthermore, such peace has a spiritual value as imperishable as internal salt. It is of greater value than fire, which as external salt could cease to have effect.

The question is, therefore, what is meant by this fire? The eternal fire which was mentioned in the preceding verses does not necessarily have to determine its meaning. The gospels provide numerous associations between paragraphs based merely on the similar sound of two words. We are, therefore, justified in attempting to find an interpretation from another context. In Luke 12:49 we read "I came to cast fire upon the earth," which must be understood in the same way as Matthew 10:34: "I have not come to bring peace, but a sword." These passages refer to the dissension and conflict Christianity has provoked in the world. This conflict manifested itself in oppression and persecution of Christians.

The gospels refer repeatedly to the reality of suffering and persecution. From other sources we know that Christians considered it a great honor to suffer in the name of Christ. They comforted themselves by identifying their fate with the suffering of their Lord. Being executed as a martyr was regarded a unique privilege by followers of Christ. A large section of the gospels remains misunderstood when the reader does not keep in mind the role of suffering during the first generations of Christendom. Many members were involved in relieving the suffering of incarcerated Christians. In the churches the martyr's crown soon became an eagerly desired honor. This drive created excesses against which already during the second century voices were raised in protest.

Taking this frame of reference into consideration we may ask whether Mark in these verses would not have given an admonition to this effect. Later on we repeatedly encounter that Christianity should take heed not to seek its highest honor in being oppressed and martyred. Indeed, fire has been kindled on earth and every Christian will be branded by it, but at some time this fire will be extinguished. If the Christians had merely found their unity in common oppression, this fellowship would be dissolved when suffering ceased. The only preservative is the inner salt creating inner peace and genuine fellowship; this salt will destroy all seeds of internal discord.

If this interpretation of Mark's metaphors is correct, it would also mean that these words would not have to be omitted by Matthew and Luke, [in case one assumes a Marcan priority. These metaphors of salt and fire] rather reveal a different era, [later than Matthew and Luke]. Mark's words are removed from the period of the eyewitnesses of Jesus' life and ministry [and reflect the situation of the early Christian Church].

Conclusion

Literary Exegetical Observations

The Theory of the Proto-Mark

We have come to a point where a summary of our total argument developed in the preceding pages is appropriate. Leaving aside the role of Luke, the question of the relation of Matthew and Mark is the following. In Matthew passages and issues occur that prevent us from regarding the first gospel as the obvious source for the second. Conversely, it is not possible simply to grant historical priority to canonical Mark. In the present stage of research no convincing objections can be made for or against either position.

The question now is, Which solution may be called the right one in this state of affairs? Accepting an Ur-gospel merely on the basis of the complicated relationship of two documents belongs to a previous era of text criticism. Contemporary scholarship requires historical research. If an exegete still wants to proceed in a nonhistorical manner, he must face up to the same critical rejection the Ur-gospel theory has experienced.[1]

Because such [a merely theoretical] approach is outdated, only two options remain. Mark could have used an earlier form of Matthew, or Matthew could have used an earlier form of Mark. Both approaches have been used by champions of the Marcan hypothesis. It became evident in our research that [Christian Hermann] Weisse and his predecessors soon had to take refuge in a Proto-Matthew in order to safeguard the unity of the second gospel.

These German scholars were forced to the assumption of a Proto-Matthew by their observation that there are places in Mark which betray a later date than their parallels in Matthew. This theory was accepted by [Heinrich] Meyer and [Bernhard] Weiss, who partially agreed at this point with [Heinrich] Ewald and his first followers. This conception was not the most popular and we may assert with some justification that the concept of a Proto-Mark was preferred by most proponents of the Marcan hypothesis. The latter theory has also basically guided us in our research. Let us summarize the pros and cons of this theory once more.

---

[1]See above, 20-26.

For its complete argumentation, the Marcan hypothesis rests ultimately on two grounds. Its advocates regarded it more likely that the shorter Gospel of Mark was the source of the longer Gospel of Matthew than vice versa. Secondly Mark has in contrast to Matthew an imagery that invites the reader to associate him as closely as possible with the early eyewitnesses.

These two considerations were the prevailing influences. The thesis of the literary imagery determined the interpretation of further details. Thus it became the strongest motivation for the assumption of a more elaborate Proto-Mark as source for the Gospel of Matthew. Later research demonstrated, however, that there was less evidence for a Proto-Mark than originally had been assumed. Only with the peculiar quantitative theory was it possible to maintain the priority of Mark. The literary imagery of Mark is of such a nature that it actually precluded an eyewitness report.[2]

The proofs for the priority of the Gospel of Mark based on the Proto-Mark theory were therefore partly invalid and partly even dangerous because of the inferences drawn from it. The proofs against the existence of a Proto-Mark are much stronger than those in favor of it. The whole distinction between a canonical Mark and a Proto-Mark is dubious. The Gospel of Mark is so much a unity and it is written with such language and style "from one mold,"[3] that the suggestion of later interpolations is not justified, without strong evidence to the contrary. Even the inauthentic concluding verses of Mark cannot be used as an argument for potential interpolations in the Gospel of Mark.

Also [on the basis of purely historical research] one is not justified in assuming that the present Gospel of Mark is an independent edition of a Proto-Mark which presumably has been lost. The reference to Papias's statement concerning such a document, if not outright improbable, is at least doubtful. Furthermore, the history of critical research has shown that the champions of the Marcan hypothesis could not do very much with the theory of a Proto-Mark. It would imply that one had lost the right to claim Papias for information on canonical Mark.

[The advocates of the Marcan hypothesis were faced with the alternative that] either their concept of the Proto-Mark or the eyewitness character of canonical Mark was invalid. Not only serious doubts concerning the Proto-Mark emerged from the studies of the adherents of the Marcan hypothesis, but also an unpleasant consequence was that canonical Mark would have to be regarded as being of a later date because of its editorial style. Even apart from these doubts and unpleasant implications, the theory of a Proto-Mark was hard to maintain.

The theological nature of the second gospel focuses on Christology, which by a wide margin surpasses the first gospel in theological development. Its

---

[2]See above, chap. 4.
[3]Quoted possibly from Heinrich Ewald: "aus einem Gusse," see above, 41.

theological perspective is of decisive importance for understanding the whole conception and outlook of the second gospel. [Its impact penetrates each level of this gospel so deeply] that even a presumed Proto-Mark could not escape having to be interpreted from the same theological perspective. As a result the so-called Proto-Mark could not be safeguarded from a late date either.

There is something peculiar in the sequence of the narratives in Mark in relation to the other two Synoptics. This peculiarity is inherent in what is left out as well as in what is included from the others.[4] [If, indeed, Matthew and Luke would have used Mark], it would be a strange phenomenon if two gospels independently of one another would have divided a common source in the way required by the Marcan hypothesis. Not only would it be a strange phenomenon, it would be improbable.

A similar remark should be made concerning vocabulary and style in the Gospel of Mark, suggesting an integration of its sources of Matthew and Luke. It would be difficult to explain the data by the opposite procedure [of separating vocabulary and elements of style]. There are those places in Mark in which we find expressions and turns of phrases integrated from parallels in Matthew and Luke. Frequently these places show a strange or inconsistent feature which can only be explained by unifying passages in Matthew and Luke. The same is true for unclear passages in Mark which need either Matthew or Luke for further clarification.

Furthermore, there are materials in Mark that can only be explained in the light of the major Marcan themes. They cannot be rescued for the Marcan hypothesis by isolating them as later components of the Gospel of Mark.

Finally, there are the uniquely Marcan materials. Several of these pericopes presuppose an acquaintance with the parallel accounts in Matthew and Luke. The position of condensation from two sources has proven to be more likely than the separation into two parallel gospels using Mark as their source. These materials are quite important for our discussion since the advocates of the Marcan hypothesis hesitate to attribute these uniquely Marcan materials to a later editor.

Considering all these observations, weighing their advantages and disadvantages, it is certainly not in doubt as to which direction the scales will tip. They would tip in the direction of the Marcan hypothesis only if conclusive force can be attached to the theses of brevity and imagery obliging one to regard all other arguments as resting on unsubstantial evidence. This would mean that ultimately the decision would be left to theological presuppositions alone.

At this point I would like to declare that the Marcan hypothesis is not tenable in any one of its three forms:

---

[4]See the chart on 152-53, above.

(a) The earlier conception that simply assigned priority to canonical Mark [on the basis of length and imagery] has been deemed superficial by a more penetrating form of biblical criticism. Even Weisse himself has given up this position.

(b) Secondly, there is a particular German form that maintains the canonical unity of the Gospel of Mark by using a Proto-Matthew as the source and explanation of Mark's later expressions. This form never became popular and had too little historical support to avoid being deemed arbitrary by its opponents.

(c) Thirdly, there is the French form that takes its refuge in a Proto-Mark and that has now become [through Holtzmann] the prevailing theory in Germany. Although confident of its prevailing position, this form still leaves too many problems unsolved in the gospels themselves to be qualified as an acceptable theory. Furthermore, one of its representatives ([Michel] Nicolas) has already pointed out its vulnerable spots.

The reader may remark that there is something inequitable in this listing of the weaknesses and strengths of the Marcan hypothesis, for we have made no reference to the arguments presented by the advocates themselves. There are, to be sure, passages in Matthew that by comparison with their parallel texts in Mark have to be assigned a secondary nature. These passages, indeed, cannot without great difficulty be harmonized with the thesis of Matthean priority.

The Theory of the Proto-Matthew

At this point we are returning to the first possibility that we had to reject in the form accepted by the proponents of the Marcan hypothesis. Our question is whether Matthew in an earlier form could have been one of the sources of the Gospel of Mark. The answer to this question is determined by two points: first by the nature of the literary expressions used by Matthew and second by the character of the total Gospel of Matthew.

The second point is the most decisive criterion, while the first point of characteristic Matthean expressions is really a phenomenon of little significance. Whenever we pursue the passages adduced as arguments against Matthean priority, it turns out quite soon that these are strongly determined by subjective motivations. By far the largest number of these passages are open to different evaluation, so that these cannot possibly be used for objective criteria concerning an early or late date. This becomes especially evident in the studies of [Albert] Réville who lists a long series of Matthean passages that are allegedly secondary to Mark. By far the largest number of them stand or fall with the presupposition assumed by the exegete. Above I have attempted to demonstrate of how great consequence a presupposition can be.[5]

However long the exegete majors on minor details, he will not be able to

---

[5]See above, 58.

prove the priority of Mark. Such details may involve a distinction between "the carpenter's son" (Matt 13:55) and "the son" (Mark 6:3) as an improvement by Matthew. Also, the question may be raised whether Matthew has corrected the Marcan text by adding the story of the virgin birth; the suggestion could be made that Matthew, in agreement with later tradition, added additional subject materials such as the sermons; arguments even have been used saying Matthew wanted to bring out more strongly than has his Marcan source the astonishment of the inhabitants of Nazareth. These exegetes blithely explain away the objectionable Matthean omission "nor the Son" from Mark 13:32 by the proposal that Matthew wanted to portray with greater profundity the inscrutable secrecy of the time of the eschaton. Such escapes should be categorized among the arguments listed above, on pages 123-25.

The phenomena we are discussing are actually of minor importance. But suppose there were many nonoriginal expressions in Matthew. We would again be confronted by the same issue discussed above in connection with the concept of Proto-Mark. The ultimate decision will have to be made in the same manner. With Mark it appeared to us that no distinction between earlier materials and their later canonical form could be made unless a strong case could be made in favor of this. The unity of Mark's Gospel was a major argument against such separation of different levels in one gospel.

If the Gospel of Matthew were an equally cohesive unity we would have to face up to the same unlikelihood [of a distinction between early and late materials]. The case is, however, that the character of Matthew is rather that of a composite of source materials. I do not need to prove my point. Holtzmann conceded that "today we argue from the concession that we start from the secondary nature of the first gospel."[6] The qualification "secondary" is of great significance for our discussion. It indicates that Matthew has not emerged from the brain of one author but rather is the result of a long history. Matthew's text points to a variety of sources. It shows evidences of editorial work and its present canonical form incorporates several interpolations. The irregularities and inconsistencies have not been wiped out by later editors either. Divergent theological conceptions point to various stages of development.

The whole question of the origin of Matthew's gospel is so obscure that only a few rays of light can guide us. We have to give up forever expecting to reach back to the sources themselves. In such a state of affairs we will never be able to analyze this gospel into its various components. Hilgenfeld has long been of the opinion that a simple distinction between an original text and an edited canonical text could explain the origin of the Gospel of Matthew. Recently, how-

---

[6]Heinrich Julius Holtzmann, *Die synoptischen Evangelien: Ihr Ursprung und geschichtlicher Charakter* (Leipzig: W. Engelmann, 1863) 36.

ever, this scholar came to recognize a still earlier source, so that the canonical gospel has been degraded by him to a tertiary text.[7]

It is clear that not only editions of an earlier text are under discussion, but also glosses and insertions must be allowed for. Professor Scholten has interpreted the words of Matthew 12:40 concerning the sign of Jonah as a gloss.[8] Let me call attention to a few other passages in Matthew. The prayer that the flight of the Christians might not take place in winter or on a sabbath disrupts the context (Matt 24:20); the coming great tribulation in verse 21 could not be a reason for such a prayer, but verse 19 with the lament about those "with child" does invoke the need [for such a prayer]. This disruption disappears when the prayer concerning the flight is inserted before the lament of verse 19 and after the instructions for the predicted flight in verses 16-18. The words of the prayer could be a gloss inserted by the copyist in an inaccurate manner.

In Matthew 15 a bitter accusation is directed against the Scribes and the Pharisees (vss. 1-9) following a question concerning the tradition. After this episode Jesus called the people to him and taught in metaphor about the real defilement of a person (vss. 10-11). When Peter asked for an explanation of this parable (vs. 15), the reader does not understand why he first should be informed that the Pharisees were offended (vss. 12-14). That offense must have been caused by the accusation of verses 1-9. Between that accusation and the information concerning the offense, however, is the message to the crowds. Also at this location the most likely explanation of verses 12-14 is that they were originally a marginal note written alongside this paragraph. These verses were then inserted after verse 11 instead of after verse 9.

Considering these phenomena in comparison with the character of Mark we will recognize that these gospels cannot be dealt with on the same basis. It is highly improbable that the canonical Gospel of Mark received its present form by way of insertions. On the other hand, it is quite probable that Matthew would show traces of later editorial work even after Mark had used it for his source.

So it is possible that the tax collector of Matthew 9:9 called "Matthew," was named "Levi" in an earlier edition. It is also possible that the words "besides the women and the children" (14:21; 15:38), were added later to the number of those present at the feeding of the multitude; a later editor of Matthew could quite well have put the question of the sons of Zebedee on the lips of their mother. Jesus' answer would rather suggest that these men expressed this request themselves (Matt 20:22). [They also responded in a personal manner saying, "We are able," namely, to drink the cup.] The editor of Matthew could have changed the original offensive words quoted in Mark 10:18: "Why do you call me good? No

---

[7]Adolf Hilgenfeld, "Das Evangelium der Hebräer," *ZWTh* 6 (1863): 345ff.

[8]J. H. Scholten, *Inleiding,* 18; later he withdrew this opinion.

one is good but God alone." Matthew's present text has "Why do you ask me about what is good? One there is who is good" (Matt 19:17).

Thus it is possible that there are long sections in Matthew that Mark has not known. Words about the keys of heaven, about binding and loosing, and about baptism could have been part of such unknown later words and phrases.[9] But I would not want to do more than just suggest this possibility. Here we have approached the borderline between exegesis and eisegesis; any step across this line might very well be a misstep.

All I want to assert is that there are many objections against a division of Mark into an early text and a canonical text. Secondly I maintain that those objections cannot be raised against the recognition of a Proto-Matthew. The less-original expressions in Matthew have therefore no conclusive power for other parts of this gospel. [They certainly are there, but they cannot provide a basis for the date of the total Gospel of Matthew.] These verses are merely the straw to which the drowning defenders of the Marcan hypothesis are reaching out.

The ratio of the strengths and weaknesses of the Marcan hypothesis is, indeed, unbalanced. I venture to stay with my opinion that this hypothesis should be rejected as inadequate. In chapter 7 several objections have been listed. Already at that stage of research it was quite evident in which direction a solution was to be found. The Gospel of Mark can best be understood as a document whose author used Matthew and Luke as his sources.

In order to substantiate my opinion I want to add a few more ways scholars have attempted to explain the origin and mutual relationships of the gospels. I am referring to the conception of those scholars who assign to Mark the same place in the development of gospel history as the early church did within the canon. Also the opinion of [Karl Reinhold] Köstlin should be evaluated. This scholar attempted a combination of the Marcan hypothesis and the Griesbach theory by assuming in Mark as well as in the other Synoptic gospels the use of a Proto-Mark.

Historical Observations

Adolf Hilgenfeld's Conciliatory Approach

I prefer not to discuss the long list of authors who since Augustine have been defenders of the canonical sequence of the gospels. They argued either on the basis (a) of tradition, (b) of theology, or (c) even on more or less critical grounds. I would rather concentrate on those scholars who in recent years have defended this position. This was the period during which one had to choose either for Griesbach or for the Marcan hypothesis.

---

[9]See Strauss, *Das Leben Jesu für das deutsche Volk bearbeitet* (1864) 1:117ff.

[Adolf] Hilgenfeld is the first to be considered in such a study. After he had developed his standpoint Hilgenfeld listed the following advantages of his theory.

Already the early church had accepted two ways for the study of the gospels. Recent research has continued along these same avenues. The first way was the assumption of a mutual relationship between the canonical gospels, while the second way studied the relation of our gospels to non-canonical writings. I have condensed both ways into one approach with the understanding that I have stressed the second.

With my approach I discovered the origin and the major results of the development of the gospels within the canon, while also the influence of noncanonical literature was of great influence on a gospel like that of Luke. The written Ur-gospel was detected within the compass of the canonical gospels, although in a different sense than [Johann Gottfried] Eichhorn had formulated. The sequence of the gospels was viewed in the same manner as [Johann Leonhard] Hug did, although again in a somewhat different way.

Also the relative justification of the Tradition hypothesis in its different forms was recognized on the assumption that the living tradition of the church exerted a continuing influence on the content of the Scriptures. The valid elements of the Marcan hypothesis have been retained by granting Mark more independence in relation to the other Synoptics. Finally, in agreement with the reasonable challenge of Tendency Criticism the gospels were studied under the aspect of the continuing development of the Christian church and her theological conflicts.[10]

It is strange that such a comprehensive theory has not received a greater response from New Testament scholars. Hilgenfeld himself repeatedly expresses his surprise that his conception of the gospels appears far from a generally accepted hypothesis.[11] He himself is certainly not to blame for not having received the desired acclaim. For years he waged an incessant battle against Baur on the one hand, and against the Marcan hypothesis on the other. Hilgenfeld's solution was presented as a conciliatory approach and he did not fail to criticize [the polarized positions of] his opponents.

The Marcan hypothesis was especially under strong attack by Hilgenfeld. He devoted a separate article to this theory in his journal,[12] in which he also dis-

---

[10]Adolf Hilgenfeld, *Der Kanon und die Kritik des Neuen Testaments in ihrer geschichtlichen Aushildung und Gestaltung, nebst Herstellung und Beleuchtung des muratorischen Bruckstückes* (Halle: C. E. M. Pfeffer, 1863) 173.

[11]"Die beiden neuesten Stimmen aus Zürich über Evangelien-Kritik," *Zeitschrift für Wissenschaftliche Theologie* 2 (1859): 252; "Die Evangelienforschung nach ihrem Verlaufe und gegenwärtigen Zustände," *ZWTh* 4 (1861): 183.

[12]"Das Marcus-Evangelium und die Marcus Hypothese," *ZWTh* 7 (1864): 287-333.

cussed the advocates of the Marcan hypothesis individually. These articles included an evaluation of [Christian H.] Weisse, [Heinrich A. W.] Meyer, and [Gustav] Volkmar,[13] of [Titus] Tobler,[14] [Daniel] Schenkel, and [Bernhard] Weiss,[15] of [Heinrich] Holtzmann,[16] and of [Karl Heinrich] Weizsäcker.[17] Three summarizing articles included these men and others in a complete history of the Marcan hypothesis.[18]

Repeatedly Hilgenfeld made known that if he were to be confronted with a choice between the Marcan hypothesis and Griesbach, he would side with the latter.[19] All this, however, did not prevent his appearance [on the critical scene] from being highly welcomed by the advocates of the Marcan hypothesis. Hilgenfeld was an ally in the conflict with Baur and his clear ideas about the relation between Mark and Luke were eagerly accepted. The proponents of the Marcan hypothesis, however, deplored Hilgenfeld's entanglement in the wiles of Tendency criticism.

Acclaim by the proponents of the Marcan hypothesis was understood by Hilgenfeld as a victory over F. C. Baur.[20] The struggle against Baur, however, lasted several years. Hilgenfeld began his research in Justin Martyr and in the *Homilies* of Clement, both benefiting his conception of the origin of the gospels. The results of this research for gospel criticism were published in his book on the Gospel of Mark in which he took the field against the Griesbach hypothesis.

Hilgenfeld's argument [in 1850] was initially against the quantitative approach by [Heinrich] Saunier who [in 1825] developed Griesbach's theory in this direction. One year later (1851) Baur reacted against Hilgenfeld in a study on the Gospel of Mark. Then (in 1852) Hilgenfeld responded by way of an

---

[13]"Die Evangelienfrage und seine neueste Behandlungen von Weisse, Volkmar, und Meyer," *Theologische Jahrbücher* 16 (1857): 381-440, 498-532.

[14]"Die beiden neuesten Stimmen aus Zürich über Evangelien-Kritik," *ZWTh* 2 (1859): 252-72.

[15]"Die Evangelienfrage und ihre neuesten Bearbeitungen," *ZWTh* 5 (1862): 3-10; "Marcus zwischen Matthäus und Lukas," *ZWTh* 9 (1866): 84-90.

[16]"Die Evangelien und die geschichtliche Gestalt Jesu," *ZWTh* 6 (1863): 311-40.

[17]"Weizsäckers *Untersuchungen über die evangelische Geschichte*," *ZWTh* 6 (1863): 171-212.

[18]"Die Evangelienforschung nach ihrem Verlaufe und gegenwärtigen Zustände," *ZWTh* 4 (1861): 1-72; "Der Kanon und die Kritik des Neuen Testaments," *ZWTh* 6 (1863): 137-204; "Die Evangelien und die geschichtliche Gestalt Jesu," *ZWTh* 6 (1863): 311-40.

[19]Adolf Hilgenfeld, *Das Markusevangelium, nach seiner Composition, seiner Stellung in der Evangelienliteratur, seinem Ursprung und Charakter* (Leipzig: Breitkopf und Härtel, 1850) 2; "Marcus zwischen Matthäus und Lukas," *ZWTh* 9 (1866): 113.

[20]"Die Evangelien und die geschichtliche Gestalt Jesu," *ZWTh* 6 (1863): 312.

article in the Tübingen "Annual." The article was written "in view of Dr. Baur's presentation" and was qualified as a "new study on the Gospel of Mark."[21]

Hilgenfeld was easily influenced by the critical method of his opponents as was already detectable in his previous publication.[22] Yet, even though Hilgenfeld was conciliatory in his attitude, Baur responded once again, in 1853, without conceding any points.[23] This exchange of ideas caused Hilgenfeld to express once more his feelings in the matter with his publication [in 1854] of *The Gospels* [note 24 below]. This final publication was merely a correction of secondary aspects of his position.

Hilgenfeld called his approach the "literary-historical" method, which is essentially different from Baur's Tendency criticism. The difference is that Hilgenfeld does not attempt to ascend to the source of the gospels, but rather is following the development of these gospels until their final form. His interpretation is less oriented to theological tendencies in the gospels than Baur's approach.[24] For our concerns we are more interested in his discoveries than in his method. We want to concentrate on his conception of the interrelatedness of the Synoptic gospels insofar as this is different [from Baur's as well as from that of the proponents of the Marcan hypothesis].

Hilgenfeld regarded Matthew as the only source for Mark, while Luke was considered independent of this development. This theory can only be brought forward on the condition that ample proofs are given to respond to the arguments for Marcan priority. His theory is for the most part based on the sequence of Matthew's stories and its way of expression, in comparison with those of the other two Synoptics. Hilgenfeld paid closer attention to the Gospel of Mark than Griesbach did in his first publications. He discovered a special design and an independent approach in Mark that could only be explained from the context and sequence in Matthew. Very little attention, indeed, had been given to Mark's design and approach by the earlier Griesbach hypothesis.

But before I formulate an evaluation of Hilgenfeld's approach, I want to mention his thesis that a certain "Gospel of Peter" had been known to Justin Martyr and to the author of the Clementine *Homilies*. According to Hilgenfeld, this gospel was an early form of Mark and, as such, a connecting link between

---

[21]Adolf Hilgenfeld, "Neue Untersuchung über das Markusevangelium, mit Rücksicht auf Dr. Baur's Darstellung," *Theologische Jahrbücher* 11 (1852): 102-32, 259-93.

[22]In his first book, *Das Markusevangelium,* Hilgenfeld majored on an argument based on imagery in the Gospel of Mark; in his article of 1852 a multiple influence of Luke on the Gospel of Mark was posed.

[23]Ferdinand C. Baur, "Rückblick auf die neuesten Untersuchungen über das Markusevangelium," *Theologische Jahrbücher* 12 (1853): 54-93.

[24]Adolf Hilgenfeld, *Die Evangelien, nach ihrer Entstehung und geistlichen Bedeutung* (Leipzig: S. Hirzel, 1854) 41ff.

Mark and Luke. I do not feel bound to express an opinion on the hypothesis of a Gospel of Peter, first because it has not been accepted by scholars of our generation,[25] second because, even for Hilgenfeld, it increasingly has lost its value. Originally, according to Hilgenfeld, this Gospel of Peter was an extensive document of which our Gospel of Mark was a condensed edition and which also was used by Luke. In Hilgenfeld's writings there remained some uncertainty concerning the way in which the editing by Mark and the use by Luke took place. The triple relationship of our Marcan gospel to Matthew, to the Gospel of Peter, and even to Luke was quite vague.[26]

After Baur's rejection of this reconstruction it was clear to Hilgenfeld that Mark could not be regarded as a simple condensation of the Gospel of Peter. Hilgenfeld changed his position on a direct condensation to an indirect relation by way of a more or less freely executed editorial process.[27] Still later, he merely assumed the possibility that a certain Gospel of Peter had been used as one of Mark's sources. At this point Hilgenfeld listed Matthew and the Petrine-Roman tradition as additional sources. The Gospel of Peter mentioned by Justin Martyr was supposedly the cause of the peculiar traits in the Gospel of Mark. These traits seemed to point to a written source.[28] Finally, Hilgenfeld changed his position once more by expressing his ideas as follows: "At least, Mark has also used the Petrine-Roman tradition" without any reference to a Gospel of Peter.[29]

Thus the assumed Gospel of Peter gradually lost its importance for the Gospel of Mark. With this decrease of importance, the recognition of an earlier more complete form of Mark has also been given up. In this connection we should remember the way in which Hilgenfeld, in an earlier publication,[30] considered the brief warning against the Pharisees (Mark 12:38-40) inexplicable. Such a warning could supposedly only be explained if at least its major points had been mentioned by Mark as well as by Luke. Similar points in Mark were considered understandable if they agreed with a Gospel of Peter, closely identical to Luke. If in our present stage of research the Gospel of Peter is no longer acceptable, such specifically Marcan texts should then be interpreted from Luke.

---

[25]Albrecht B. Ritschl, "Über den Gegenwärtigen Stand der Kritik der synoptischen Evangelien," *Theologische Jahrbücher* 10 (1851): 482ff; F. C. Baur, *Das Markusevangelium nach seinem Ursprung und Charakter, nebst einem Anhang über das Evangelium Marcions* (Tübingen: L. F. Fues, 1851) 124ff.

[26]Cf. Hilgenfeld, *Das Markusevangelium*, 98, 100, 101.

[27]Hilgenfeld, "Neue Untersuchung über das Markusevangelium, mit Rücksicht auf Dr. Baur's Darstellung," *Theologische Jahrbücher* 11 (1852): 291.

[28]Hilgenfeld, *Die Evangelien*, 147.

[29]Hilgenfeld, "Das Markus-Evangelium und die Markus-Hypothese," *ZWTh* 7 (1864): 329.

[30]Hilgenfeld, *Das Markusevangelium*, 98.

Consequently, if there had been no Gospel of Matthew, Hilgenfeld would have suggested the origin of Mark later than Luke.

Hilgenfeld, however, had a too independent and structured plan for Mark, which caused him to leave ample room for creative work by the author himself. Hilgenfeld even felt urged to consider Matthew the major source for Mark. Let us investigate whether the independence of Mark is of such a nature that its text variations can, indeed, be better explained from Matthew than from Luke.

One point must immediately seem suspicious. Why was it so difficult for Hilgenfeld to explain his position to others, in spite of repeated efforts on his part? When we read his description of the nature of Mark's gospel, we are told, first of all, that immediately Jesus caused amazement by his teaching and miracles in Capernaum. Hilgenfeld portrays how Jesus' fame spread throughout Galilee; how he performed several healings in the evening; how the people could hardly do without him when he wanted to preach and perform healings in the surrounding towns; and how people flocked to him from all directions (Mark 1:14-45).

Thus the first impression Jesus made was favorable. The next five sections of the Gospel of Mark show a totally different situation. The Scribes and Pharisees were offended by Jesus' claim to forgive sins, by his association with tax collectors and by his commonsense approach to fasting and Sabbath observance. Together with the Herodians these leaders devised a plot to kill him (2:5–8:6). At this time the opposition was already in full force.

According to Hilgenfeld it is in this sequence of [positive and negative] events that Mark's predilection for literary contrast is revealed. This endeavor to present the light and dark side of Jesus' ministry was also the reason why he rearranged the materials he adopted from Matthew. For example, he inserted a second absence from Capernaum before the crossing of the Lake to Gadara (Mark 5:1-20). His teaching at the lakeside away from Capernaum brings him praise by the people (Mark 4:1-41). This light side was balanced by a dark side reflected in the request by the Gadarenes that the dangerous miracle worker leave their area (Mark 5:17). The same literary contrast of acceptance and rejection is allegedly the reason the two rebuttals about breaking the sabbath (Mark 2:23-28 and 3:1-6) immediately follow the discussion about fasting (Mark 2:18-21). In Matthew these rebuttals occur namely in a much later context.

Response to Adolf Hilgenfeld

This pattern of contrasting impressions is not altogether unlikely, but a closer look leaves us with many questions. In the first place this contrast motif alone is not sufficient to explain Mark's divergence from Matthew. According to Hilgenfeld, the events at Capernaum take the place of the Sermon on the Mount. The positive response in Capernaum, the city of Peter, is derived from a questionable veneration for Peter in the Marcan gospel. Secondly, Jesus' better moments appear to be his moments of popularity with the crowds leaving aside any other aspect.

The performance of great miracles could have demonstrated a high point, which would have allowed Hilgenfeld to depict the silencing of the storm as a high point rather than a low point because of the little faith of the disciples. Similar remarks about Hilgenfeld's view can be made in connection with the event in Gadara which in Hilgenfeld's reconstruction is marred by the unusually negative request of its inhabitants. There is often light during the periods of darkness. While the Pharisees made their plans to kill Jesus, the crowds are gathering in front of his temporary home in astonishment and gratitude (2:1); they gather again in 2:13; and in 2:15 even the tax collectors follow him. It is difficult to maintain that the radiance of Jesus' first appearance would have been diminished because of the scheming of the Pharisees. The contrast between light and dark becomes quite diffused when all aspects are brought into play. Finally, it all amounts to this: five similar pericopes, which occur separately in Matthew, are united in Mark as well as Luke (see the chart above, on page 152, referring to Mark 4:35-5:43).

The first divergence by Mark from Matthew, therefore, cannot be explained by any endeavor for contrast. The question remains, who brought the five pericopes together, Mark or Luke? It would be Mark if, indeed, this pattern of contrast were evident in later parts of his gospel. But unfortunately Hilgenfeld's strongest case for contrast is based on the first two chapters in Mark, discussed above.

Hilgenfeld naturally continues to find bright moments in chapter 3. The many crowds surrounding Jesus and the many demons who know him must serve this emphasis. Also the appointment of the twelve apostles is presented in contrast to the plot of the Pharisees and points to a greater expansion of Jesus' ministry (3:7-19). Immediately after this Jesus is declared a demented person by his own friends, and the scribes claim that he is possessed by Beelzebul (3:18-30).

In this connection we already get premonitions that we will soon lose the theme of Mark's narrative. The opposition of praise and hostility has been adjusted in order to make place for another contradistinction: resistance and perseverance. Such a contrast is to be detected with great difficulty in the general description of 3:7-12. As we found light during dark periods, above, so we find here a similar confusion of contrast. In the home where Jesus is called demented the thronging is so great that there is no opportunity to eat (3:20).

Gradually we have arrived at totally different contrasts. On the occasion of the visit of his relatives, Jesus pointed to a wider group of followers who would be open to his teaching. The contraposition of receptivity and inability to understand comes now into focus. In the series of parables both these attitudes occur next to one another. The crowd, which again is present in large numbers, belongs to the group for whom every teaching has to be enveloped in parables. The disciples, on the other hand, are those to whom it is given to understand the mysteries of the Kingdom (4:11). But even the disciples do not measure up to expectations. [Since the disciples do not understand the meaning of the first parable,] the contrast between ability and inability to understand is also diffused and shadows mix with the light.

The shadows become dark during the period in Gadara (Mark 5:1-20), according to Hilgenfeld. The reason was the request by the Gadarenes to leave their territory. This story had been left out by Mark in an earlier connection,[31] because, at that location, the editor needed a favorable response. At this time there is a place available for a dark moment, so Mark inserts the total episode of Gadara in chapter 5. However, the remarkable thing is that the editor adds a request by the previous demoniac to become a disciple, which is a moment of light; also, there was a general awe about Jesus' miraculous work among the crowd when Jesus proclaimed his message in the Decapolis. Again favorable features are mixed in with unfavorable events. [The positive response of the demoniac is followed immediately by another positive response, namely,] the thronging of the crowds which are depicted with great emphasis (5:21-31).

Another combination of contrasts is seen by Hilgenfeld in Mark 6:1-12, where the rejection at Nazareth is balanced by the sending out of the disciples. To be sure, the sequence of the contrast is immediate. One is allowed to ask, however, whether the unbelief of the people of Nazareth should be called an "absolute rejection" and whether the mission of the disciples two by two has anything to do with the impossible mission in Nazareth. The evangelist does not inform us about such a change in policy by Jesus. The question is whether there is a contrast at all in this context.

Hilgenfeld points also to the low level of understanding among the disciples (6:52; 7:17; 8:17), which stands in strong contrast to the well-articulated profession of faith by Peter. Hilgenfeld remarks that the enthusiastic throngs in these chapters decrease, that the miracles receive a more mysterious character, and that everything is preparing for the final catastrophe. In the midst of these looming shadows the profession of faith by Peter and the transfiguration are points of light. There no longer is a reference to a contrast. The motif has now become "a striving for historical consistency." With this motif we have totally left the initial thesis of contrast.

It may be that the contraposition between the inability to understand among the disciples and their clear insight is inherent in the nature of their master. At least, Hilgenfeld would have to demonstrate that the author betrays his intention to bring out that clear insight. The opposite is the case when the editor describes

---

[31]See above, 218.

in later verses that the disciples still do not give evidence of a higher level of understanding (9:6, 10, 32; 10:32). Finally, Hilgenfeld assures the reader that whatever contrasts may be present in chapters 8 and 9, they were already existent in Matthew and were adopted by Mark without any change.

In summary, it is hardly possible to get a clear picture of Hilgenfeld's ideas. He first seeks for a contrast between the praise of the crowds and the opposition of the hostile parties, although the portrayal of thronging crowds is a consistent peculiarity in Mark. Then he pursues the crowd's inability to understand in distinction from the insight of the few initiated men. But this is a distinction that is mentioned by Mark only in passing, and certainly has no influence on the total gospel. Repeatedly Hilgenfeld asserts that opposition on the one hand leads to a more intensive ministry on the other hand. But also concerning this contrast it is difficult to form a notion of what is meant.

Finally, Hilgenfeld points to the structural unity of Mark, which portrays the spiritual growth of the disciples culminating in their profession of faith, on the one hand, and which spurs the opposition against Jesus ending in the crucifixion, on the other. It is clear to me that the former development is hardly present in Mark, while the latter development leading to the crucifixion is not specifically of Marcan origin.

It is a difficult assignment to create a unity of all these motifs and to see this dialectic unity as a characteristic feature of Mark. It would be even more difficult to explain the organization of these materials on the assumption that Mark is simply dependent on Matthew. At first, according to Hilgenfeld, it was an established fact that Mark did not know our third gospel and had to be explained only from Matthew. The reader should keep this in mind, says Hilgenfeld, in interpreting the occasional changes in sequence. However, Hilgenfeld's criteria are far from adequate. They cannot provide a basis for the proof that Mark would not need the Gospel of Luke for its interpretation.

Hilgenfeld's merit is mainly that he emphatically affirmed the independence of Mark over against the early form of Griesbach's hypothesis which denied to Mark any type of individuality. But it is an exaggeration when he claims to discover so much structure and design in the creative effort of the second gospel that Mark's work can only be explained from Matthew. For me, at least, Hilgenfeld has not demonstrated that the origin of Mark can be traced better from Matthew alone than from the texts of both Synoptics.

Theological Observations

Gustave d'Eichthal's Traditional Approach

One more scholar needs to be discussed, who considers the sequence of the gospels along the same lines as Hilgenfeld. I am referring to Gustave d'Eichthal whose work *The Gospels,* was published during the early 1860s.

There is a certain dignity in his personality. D'Eichthal was born a Jew. In his younger years he joined the Roman Catholic Church. As a young man he became a disciple of [the socialist] Saint-Simon [Claude de Rouvroy] and continued his work together with other followers. Gradually d'Eichthal came to the conviction that only in and through the world at large could the work of the Kingdom be completed which had been started within a small circle. At the same time it became clear to him that the development of Christendom would introduce those changes that society needed.

D'Eichthal's newly gained convictions did not ask anymore for a "New Christianity" in the sense of Saint-Simon. Jesus had already formulated the criterion: "Render to Caesar the things that are Caesar's and to God the things that are God's" (Mark 12:17). As this provided a common basis for Israel and the Roman world, it would also create a common task for religious and social existence in our day. D'Eichthal dedicated himself totally to the history of antiquity in order to discover that our contemporary civilization is nothing else than the melting pot of Jewish, Greek, and Roman culture. He then continued to study early Christian literature, discovering that the mystic and spiritualistic outlook, to which Saint-Simon reacted so vehemently, was a later development and that it was not indigenous to original Christianity as it emerged from Jesus and from Israel.

This last conviction was the fruit of his gospel studies, the conclusions of which we will discuss here. Before d'Eichthal began his research he had consulted the introductions that had been provided for the translations of the gospels in an edition of the New Testament made in the city of Mons during the seventeenth century. He then read Augustine's "On the Harmony of the Gospels." Both studies assured him that Mark had used Matthew and that Luke had used both Matthew and Mark as his sources. This provided him a starting point as well as his ultimate result.

D'Eichthal compared Matthew and Mark carefully and discovered that Mark in the parallels always shows a later reading.[32] He also discovered that Mark omitted Jesus' theological expositions which were most essential for the religious Jews and proselytes of Jesus' day. Instead, Mark gave detailed information on

---

[32]Gustave d'Eichthal, *Les Évangiles, Examen critique et comparatif des trois premiers évangiles* (Paris: Hachette, 1863) 1:39.

Jesus' miraculous work. Consequently, for d'Eichthal the objective of Mark seemed to be a promotion of Christianity for the lower class of pagan society.[33]

Then he continued to compare Luke's text with both Matthew and Mark in order to find the motivations that had led Luke to his project. Specifically, d'Eichthal's study of Luke's travelogue is important. He called this a "theological section" partially drawn from Matthew. Luke applied his critical mind, in the sense that he interrogated Matthew concerning various occasions and often received contradictory answers, which he wrote down without further editorial harmonization.

Furthermore, Luke developed in the same travelogue his own Pauline theology.[34] The sections that precede the travelogue and those that follow are called "historical sections," which mainly follow Mark's text although there are rearrangements, insertions, and omissions. It is striking how d'Eichthal sets apart a whole series of pericopes and verses from Matthew, which do not occur in Mark and Luke. He categorizes these parts as "annexations" from later times. Some of these he later discovered in Mark and finally he recognized their presence also in Luke.

However much d'Eichthal's conception is the result of extensive and conscientious research, however much his studies abound in mature considerations and minute observations, I cannot view his exposition as a proof that Luke has known the Gospel of Mark. His convictions are so speculative that I would deny this study any academic value.

I would like to assess d'Eichthal's work in comparing it with Renan's work. Why did Renan, for instance, fail to make adequate use of the gospels as sources for the history of Jesus and of original Christianity? Since his scholarship was uncontested, Renan could not be accused of a lack of scholarly concern. As far as I can see the reason is the following: The various critical schools, which have investigated canon history as well as the theories in this field of study, have their own reason of existence. They came into being partly because of the peculiar nature of gospel literature, partly because of the development and capacity of the human mind [at a particular moment in history].

The history of the critical schools is parallel to the development of each person involved in biblical criticism. There will always remain an interest in harmonization among critically inexperienced scholars. A naturalistic interpretation will always find representatives among those who have objections against the miracles and who have not followed this history of criticism in its latest stages. Whoever has not studied the Tübingen critics will always have difficulty keeping in mind that ultimately the authors themselves are the sources of their

---

[33]Ibid., 1:55, 68.
[34]Ibid., 1:157ff.

books. Their ideas and circumstances are the backdrop against which the form and content of their gospels must be explained.

If it would be possible to start all over again, all the schools and hypotheses would have to be revived and maybe even in the same sequence! In other words, the history of literary criticism with all its assertions is a continuously developing movement. This truth is easily overlooked, so that the various hypotheses are regarded as arbitrary attempts to resolve the question of gospel history, where everyone and every new direction has the same rights. [History demonstrates, however, that there is a necessary concatenation of theories.]

For instance, when Renan attempts to contribute a solution to the question of canon history on the basis of scholarly research, it still remains to be seen what level of criticism he has reached before. If he ventures to set up a theory without first having been seated as a disciple at the feet of the great masters in historical criticism, he will of necessity fall into a position that has long been overcome by the development of criticism. This means that Renan accepted the naturalistic explanation of gospel history, because unbelief in miracles was current in his day.

This also is the case with d'Eichthal, although in a modified sense. When he set himself the assignment to investigate the truth of Augustine's concept of the gospel he was already lost for the cause of higher criticism. Such research is as irrelevant as the justification of the Ur-gospel hypothesis is today. D'Eichthal decided to make a new effort after he had learned that the German scholars had not come to a unanimous position.[35] At that point he made his first error by not considering what had been achieved by canon criticism and what was to become the next stage of research. Because of this ad hoc approach his work is not quite aware of current issues, no matter how many correct viewpoints he adopted from his predecessors and whatever good insights into the essence of the gospels he obtained.

There is namely a difference between the way in which d'Eichthal assigned a place to Mark in the development of gospel literature and Hilgenfeld's approach. The many arguments developed for either Matthean or Marcan priority have caused no problem for d'Eichthal at all. Hilgenfeld, at least, attempted to refute the arguments of both schools. D'Eichthal gives no evidence that he has overcome these arguments in the privacy of his study.

Mark is simply the second author in the sequence of time. This is the consequence of d'Eichthal's starting point, namely, the conceptions of Augustine and of Lemaitre de Sacy. It is merely a matter of coincidence when he is found in agreement with Hilgenfeld. In the endless succession of hypotheses, the old Augustine and the accepted tradition again have taken their turn.

---

[35]Ibid., "Preface," lii.

Karl Reinhold Köstlin's Mediating Approach

Finally a brief statement about a second mediating position, that of Köstlin, who attempted to unite the two opposite hypotheses of Griesbach and the Marcan hypothesis. His work was published in *The Origin and Composition of the Synoptic Gospels*. He first demonstrated the late origin of the canonical Gospel of Mark and its use of the sources Matthew and Luke. As a correction to the followers of Griesbach, he maintains that the Synoptics are not sufficient to explain Mark.[36]

In order to clarify his position Köstlin points to the many specific references to names of persons and places, which we discussed above.[37] He also mentions other smaller features, such as the reference to the Herodians, Pilate's astonishment about Jesus' early death, the frequent occurrence of names like Decapolis, Bethsaida, and so forth. Some of these features are too insignificant or too widespread to be derived from a specific tradition.

We are touching here on the question of how much freedom in theological formulation and editing one may assume from an evangelist. Baur, for instance, did not think he needed an additional document in interpreting Mark. Köstlin had the opposite opinion. I do not mind his views, but I do object to his method of implementation. After Köstlin has recognized the need for a third source document, he discovers its influence at points where no one else would have expected it.

For example, Köstlin is of the opinion that it is unclear in Mark 2:18 who the persons are who ask for the reason why Jesus' disciples do not fast. In Luke the scribes raise the question (Luke 5:33) and in Matthew the question is attributed to the disciples of John (Matt 9:14). Since Mark refers to "people" in general, Köstlin assumed that Matthew and Luke have each, independently, corrected Mark's third source. Mark himself, however, did not improve his source at this point.[38]

Another example of the third source is seen in Mark 3:9, where a boat is available to avoid the throngs of the crowd. Other traces of the third source can be found in the reference to Jesus' inability to perform miracles in Nazareth, and in the expression of amazement over the unbelief of its inhabitants (6:5, 6).[39] Finally, the typical biographical description "from childhood," in the story of the deaf and dumb boy (9:21), was considered by Köstlin as additional evidence of

[36]Köstlin, *Der Ursprung und die Komposition der synoptischen Evangelien* [*The origin and compostion of the synoptic gospels*] (Stuttgart: Mächen, 1853) 334.
[37]See above, 199.
[38]Köstlin, *Der Ursprung,* 339.
[39]Ibid., 343.

that third source.[40]

These and similar features leave no doubt of the influence of an Ur-Mark, according to Köstlin. However, these features are indistinguishable from Köstlin's description of materials that are intrinsic to Mark and do not require a third source document. Among these intrinsic features are the distinction between teaching for the initiated and for the uninitiated; the division of the pericope about the fig tree; the many geographical identifications; and the graphic details.[41] Such a listing of indigenous Marcan materials makes it difficult [to establish a logical distinction between material from Mark himself and material from the third source]. The borderline seems to have been drawn arbitrarily.

The idea of the third document is at least dubious. Köstlin's hypothesis becomes even less acceptable when we see how much he derived from these few data. His Ur-Mark was allegedly a Petrine gospel because Jesus' ministry begins with the vocation of Peter. It is Peter who urges Jesus to return to Capernaum after his first departure from that town. Peter also remembers the curse over the fig tree pronounced during the preceding day; and it is Peter who, more so than in the other gospels,[42] takes the initiative in the discussions with Jesus.

According to Köstlin, this third source was a Galilean gospel as well, for in Mark 14:28 Jesus assures his disciples that he will go ahead of them to Galilee.[43] This gospel must have originated in Syria, for Capernaum is supposed to be so familiar to the readers that the author must have lived in that vicinity. The readers must have lived outside Palestine since this gospel was written in the Greek language. The Canaanite woman is expressly identified as a Syrophoenician.[44]

This third and Petrine source from Galilee was allegedly the same gospel mentioned by Papias, because it showed a great lack of order. The exclamation of the people proves that Ur-Mark must have had more similar miracles of healing. These included Jesus' making the deaf hear and causing the dumb to speak (see 7:37). On page 171 above we discussed these miracles of healing from Matthew's general account in 15:30, 31. Our proposal was that Mark selected a specific example for further elaboration. Köstlin, however, states,

> In the original document as well as in the canonic Gospel of Mark we find minutely described healings (Mark 7:31-37 and 8:22-26) interspersed between the teaching of Jesus (Mark 7:1-13) and the feeding of the multitudes (Mark 8:1-10). No wonder that Papias would take note of a lack of order (τάξις) in this document. Matthew, for instance, transferred these miracles

[40]Ibid., 349.
[41]Ibid., 335.
[42]Ibid., 366.
[43]Ibid., 358.
[44]Ibid., 365.

to his chapters eight and nine.[45]

As the reader will agree, Köstlin's assurances are made so boldly that one cannot follow him anymore. Many questions remain. What justification allows us to identify this Ur-Mark with the document mentioned by Papias? The only arguments for Köstlin are a lack of order, and his conviction that neither Mark nor the teachings of Peter have been its source.[46]

When the context is so loose, with what justification can one assume the presence of so many "logia" in this Ur-Mark[47] The words of Papias concerning Peter, "who placed the teachings in his hand," would supposedly refer to these "logia." What notion should we have of somebody who wants to redeem the Ur-Mark from imperfection and disorderliness? Why would such a large quantity of "logia" be eliminated merely because this arrangement was to be modeled after Matthew and Luke? Why would he grant so much influence to Matthew and Luke that the original so-called "third source" would be totally lost except for a few features?[48]

The iron statue of Köstlin has been erected upon feet of clay. Too many conclusions are drawn from too few factual data. I have no objections if one wants to claim a third source in addition to Matthew and Luke, as long as one does not make special claims about the nature and form of such a source. Köstlin's attempt to combine Griesbach's hypothesis with the Marcan theory has failed to convince his readers.[49]

The Present State of Canon Criticism

With these last representatives I trust to have demonstrated that there is no adequate mediating position in the present state of canon criticism. The leading scholars have presented us with a dilemma concerning the Gospel of Mark. It is either the source or it is a reworked edition of the two other Synoptic gospels. The consequences emerging from a conclusion in this matter are far from insignificant.

Both hypotheses have produced their own results for gospel history. On the one side stands *A Sketch of the Character of Jesus* by [Daniel] Schenkel, on the other side *The Life of Jesus* by Strauss. The former represents the Marcan hypothesis while the latter basically agrees with Griesbach. I have attempted to

---

[45]Ibid., 347; a similar proof on 351.
[46]Ibid., 359ff.
[47]Ibid., 102-103, 358ff.
[48]Cf. Ibid., 356.
[49]Köstlin rejected the Marcan hypothesis in Ewald's version of it: ibid., 357.

prove the weakness of the Marcan hypothesis. Together with Strauss, I cannot consider it anything else than the "swindle of the century." And, with Hilgenfeld, I would like to apply the old Roman dictum to this hypothesis: "I am of the opinion Carthage has to be destroyed."

In this thesis I have tried to detect the motives of the advocates on both sides of the fence. I have asked how they could speak with so much conviction, and which preconditions must be present in the critic if he wants to choose either one or the other of these hypotheses. It is still too early to determine what the future will bring. The most decisive factor in the further development seems to be the theological factor. The giants of Tübingen and Heilbronn have not been able to stem nor change the tide in favor of the Marcan hypothesis in Germany.

In our country [the Netherlands], the question of canon history has not been considered with a view to its theological consequences. The destiny of the Marcan hypothesis [in the Netherlands] is therefore not so much in the hands of theologians as in the hands of the biblical critics. I will feel richly rewarded for my efforts, if in addition to my doctor's degree, I will have gained at least one reader who has carefully read my exposition up to the last page. I hope that the conviction will have taken root in the mind of the reader that the proponents of the Marcan hypothesis do not deserve the wreath of victory awarded to them by their admirers.

Indexes

Index of Topics

Topics are arranged alphabetically; subtopics follow the sequence of Meijboom's presentation and of the introductions by Kiwiet and Farmer. (See also "An Outline of the Translation," xxxv-xl, above.)

Tendency Criticism (Theological Analysis)

Index of Persons

Agricola, Rudolf, xxvi
Augustine, xvi, 213, 222, 224
Bauer, Bruno, xxviiin, 32-36, 66, 83, 85, 91
Bauer, Walter, vii
Baur, Ferdinand Christian, xx, xxi, xxii, xxiiin, xxv-xxviii, 24, 31n, 34-37, 62, 66, 90-91, 110, 132n, 215, 216, 217
Bengel, Johann Albrecht, xviii
Bengel, Ernst Gottlieb, xviii
Bigler, Robert M., xvn, xviii, xxiin, xxiiin,
Bismarck, Otto von, xvi, xxin, xxiv
Bleek, Friedrich, 176n
Clement of Alexandria, xxv, xxxiii, 200n
Colani, Timothée, 45, 52
Conzelmann, Hans, vii
Cranford, Lorin L., xi
Credner, Karl A., 17-18, 62, 117, 121n
de Groot. *See* Groot, B. P. Hofstede de
D'Eichthal, Gustave, 222-24
De Wette, Wilhelm Martin, 121n, 186
Droz, Jacques, xvn, xviin
Dungan, David, vii, x
Eichhorn, Johann G., 22, 24, 26, 214
Ellis, E. Earle, xi, xxviiin
Erasmus, Desiderius, xxvi
Eusebius, xxv, xxxi, 124n
Eylert, R. F., xvn
Ewald, Heinrich A. von, xvii, xx, xxi, xxii, xxvi-xxx, 3, 38-43, 65-70, 110, 115, 170n, 208n, 227n
Farmer, William R., viii, xi, xvin, xviin, xxn, xxiiin, xxiv, xxviii-xxxi
Felix, Minucius, xxv
Francis II, xv
Friedrich Wilhelm III, xiv, xv
Gansfort, Wessel, xxvi
Gerlach brothers, xvn
Griesbach, Johann Jakob, xvin, xxxii, 23-24, 37, 73, 78, 155-57, 162, 164-66, 175, 183, 214, 215, 216, 225, 227

Groot, B. P. Hofstede de, xxxiv
Gutzkow, Karl, xx
Harnack, Adolf von, xvi
Harris, Horton, xviii, xixn, xxn, xxi, xxiin, xxviiin, xxvn, xxvin, xxviin
Hasert, Christian Adolf, 36n
Hegel, Georg Friedrich Wilhelm, xiv-xvi, xix
Hengstenberg, Ernst W., xxvii
Herder, Johann Gottfried, xxix, xxx, 16-17, 19
Hilgenfeld, Adolf, xvii, xxn, 85, 93, 118, 132n, 145, 211, 212n, 213-221, 224, 228
Hippolytus, xxv
Hitzig, Ferdinand, xxxn, 27-31
Holtzmann, Heinrich Julius, viii, ix, xxiii, xxiv, 3, 22n, 26n, 71-82, 92, 121n, 129, 156n, 160, 184n, 210, 211n, 215
Hug, Johann L., 60, 214
Hutten, Ulrich von, 37
Irenaeus, xxxn
Jansen, John J., xi
Justin Martyr, 216, 217
Kee, Howard Clark, vii
Kingsbury, Jack Dean, viii
Koppe, J. B., xviiin, xxxin
Köstlin, Karl R., 124, 132n, 213, 225-27
Kotzebue, August, xvii
Kraft, Robert, vii
Krodel, Gerhard, viii
Kuijper, Abraham, xxvi
Küng, Hans, xivn, xixn
Lachmann, Karl F. W., xvin, 17-18, 165
Lambrecht, Johannes, 89n, 90n, 92, 161n
Lessing, Gotthold Ephraim, xvin, xxxi
Luther, Martin, xvii
Marcion, xxv, xxxiii
Massey, Marilyn Chapin, xvii, xix, xxn, xxiin
Metternich, Klemens W. N. L., xxi

New Gospel Studies
A Monograph Series for Gospel Research

Titles in the New Gospel Studies Series

1. David Barrett Peabody, *Mark as Composer* (1987)
2. Dennis Gordon Tevis, *Matthew as Composer* (forthcoming)
3. Franklyn J. G. Collison, *Luke as Composer* (forthcoming)
4. Thomas R. W. Longstaff and Page A. Thomas, eds.,
The Synoptic Problem. A Bibliography, 1716–1988 (1988)
5/1 5/2 5/3. Édouard Massaux, trans. Norman J. Belval and Suzanne Hecht,
ed. Arthur J. Bellinzoni, *The Influence of the Gospel of Saint Matthew
on Christian Literature before Saint Irenaeus* (1991, 1992, 1993)
6. Ben F. Meyer, ed., *One Loaf, One Cup. Ecumenical Studies
of 1 Cor 11 and Other Eucharistic Texts* (1993)
7. David J. Neville, *Arguments from Order in Synoptic Source Criticism.
A History and Critique* (1993)
8. Hajo Uden Meijboom, *A History and Critique of the Origin of the Marcan
Hypothesis, 1835–1866. A Contemporary Report Rediscovered,*
trans., ed., and intro. John J. Kiwiet (1993)

Related Titles from Mercer University Press

Hans-Herbert Stoldt, *History and Criticism of the Marcan Hypothesis,*
trans. and ed. Donald L. Niewyk (1980)
William R. Farmer, ed., *New Synoptic Studies. The Cambridge Gospel
Conference and Beyond* (1983)
Bruce C. Corley, ed., *Colloquy on New Testament Studies.
A Time for Reappraisal and Fresh Approaches* (1983)
Bernard Orchard, *A Synopsis of the Four Gospels in a New Translation* (1982)
Bernard Orchard, *A Synopsis of the Four Gospels in Greek* (1983)
Bernard Orchard and Harold Riley, *The Order of the Synoptics.
Why Three Synoptic Gospels?* (1987)
Ed Parish Sanders, ed., *Jesus, the Gospels, and the Church* (1987)
Harold Riley, *The Making of Mark. An Exploration* (1989)
David L. Dungan, ed., *The Interrelations of the Gospels. A Symposium* (1990)
Harold Riley, *The First Gospel* (1992)
Harold Riley, *Preface to Luke* (1993)

(d) William R. Farmer, *The Synoptic Problem. A Critical Analysis*
(Macmillan, 1964; Western North Carolina, 1976)
(d) William O. Walker, Jr., ed., *The Relationships among the Gospels.
An Interdisciplinary Dialogue* (Trinity, 1978)

*Titles marked (d) are from other publishers and distributed by Mercer University Press.
Most titles are available in Europe from Peeters Press, Leuven.*